Swantje van Mark, Leonore Sell, Norbert Lennartz (Eds.)

Boundaries, Limits, Taboos: Transgression in Romanticism

Selected Papers from the Vechta Conference
of the German Society for English Romanticism
and the International Association of Byron Societies

D1662273

Christoph Bode, Jens Martin Gurr, Frank Erik Pointner (Hg.)

STUDIEN ZUR ENGLISCHEN ROMANTIK

(Neue Folge)

Band 23

Swantje van Mark, Leonore Sell,
Norbert Lennartz (Eds.)

Boundaries, Limits, Taboos: Transgression in Romanticism

Selected Papers from the Vechta Conference of the German Society for English Romanticism and the International Association of Byron Societies

ᴜᴜᴜᴛ Wissenschaftlicher Verlag Trier

Boundaries, Limits, Taboos: Transgression in Romanticism.
Selected Papers from the Vechta Conference of the German Society for English
Romanticism and the International Association of Byron Societies. -
Swantje van Mark, Leonore Sell, Norbert Lennartz (Eds.)
WVT Wissenschaftlicher Verlag Trier, 2021
(Studien zur Englischen Romantik, 23)
ISBN 978-3-86821-918-0

Cover illustration: Artwork: The Lament for Icarus, exhibited 1898, by Herbert Draper
(1863-1920), presented by the Trustees of the Chantrey Bequest 1898
Photo: Tate

Cover design: Brigitta Disseldorf

© WVT Wissenschaftlicher Verlag Trier, 2021
ISBN 978-3-86821-918-0

WVT Wissenschaftlicher Verlag Trier
Postfach 4005, 54230 Trier
Bergstraße 27, 54295 Trier
Tel. (0651) 41503, Fax 41504
Internet: http://www.wvttrier.de
E-Mail: wvt@wvttrier.de

Contents

List of Figures

Acknowledgements

Tourneys, masques, theatres, better become
Our halcyon days
Thomas Carew, 'In Answer of an Elegiacal Letter,
upon the Death of the King of Sweden …' ll. 96-97.

This collection of essays stems from the joint conference of the International Association of Byron Societies (IABS) and the German Society for English Romanticism (GER) held at the University of Vechta in September 2019. When scholars from the US, Canada, Britain, France, Italy, Sweden, Lebanon, Japan, South Korea and Germany convened on the campus of our small university in Lower Saxony, nobody could have known that this meeting was to be the last gathering for many of us and that fewer than six months later the academic world came to a standstill due to Covid-19.

In seventeenth-century literature, the Cavaliers used the term 'halcyon days' to describe the few convivial days that Royalists enjoyed before the onset of the rigorous Puritan Interregnum. Unwittingly, we were also enjoying halcyon days in September 2019, partaking of the pleasures of academic life, sitting closely together at conference dinners in Bremen and Vechta and listening (with a few glasses of wine) to Robert Schumann's fabulous *Kreisleriana* played by the pianist, colleague and our dear friend Wolfgang Mechsner. Today, after more than a year of intermittent lockdowns, it seems almost inconceivable that people from all over the world were able to come to Vechta, to sit together in rooms without restrictions, to talk to each other without wearing face masks and to spend a wonderful time without being constantly alerted to pandemic spikes, R-numbers and rates of infection. The fond memories that we have of the conference have helped us to deal with the hard and often challenging periods of isolation (for quite a long time Vechta was one of the hotspots of the pandemic in Germany) and to look forward to new post-covid conferences where Romanticists meet in person (and not via Zoom), engage in lively conversations and recollect in tranquillity the time when a little, but pernicious virus became the transgressor of boundaries, limits, taboos and bodies.

Our heartfelt thanks go to the German Research Foundation (DFG) that supported the conference and the project of transgression in Romanticism as generously as the University of Vechta. We are very grateful for the wonderful selection of essays that renowned scholars in the field of Romanticism submitted to us and to these authors who responded to all our nit-picking queries with patience and benevolence in spite of current circumstances. We are very happy and grateful that in these times of pandemic restrictions and ever-recurring lockdowns we were able to rely on flexible and cooperative contributors who eventually made this collection possible as a lasting tribute to those halcyon days in Vechta in 2019.

Vechta, in April 2021

Swantje van Mark   Leonore Sell   Norbert Lennartz

Swantje van Mark and Norbert Lennartz

Transgression in Romanticism: Some Introductory Remarks

The arts have always attracted and even invited transgressions, and at least since Christopher Marlowe's *Doctor Faustus* readers of all generations have known that neat compliance with norms, rules and regulations is liable to create fatal boredom and leave the avid scholar "glutted with conceit of this" (*Doctor Faustus* 1.1.77). When Alexander Pope considers it advisable to remind his contemporaries of the fact that to probe into God's plans is presumption and that the "proper study of mankind is Man" (a maxim still duly repeated by the law-abiding and tragic protagonist of Goethe's *Elective Affinities*, Ottilie) ("Essay on Man" 2:2, *Major Works* 281; *Wahlverwandtschaften* 417) he seems to be responding to man's ongoing unruliness in allegedly serene Classicism in the same way as John Donne did more than a century before when he lamented that seventeenth-century Faustian man wanted to be as unique as a phoenix ("The First Anniversary" l. 217).

While in early modern times overreachers rebelled against limitations imposed on them by religion and convention and in their outrageous complaints focused on the Chain of Being as a God-given instrument of clipping the wings of their Icarian aspirations, Romantics saw themselves thrust into a world in which the opprobrium attached to transgression changed into fascination, awe-inspired admiration and an unprecedented celebrity cult. Reverting to Milton's singular idea of restoring Lucifer to his pristine angelic splendour in *Paradise Lost*, Romantics such as Percy Bysshe Shelley not only courted the idea of being blasphemers or followers of the Satanic school of poetry, but also sought scandal when they turned the foremost Luciferic sin of pride into a new transgressive virtue. Although burdened by a "heavy weight of hours" and suffering from the dreariness of the human condition, the speaker in "Ode to the West Wind" (1819) feels himself akin to the destructive sublimity of the wind and characterizes himself as "tameless, and swift, and proud" ("Ode to the West Wind" ll. 55-56), giving the last word full stress and turning it into a byword for positive transgression.

The fact that Shelley was a political radical who was actuated by transgressive pride against the *ancien régime*, in particular at the time of the traumatic Peterloo massacre in 1819, is not new; neither is the fact that in just one line – "I fall upon the thorns of life! I bleed!" ("Ode to the West Wind" l. 54) – he conflates bleeding Christ with Icarus and thus creates a new syncretistic type of (thwarted) transgressor. What is, however, intriguing and underlines the Romantics' tendency to contradiction and paradox is that this eulogy of transgressive power is subjected to the rigorous demands of an intricate form that coerces the wind into the double grid of the Dantean *terza rima* and the fourteen-line sonnet. While even Shakespeare tends to give his overreachers the partial freedom of showing their high-flown rhetorics in rhymeless blank verse, Romantics seem to negate their transgression when they prefer to confine their manifestations of unbounded strength to the conservatism of traditional forms.

This contradiction permeates most of the Romantics' works and, to a certain extent, tempers the transgressiveness of their overriding subjects. Read from this perspective, even Byron, after his Faustian spell in *Manfred* (where he, however, refrains from giving his ranting hero a flamboyant Wertherian death), reverts to the discipline of the comic epic in *ottava rima*, a stanzaic form which is instrumental in belittling the former metaphysical rebel Don Juan and transforms him into a *picaro* buffeted around by his mother, harassed by voracious women and even laughed at as a drag queen *avant la lettre* in an Oriental seraglio. While, in Byron's poem, the world is transgressively turned upside down, making the boyish Don Juan bear the brunt of an unleashed Hobbesian wolfishness, Juan's rebellion and transgression are made alarmingly redundant in the absence of a punitive God. In this context, it is interesting to see that, in the scandalous Canto 2 of *Don Juan* (*DJ*), Byron shows his (anti-)hero's disconcerting shift from Prometheus, the relentless and vindictive rebel against Jupiter's tyranny, to the carnivorous vulture that daily devoured the Titan's liver and now stands for man's bestialization and reduction to an instinct-driven nonentity. When the "savage hunger" demands, "[l]ike the Promethean vulture, this pollution" (*DJ* 2.595-96) man's identification with the predatory bird is almost complete. With the ship of the holy trinity (*Trinidada*) turned into a small boat of cannibalistic fools, Byron seems to insinuate that transgression has lost its way and that even the breach of the last taboo, cannibalism, has been deprived of its momentum when all myths of order have come to be replaced by chaotic arbitrariness. The fact that Juan refrains from partaking of this cannibalistic excess – "'Twas not to be expected that he should, / Even in extremity of their disaster, / Dine with them on his pastor and his master" (*DJ* 2.622-24) – and that he is consequently spared the horrid convulsions with which the devourers of Pedrillo are afflicted is certainly not due to an act of metaphysical justice, but rather the result of both a desultory stroke of luck and a lingering feeling of humanity in a post-human world.

Despite the fact that Goethe was like Byron a "bad metaphysician" (*Byron's Letters and Journals* 3:135; cf. Conrady 2:487), he seems to have checked his overreacher's designs by embedding the tragedy of the disgruntled Faust into the framework of a wager between God and Mephisto. And when Mephisto even defines his role as being part of a power that by wreaking havoc intends to effect good things ("Teil von jener Kraft, / Die stets das Böse will und stets das Gute schafft"; *Faust* ll. 1335-36),[1] Goethe leaves his readers in no doubt that Faust's transgression follows the pattern of a dialectic gravitating towards a meaningful end (eventually discernible in the *deus ex machina* interference in Gretchen's dungeon). The Faust syndrome (see Lansdown) is thus doubtlessly inscribed into many Romantic works, but while Goethe's play seems to imply that transgression is an integral part of a Calderonian *theatrum mundi*, British Romantics insinu-

---

1   See also Coleridge's rather wooden translation: "a portion of that power / Whose wills are evil, but whose actions good" (Burwick and McKusick 21).

ate that all Faustian transgression is on the point of becoming absurd when the transgressor's antagonist (Jupiter, Jehovah) is either an inveterate *deus absconditus* or even fading away into non-existence. It is this sudden meaninglessness that Frankenstein's monster is ultimately faced with when its dilettantish creator dies and provocative confrontations between creature and creator (modelled on disputes between God and Satan in *Paradise Lost*) have irretrievably come to an end.

In the first generation of Romanticism, for Wordsworth and Coleridge, even small-scale transgression immediately triggered self-censorship and corrective intervention. For generations, critics have been trying to lift the mysterious veil of the (genderless) person from Porlock and inadvertently contributing to its myth rather than explaining its untimely arrival to truncate the surreal poem "Kubla Khan" (see also Wu 108-14). That "Kubla Khan" is a poem about transgression is evident and that the eruption of the mighty fountain is suggestive of an orgasmic ejaculation and predictably the result of suppressed auto-erotic fantasies can also be proved by textual evidence. The more the poem seemed to be getting out of control and the sexual subtext was on the point of surfacing, the more urgently Coleridge seems to have felt the need to apply what Eve Kosofsky Sedgwick, in a related context, was to call the "sphincter of the will" (Sedgwick 818-37), the proto-Victorian application to an instance of self-censorship later personified by an invisible character from a Romantic play, Mrs Grundy in Thomas Morton's forgotten melodrama *Speed the Plough* (1798). In "The Rime of the Ancient Mariner", the transgression is arguably less sexual than a good example of the "motiveless malignity" that Coleridge associated with Shakespeare's Iago. As soon as the Mariner shoots the albatross and thus arbitrarily interferes with the sentimental ring of sympathy between man and animals, there is, however, an immediate reaction from an ontological Mrs Grundy, repaying the Mariner's purposeless transgression with the death of the ship's crew, with the curse of the Mariner's Ahasverian existence and forcing him to overcome his aversion to the thousands of "slimy things" ("Rime" l. 238) and to extend his love even to the ambiguous ugly water-snakes (see Böhm). To what extent this transgression loses its impact and turns into a banality in the pre-Darwinian struggle for survival is shown in Byron's *Don Juan* when the beautiful webfooted "bird of promise" (*DJ* 2.754) only whets the cannibals' appetite, and eventually it is by chance that the bird escapes and leaves the few survivors of the *Trinidada* still famished and longing for their elusive food: "They would have eat her, olive branch and all" (*DJ* 2.760). Considering the fact that man is, according to Byron's sardonic narrator, "a carnivorous production" (*DJ* 2.529), only crude necessity is paramount, but Coleridge's divine and punishing antagonist, so indispensable for the concept of transgression, has fallen out of Byron's poem.

Even Wordsworth is unable to escape the emergent Mrs Grundy whose correction he seems to solicit even for minor transgressions in his youth and for his Icarian flight into the Alps. Before the speaker of *The Prelude* yields to the temptation of the soul-liberating feeling of the sublime, he introduces a peasant, who, like an ontological signpost, exhorts the mountaineers to descend and to be aware that "our future course ... / Was downwards" (*Prelude* 6:581; 6:584-85). When they still entertain hopes that "pointed to the clouds" (*Prelude* 6:587) and are loath to believe that their aspirations are futile, Wordsworth and his crew are compelled to come to terms with the sobering and castigating truth the peasant so insistently reiterates: "*that we had crossed the Alps*" (*Prelude* 6:591; italics in the original).

With transgression eliciting responses that range from the censorious application of the volitional sphincter to the conviction that man is fatalistically thrust into an absurd universe in which transgressions have ceased to be transgressive, some of the Romantics, more often than not those writing off the beaten track of the canonical 'big six', tried to tackle the boundaries, limits and taboos that persistently keep the individual locked in "mind-forg'd manacles" (Blake *Songs of Experience* 8:8). As if to escape the ever-tightening grip of an imaginary Urizen, Godwin is in line with his son-in-law Shelley when he predates *The Cenci* by a few years with an action-packed novel about incest (a work that might not have passed muster with Wordsworth who, on the one hand, was exposed to allegations of incestuous love for his sister, and, on the other, saw British culture flooded by a deluge of trashy and immoral novels) (see Möllers). Others follow Byron's cue, pop star, *enfant terrible* and alleged practitioner of incest, who not only transgressed boundaries of taste and decorum in his anarchic *Don Juan*, but also transgressed real geographical boundaries and introduces his bewildered British audience into the exotic and passionate realm of the Orient. *The Giaour*, *The Corsair* and various other Oriental tales suck their readers into the vortex of passion, jealousy and death (see also Reimann), but they also give them insight into forms of otherness which Regency society – despite its ubiquitous display of flippancy – recoiled from. The anonymous epistolary novel *The Lustful Turk*, fuelled by the transgressive potential of preceding works of clichéd Orientalism such as Beckford's *Vathek* and Byron's seraglio episode in *Don Juan*, makes use of the transgressive power of pornography which, present in Romantic literature at least since Matthew G. Lewis's *The Monk* (1796), channels sentimental feeling, introspective narration and the generic freedom of the novel into a liminal area where lustful Oriental man coalesces with machines, displaying ever-erect genitals as instruments, engines and weapons (see Saglia). The anonymous writer of this titillating story ostensibly goes beyond the boundaries imposed by Romantic Platonism and counteracts the disembodied growth of poets' minds with the daunting heritage of the eighteenth-century *homme machine* and its genital sublime as paraded in John Cleland's *Memoirs of a Woman of Pleasure* (Blackwell 39-63). Yet, it was to take another century before D. H. Lawrence was able and audacious enough to transgress the linguistic boundaries which hedged in nineteenth-century pornographic forays (from *The Lustful Turk* to Bram Stoker's *Dracula*) and to free literature from the clutter of metonymies and metaphors (see also Domsch). Although "transgressing logocentric perspectives that dominated Western culture from the first", as Larry H. Peer maintains (Peer 5), even the transgressive genre such as burgeoning pornography seems to be peculiarly hampered by a linguistic codification that can pass muster in the face of a stern and ever-vigilant Mrs Grundy.

While the spirit of the perverse propels many Romantic works, from Beethoven's late piano sonatas to ramified novels of the Gothic tradition, it never reigns supreme, but rather proves to be perpetually locked in an antinomian or pseudo-dialectical dichotomy (Kershaw 92-114) between the perverse transgressor and a demonic nemesis (see Duncan). In Edgar Allan Poe's unsettling story "The Black Cat", the murderer is eventually tracked down by the ruses of his feline antagonist, the eerie epitome of fate's vindictiveness. Lewis's Ambrosio is lured into perdition by the erotic traps that the devil puts in his way in the shape of seductive Matilda, and E. T. A. Hoffmann's universe, in which Gothic implausibilities from Horace Walpole's and Lewis's stories converge, is ultimately swayed by the ruthless influence that the ominous dead wield over the living (see Schlutz). It is this dualism that keeps Romantic transgressors in check and shows them nullified by an indefinable antagonistic power which defies expression in the same way as the unleashed erotic force that writers preferred to demonize or to domesticate in a language of vexing ambiguity.

Considering the fact that Regency society vociferously called for a counterpoise of smug domesticity where Thomas Bowdler hoped to familiarize his audience with an adulterated Shakespeare that could freely be read aloud in family circles, readers are scarcely surprised to find Romantic transgressions repeatedly mitigated by stunning depictions of the petty bourgeois world. It is in this context that Byron's *Don Juan* has to be read as a story that reduces Mozart's metaphysical rebel to a boy whose books are mercilessly bowdlerized and who, instead of flamboyantly descending into hell, grows up in the trite matrimonial hell of his parents. This atmosphere of inane domesticity, which to a certain degree is bolstered by the gossipy style of the prevalent gazettes, not only clashes with the *ottava rima* of the Italian epic tradition, it is also held together by what Gottfried Benn calls the "form-demanding power of nothingness" (Benn 8:1913) without which the whole poem would fall apart or dissolve into utter contingency (see Sha). Reverting to a style of meandering loquacity (so much at odds with the elegiac *ubi-sunt* tone about dying cultures in *Childe Harold's Pilgrimage*) (see also Kasahara) and inducing his readers to transgress the boundaries of decorum by filling the gaps created by the odd, allegedly shamefaced hyphen, Byron adroitly shifts the transgression from poet to reader, who from behind the façade of sentimental priggishness hoped to peep through the various keyholes of Juan's life.

In particular, in these private spaces newly created as buttresses against the public mode of eighteenth-century culture, in libraries, boudoirs and salons, readers were quietly introduced to the new transgressive art of taste-making (see Gigante). Books, formerly the pillars of masculine culture in monastic-looking rooms of authoritative knowledge, now turn into objects in which women such as Byron's hectoring Donna Inez not only censor juicy passages but which have also become decorative things standing next to tea dishes, vases and other ornaments. Books themselves (some of them exploring new provinces such as gastronomy) are no longer containers of sacrosanct and hermetic knowledge, they turn into objects that, in their sheer materiality, are violated, commodified, roughhandled and used as sites of intellectual conversation, Swiftian battles or even fierce and sardonic games of 'crambo' (see Gross). Not only does Charles Lamb's bibliomaniacal library seem to be one of the prime examples of the way books, in the private sphere of domesticity, turn into tools, instruments and receptacles whose aesthetic boundaries are disregarded and whose contents are treated as intellectual food, but more often than not as baits that tend to make the taker mad. In this respect, Byron not only weaponizes books to engage in fierce conversations with the Lake Poets, allied with Beckford, he also seems to pounce on Southey's unctuous *Vision of Judgement* and to hold the Poet Laureate, the "dry Bob" (*DJ* "Dedication" l. 24) and slavish imitator of Kotzebue, accountable for his pompous acquittal of sinners, traitors and decadent regents.

Southey, nowadays seen as a minor poet, but in the early nineteenth century the butt of hatred for the younger generation, is part of the Lake triumvirate that, for Byron and his ilk, epitomizes stagnation, turn-coat conservatism and collusion with the corrupt Establishment. While Byron paraded the "pageant of his bleeding heart" through post-Napoleonic Europe, the Lake Poets were accused of withdrawing into the remote nooks of their native villages, there to start a long process of self-observation, to vent ever-increasing opinionated views and to become as "dispensable" as the late Wordsworth is for Jonathan Bate (Bate 427). Despite the fact that Wordsworth increasingly became monumentalized and as the "sage of Rydal" savagely lambasted works of ostensible loose and transgressive morals such as Goethe's *Wilhelm Meister* (translated by Carlyle in 1824-27), Wordsworth preceded Goethe in writing his autobiography and thus in transgressively placing his ego at the centre of a "secular theodicy" (Abrams 95). Although Wordsworth was pre-Victorian enough to keep the objectionable facts of his French liaison with Annette Vallon out of the *Prelude* and like Goethe in *Truth and Fiction* (*Dichtung und Wahrheit*, 1811-31) liberally mixed truth and fabrication, he touched upon an area that was suspected of being a kind of anatomy, of laying bare the innermost recesses of the poet's mind. While Romantic poets thus readily gave insight into their private lives and willingly contributed to the commodification of their vulnerable personalities, they took advantage of a transgressive longing for biographical information and savoury voyeuristic details that had first gathered its momentum in the eighteenth century and flourished with James Boswell's *Life of Samuel Johnson* (1791). What in the Romantic autobiographies came to be seen as an unhampered form of exhibitionism, in post-Boswellian biographies, became synonymous with body-snatching, with the obscene rummaging in the entrails of a dead body, clandestinely done in the Frankensteinian "workshop of filthy creation" (*Frankenstein* 55) (see Roe).

Seen in this context, the transgression of boundaries, limits and taboos is something which is deeply inwoven into all areas of Romantic literature, even though the life span of arch transgressors such as Prometheus, Faust, Icarus or Don Juan was relatively short, consumed like a spark – "Der lohe Lichtfunke Prometheus ist ausgebrannt" (*The Robbers / Die Räuber* 1781, 1.2.3) – and more often than not nullified by the worm-like representatives of what Friedrich Schiller indignantly dismissed as the "century of limp eunuchs" ("das schlappe Kastraten-Jahrhundert"; *The Robbers / Die Räuber* 1.2.27). While too much attention has been devoted to aspects of Promethean rebellion over the past decades, critics have tended to overlook the fact that transgression in the Romantic age is more variegated, covers all manner of things such as Orientalism, pornography, gastronomy, bibliomania and (auto)biography and that it also tentatively affects a language that is for a long time fuelled by the Miltonic sublime, but so glaringly fails to shake off its inhibitions in the realm of backward *homme-machine* pornography.

It might be a coincidence, but also provoke further research that in this study of Romantic transgressions women are conspicuously underrepresented. Although Byron seems to hint that a weak and malleable Don Juan is on the point of being replaced by transgressive women such as Gulbayez or the larger-than-life Empress Catherine of Russia, the countless women in the position of meek Gretchens are still shepherded into the roles of the transgressors' victims and eventually pave the way for the nondescript Sibyl Vane, a specimen of the "decorative sex" in Oscar Wilde's *The Picture of Dorian Gray* (38) – a late nineteenth-century novel still propelled by the Faust theme. Women are either immured by psychopaths, used as gender-bending tools of Satan (as Matilda in *The Monk*) or turned into the ravaged bodies battered by the Lustful Turks' genital machines. Even Lucy Westenra in *Dracula,* who as a vampire temporarily dares to defy the regime of Victorian Grundyism, is later ruthlessly subjected to patriarchal order by her fiancé Arthur when he, like the Germanic god Thor, drives "the mercy-bearing" stake through her riotous body (*Dracula* 201). It is to the merit of Lawrence's *Lady Chatterley's Lover*, albeit amply vilified by feminists, that women are increasingly shown in the role of Romantic transgressors, disregarding the time-honoured boundaries between culture and nature and slackening the volitional sphincter by enjoying eurhythmic dances naked in the pouring rain. The fact that Lady Chatterley dislikes men in the role of raffish Don Juans not only makes the history of transgression featuring prominently Byron's *Don Juan* come full circle, it also proves that since the twentieth century Byron's deplored lack of heroes has been compensated for by new and transgressive heroes of all genders.

Works Cited

Abrams, M. H. *Natural Supernaturalism. Tradition and Revolution in Romantic Literature*. New York: W. W. Norton, 1971.

Bate, Jonathan. *Radical Wordsworth: The Poet Who Changed the World*. London: William Collins, 2020.

Benn, Gottfried. *Gesammelte Werke*. Ed. Dietrich Wellershoff. Wiesbaden: Limes, 1960-68.

Blackwell, Mark. "'It stood an object of terror and delight': Sublime Masculinity and the Aesthetics of Disproportion in John Cleland's *Memoirs of a Woman of Pleasure*". *Eighteenth-Century Novel* 3 (2003): 39-63.

Blake, William. *The Complete Poems*. Ed. W. H. Stevenson. London: Longman, 1989.

Burwick, Frederick and James McKusick, eds. *Faustus. From the German of Goethe*. Oxford: Oxford UP, 2012.

Byron, Lord [George Gordon]. *Don Juan*. Ed. T. G. Steffan, E. Steffan and W. W. Pratt. Harmondsworth: Penguin, 1986.

---. *Byron's Letters and Journals*. Ed. Leslie A. Marchand. 12 vols. Cambridge, MA: Harvard UP, 1973-82.

Coleridge, Samuel Taylor. *The Complete Poems*. Ed. William Keach. London: Penguin, 1997.

Conrady, Karl Otto. *Goethe: Leben und Werk*. 2 vols. Frankfurt: Fischer, 1992.

Donne, John. *Poetical Works*. Ed. Herbert J. C. Grierson. Oxford: Oxford UP, 1979.

Goethe, Johann Wolfgang von. *Werther, Wahlverwandtschaften*. Ed. Waltraud Wiethölter and Christoph Brecht. Frankfurt: Deutscher Klassiker Verlag, 2018.

---. *Faust*. Ed. Erich Trunz. Munich: C.H. Beck, 1989.

Kershaw, Matt. "Transgressive Dialectic: Kant, Hegel, and Beethoven's Late Piano Sonatas". *Transgressive Romanticism*. Ed. Larry H. Peer. Newcastle: Cambridge Scholars Publishing, 2018. 92-114.

Marlowe, Christopher. *The Complete Plays*. Ed. J. B. Steane. London: Penguin, 1986.

Peer, Larry H. "Introduction: The Sweep of Transgressive Romanticism". *Transgressive Romanticism*. Ed. Larry H. Peer. Newcastle: Cambridge Scholars Publishing, 2018. 1-9.

Pope, Alexander. *Major Works*. Ed. Pat Rogers. Oxford: Oxford UP, 2006.

Schiller, Friedrich. *Die Räuber, Fiesko, Kabale und Liebe*. Ed. Gerhard Kluge. Frankfurt: Deutscher Klassiker Verlag, 2009.

Sedgwick, Eve Kosofsky. "Jane Austen and the Masturbating Girl". *Critical Inquiry* 17 (1991): 818-37.

Shelley, Mary. *Frankenstein, or The Modern Prometheus*. Ed. M. K. Joseph. Oxford: Oxford UP, 1998.

Shelley, Percy Bysshe. *Poetical Works*. Ed. Thomas Hutchinson. Oxford: Oxford UP, 1986.

Stoker, Bram. *Dracula*. Ed. Roger Luckhurst. Oxford: Oxford UP, 2011.

Wilde, Oscar. *The Picture of Dorian Gray*. Ed. Isobel Murray. Oxford: Oxford UP, 1998.

Wordsworth, William. *Poetical Works*. Ed. Thomas Hutchinson and Ernest de Sélincourt. Oxford: Oxford UP, 1988.

Wu, Duncan. *30 Great Myths about the Romantics*. Oxford: Wiley Blackwell, 2015.

Richard Lansdown

Appetite and Deeds, War and the Will: Faustian Transgression in Byron's *The Deformed Transformed*

"En tirant sur la grappe, on fait tomber les grains à terre."
Simone Weil, *La Pesanteur et la grâce*

This chapter inserts Lord Byron into the history of Anglo-Germanic Faustianism, from the English *Faust Book* published in 1592, via Marlowe and Goethe to Thomas Mann's *Doctor Faustus*, published 360 years after the originary *Historia von Johann Fausten* (based on the life of a historical charlatan dead some fifty years before) was printed in Frankfurt in 1587. In doing so it takes account of matters historical (the Sack of Rome of 1527, where and when *The Deformed Transformed* is set) and philosophical (the will, the hypertrophied exercise of which has often been seen as central to the Faustian legend).

Byron wrote three Faustian poems: *Manfred*, started in the *Frankenstein* summer of 1816 but completed in Rome in May 1818; *Cain* of 1821, where he interpreted events from the fourth chapter of Genesis in terms of a Mephistophelean temptation; and *The Deformed Transformed*, started in January 1822 and abandoned around a year later. *Cain* is a special case, couched as it is in Miltonic terms, and complicated as it is by the preceding incident of the temptation of Eve. But the first and the third poems are clearly influenced by Goethe. The seed of *Manfred* was planted by the Gothic novelist Matthew Lewis, who had translated passages from *Faust* to the poet "by word of mouth" (*Byron's Letters and Journals* [*BLJ*] 5:26) at Diodati in August 1816 – though the hero of that poem is "his own dupe and destroyer", as Anne Barton suggests (Barton 204), without a Mephistopheles to bring him to perdition. The Faustian atmosphere amidst the Shelley circle at Pisa in 1822 was even thicker. By then Byron's publisher had sent him the anonymous *Analysis of Goethe's Tragedy of Faust*, published in 1820, which involved a brief introduction, sixty pages of translations from the drama, and twenty-six engravings of Friedrich Retzsch's illustrations for it, originally issued in Germany in 1818.[1] Shelley had also been impressed by these engravings, and by April 1822 had translated the Prologue in Heaven and the *Walpurgisnacht* scene from Goethe. We can be fairly

---

1   Text and plates are reprinted in Burwick and McCusick. A month after his arrival at Pisa, on 4 December 1821, Byron asked John Murray: "Are there not designs from *Faust*? send me some – and a translation of it – if such there is …." (*BLJ* 9:75). On 22 May 1822 we have record of him giving the book to the wife of a visiting American naval officer, Mrs Catherine Potter Stith (*BLJ* 9:161-62). Shelley had his copy by 12 January 1822 (Jones 2:376 and 406-07).

certain that he shared his efforts with Byron.[2] If Thomas Medwin is to be believed (153), Byron showed Shelley some papers in January 1822, saying they contained "a *Faustish* kind of drama", and in any event Byron himself acknowledged his debt to "the 'Faust' of the great Goëthe" in a prefatory note to *The Deformed Transformed* (Byron *Complete Poetical Works* [*CPW*] 6:517), eventually published by John Hunt in February 1824.[3] Manfred is a Faust-figure, and Cain is another such disgruntled intellectual, but only in the later fragment do we find the Mephistophelean theme fully developed – and transformed by creative circumstance and the literary tradition.

Faust: 1587-1947

Byron made it clear in 1817 that he did not know *Doctor Faustus*, and makes no further reference to it.[4] Marlowe's tragedy had fallen into disfavour in the mid-seventeenth century, from which it began to recover in the hands of Charles Lamb and William Hazlitt, even if no full text was back in print until 1826. Its source, the *English Faust Book*, merely asks its readers to "take example" (Marlowe *Faust Book* 74) from the "miserable and lamentable end" (Marlowe *Faust Book* 146) of a sinner given to "amorous drifts … delicate fare, and costly apparel", and who accused himself mostly of "gross understanding and wilful will" (Marlowe *Faust Book* 79, 145). Marlowe converted this sometimes powerfully written morality tale into a Renaissance tragedy – and a tragedy *about* the Renaissance – in part by bringing Lutheran fundamentalism (i.e. the devil really is flying overhead, listening for sinners taking the name of God in vain) into fruitful conflict with early modern psychology (i.e. Hell is a state of mind, and good and bad angels are embodiments of conscience). In the *Faust Book* Faustus's "mind was so inflamed that he forgot his soul" (Marlowe *Faust Book* 73); in Marlowe the hero's gross understanding and wilful will is reconfigured as something quintessentially human rather than sinfully anomalous. He may be "swoll'n with a cunning of a self-conceit" and a dabbler in "cursèd necromancy" (Marlowe *Doctor Faustus* 1.1.21, 26), but the end of all his academic triumphs is only to remind him he is "still but Faustus and a man" (Marlowe *Doctor Faustus* 1.1.53). "Yet all things far, and all things near, are vain", as Shelley put it in his

---

2   Edward Trelawny recorded Shelley reciting his translations to Byron (Lovell 271).

3   Byron's detailed knowledge of *Faust* emerges in a number of informal sources. At Cephalonia in 1823, for example, he told James Kennedy that he regarded Mephistopheles as "one of the finest and most sublime specimens of human conception", and in conversation with George Finlay at the same time "He said nothing could be more sublime than the words of the Spirit of the Earth to Faust, 'Thou resemblest the spirit of thy imagination, not me.' I involuntarily repeated it in German, and he said, 'Yes, those are the words'" (Lovell 440 and 458).

4   Regarding *Manfred* Byron wrote to Murray on 12 October 1817: "I *never read* … the 'Faustus of Marlow' and had & have no Dramatic works by me in English … but I heard Mr. Lewis translate verbally some scenes of *Goethe's Faust* … last summer – which is all I know of the history of that magical personage …" (*BLJ* 5:268).

translation of Goethe's version (Shelley *Complete Poetical Works* [*CPW*] 742), "To calm the deep emotions of his breast".

So it is that throughout literary history Faust remains essentially an everyman, and "the world of profit and delight" he dangles before himself is one it seems we all crave, in terms "Of power, of honor, of omnipotence" (Marlowe *Doctor Faustus* 1.1.83-4). Faust is "a man who stands", as Thomas Mann put it in "Germany and the Germans" (*Thomas Mann's Addresses* 51), "at the dividing line between the Middle Ages and Humanism", caught forever between Pico della Mirandola's idea that the individual is the moulder and maker of himself and Luther's idea that we have no free will to exercise in our relation to God. "Faustus is a rude sketch", Hazlitt suggested in his *Lectures on the Dramatic Literature of the Age of Elizabeth*, "but it is a gigantic one":

> a personification of the pride of will and eagerness of curiosity, sublimed beyond the reach of fear and remorse. He is hurried away, and ... devoured by a tormenting desire to extend his knowledge to the utmost bounds of nature and art, and to extend his power with his knowledge. (Hazlitt 6:202)

Marlowe's extension of the *Faust Book* in this direction is most famous in the Helen scene (Marlowe *Doctor Faustus* 5.1). In the prose original, the exhibition of the Homeric heroine to some students – on a *Sunday*, indeed – is only another trivial exercise of thaumaturgic power, alongside eating a load of hay and conjuring away the wheels of a cart: "fair Helen" is the lascivious possessor of "a rolling hawk's eye" and a "smiling and wanton countenance" (Marlowe *Faust Book* 134), and that is all. In Marlowe she becomes a rapturously tragic emblem of Renaissance neoclassical infatuation, launching a thousand ships and burning the topless towers of Ilium.

Philosophical and tragic alterations such as these notwithstanding, Marlowe was too instinctive a man of the theatre to cast out the stagier elements in his original, such as the slapstick scenes and the twenty-four-year compact signed in blood. It is a remarkable historical irony that English theatrical troupes took *Doctor Faustus* back to Germany in the early seventeenth century and helped spawn new versions of the drama in the popular theatre there in the next two hundred years. In the Enlightenment the German *Faustbuch* almost disappeared, but theatrical versions of the legend persisted, adding, above all, the Gretchen story of seduction and infanticide to the brew alongside the bloodcurdling contract with the Devil and Faustus's famous opening soliloquy of academic disenchantment. This was the tradition that Goethe consolidated and crystallized as a Romantic myth, as opposed to a Renaissance one, in the period in which the first part of his tragedy was incubated, from the early 1770s to 1806.[5]

In effect Goethe did what Marlowe had done before him: he brought the legend out of one zone (prosaic and pious in the sixteenth-century instance, theatrical and popular in the eighteenth-century one) up to the level of tragic art. But the tragedy of Romantic human aspiration is less religious and more existential, and it converts the materials from

---

5   See Williams, chapter 1: "The Sources and Transmission of the Faust Legend".

which it derived, turning Faust from an over-ambitious necromancer and magician into an emblem of humanity at large. Margareta becomes an embodiment of romantic and existential desire with no parallel in the sixteenth-century versions. The slapstick fades away, retained only in the Leipzig tavern scene, and Mephistopheles's entrance and involvement is delayed by dialogues with the Earth Spirit and an intellectual mediocrity (clearly representative of the Enlightenment), so that Faust's suicidal despair is more fully contextualized:

> I am not like a god! Too deeply now I feel
> This truth. I am a worm stuck in the dust,
> Burrowing and feeding, where at last I must
> Be crushed and buried by some rambler's heel. (Goethe *Faust* 1 ll. 652-55)

In short, "Wings, alas, may grow / Upon our soul but still our body is / Earthbound" (Goethe *Faust* 1 ll. 1090-92).

Accordingly the compact with Mephistopheles takes a new form in Goethe. There is no referral to Lucifer, the signature in blood is a sideshow ("a farce," according to Faust; Goethe *Faust* 1 l. 1739), and the entire proposal is couched in business-like terms, with no mention of eternal damnation. "I'm not exactly a grandee", Mephistopheles admits:

> But if you'd fancy getting through
> Your life in partnership with me,
> I shall with pleasure, without more ado,
> Wholly devote myself to you.
> You shall have my company,
> And if you are satisfied,
> I shall be your servant, always at your side! (Goethe *Faust* 1 ll. 1641-48)

In Faust's view the most important element in the arrangement is a bet. "If ever I lie down in sloth and base inaction", he says, "Then let that moment be my end!" (Goethe *Faust* 1 ll. 1692-93). If ever, that is, an experience Mephistopheles is able to deliver has Faust say, "Beautiful moment, do not pass away!" – if ever he is brought to a state of satisfied repletion – "Then you may forge your chains to bind me", and not before (Goethe *Faust* 1 ll. 1700-01). Rather than being the product of either gross understanding or a wilful will, the wager is a Romantic challenge – asking whether the world can offer anything that would finally satisfy humanity's "eagerness of curiosity". Thus, there is no need for a twenty-four-year compact, and the signature in blood is only an insurance policy. Mephistopheles trusts the world itself to bring Faust to perdition. "Fate has endowed him with the blind / Impatience of an ever-striving mind", he says, and "Even without this devil's bond that he has signed / He's doomed to perish nonetheless!" (Goethe *Faust* 1 ll. 1857-58, 1866-67). Indeed, John Williams argues that Mephistopheles is indifferent to Faustus's wager: "He will feed Faust with illusions and trivial banality …; but, far from satisfying Faust's highest aspirations, he will simply be fuelling his insatiable appetite for experience and will thereby involve him in such a morass of guilt that he will be beyond the pale of salvation" (Williams 89). Eudo Mason agrees: Mephisto "sets about procuring Faust's damnation by the good, old-fashioned, and well-tried method of involving him in guilt, crime and sin – just like any other normal devil" (Mason 307). For readers, Faust's aspiration for experiences so beautiful that he wants them to last forever is a cardinal issue in the drama, and a cardinal issue in Romantic thought – trailing back, it is true, to Doctor Faustus asking Helen to "make me immortal with a kiss" (Marlowe *Doctor Faustus* 5.1.1359). But for Mephistopheles such things are procedurally and contractually nondescript. So it is that John Williams is right to describe Goethe's tragedy as fundamentally a drama of *perspectives*: Faust's, Mephisto's, and The Lord's:

> Mephisto's perspective is partial, and limited; he is aware of his creative function for good ... and yet he must be committed to the aim of dragging Faust down his path to perdition. Faust's perspective is on the one hand more limited than Mephisto's, in so far as he is quite unaware of the issues discussed in the scene in heaven .... On the other hand his perspective is superior to Mephisto's in that ... he is aware of and believes in his higher spiritual urge, aware of a conscience that will, for all the confusion and criminality of his subsequent career, assert itself sufficiently to prevent him from falling hopelessly into the devil's clutches .... The Lord's perspective embraces both the others: he allows for the perpetual error involved in human striving, and he also sanctions the creative function of the [Mephistophelean] "Schalk" ("rogue") in his cosmic scheme. (Williams 89-90)

As Shelley has the Lord say in his translation of the Prologue in Heaven: "The active spirit of man soon sleeps, and soon / He seeks unbroken quiet; therefore I / Have given him the Devil for a companion, / Who may provoke him to some sort of work, / And must create forever" (Shelley *CPW* 743).

Perhaps this is the most significant development of *Faust* to come out of the *Doctor Faustus* tradition. Marlowe's slapstick becomes philosophically self-aware, and it is what John Williams calls "the world of 'Lust und Taten' ... the hurly-burly of life" (Williams 86) that will destroy the hero's soul, rather than an ungodly compact with the Devil:

> action, "Taten", is precisely what Mephistopheles aims to provide for Faust: active involvement in life, not abstract contemplation, "joy and deeds" in place of "reason and learning" – that is, the kind of involvement that can, indeed will, bring with it the error and guilt that the devil must exploit if he is to have any chance of Faust's damnation. (Williams 83)

Satan tempted Christ in the wilderness, but Mephistopheles tempts Faust in the world. "Let us plunge into the rush of things", therefore, as Faust says, "Of time and all its happenings!" (Goethe *Faust* 1 ll. 1754-55).

This lure of *Lust und Taten* – "appetite and deeds" – is a part of what the Devil holds out to Thomas Mann's Faust, the hubristic composer Adrian Leverkühn – whose surname itself suggests "living boldly". (Mann read Marlowe in the early months of work on *Doctor Faustus*, and said that his novel "always stood with one foot" in the sixteenth century. In due course he also came across a compendium of *Faust* chapbooks and dramas from the popular tradition; T. Mann *Genesis of a Novel* 54, 112.) This time there is no need for Mephistopheles to contrive a *Teufelspakt*; it is already in place, via the syphilis the composer contracted with a prostitute years before. "Time is what we sell", the Devil tells Leverkühn – "twenty-four years, shall we say"; but "betwixt us there need be no four crossways in the Spesser Forest and no circles … this visit of mine is intended merely for confirmation" (T. Mann *Doctor Faustus* 245, 263-64). As Martin Swales points out, "cynicism and doubt" are by no means what the Devil depends upon in Mann's case (Swales 87), any more than Marlowe's or Goethe's. Mephistopheles has neither time nor need for what he disparagingly calls "*zersetzende Kritik*" ("ravaging criticism": "one of the key terms of Nazi propaganda", Swales reminds us [88], and frequently associated with so-called cultural Bolshevism).[6] "The Devil, I believe", he says,

> is held to be the man of ravaging criticism? Slander …! God's bodykins! If there be some-thing he hate, something most contrary in all the world, it is ravaging criticism. What he wishes and spends, that is verily the triumph over and beyond such, the shining want of thought [*die prangende Unbedenklichkeit*]. (T. Mann *Doctor Faustus* 252-53)

What Mann's Mephistopheles promises this Faust is "the vital efficacy needed for what you will accomplish with our help" (T. Mann *Doctor Faustus* 258) – with the terrible codicil that Leverkühn "may not love": "Your life shall be cold" (T. Mann *Doctor Faustus* 264). So it is that Mann's novel, like its predecessors, "ends with the Faustian question as to whether man is to be justified in his quest for intensity of being, for crea-tivity" (Swales 90) – that ambiguous urge the Lord speaks of in Goethe's Prologue.

In these ways the Faust myth was transformed in the literary tradition. Goethe added the Margareta motif, the Earth-spirit, and the *Walpurgisnacht*; he retained the opening study soliloquy that was itself Marlowe's addition to the *Faust Book*, but he abandoned Faust's valedictory confession to his students that Thomas Mann reintroduced in Chapter 47 of *Doctor Faustus* before Leverkühn takes his leave of the world. So, too, the nature of Faust's perdition changed over time, from the theological to the existential. We no longer "see where Christ's blood streams in the firmament", one or half a drop of which would save Faustus's soul in Marlowe (Marlowe *Doctor Faustus* 5.2.1463). Of the greatest dramatic significance, perhaps, is the changing relationship of Faust to Mephistopheles, from the spirit "that ever was diligent at Faustus' command" in the *Faust Book* (Marlowe

---

6   The relation of Faustianism to Nazism is developed not just by Thomas Mann but by his son Klaus, in his *Mephisto* of 1936. The central character, Hendrik Höfgen, plays Mephisto in Goethe's tragedy, but essentially is yet another Faust who seals a pact with "the potentate", Hermann Göring, for professional advantage (K. Mann *Mephisto* 180). Göring himself discusses Mephistopheles: "isn't there a little of him in us all? I mean, hidden in every real German isn't there a bit of Mephistopheles, a bit of the rascal and the ruffian? If we had nothing but the soul of Faust, what would become of us? It would be a pushover for our many enemies! No, no, – Mephisto, too, is a German national hero" (K. Mann *Mephisto* 189). Eventually a poetaster, Benjamin Pelz (who boasts of his "bound-less hatred of the dreary tyranny of reason and the bourgeois fetish concept of progress"), spells out a kind of travesty of Adrian Leverkühn: "Our beloved Führer is dragging us toward the shades of darkness and everlasting nothingness. How can we poets, we who have a special affinity for darkness and the lower depths, not admire him?" (K. Mann *Mephisto* 203).

77), to the passive-aggressive co-dependency of Marlowe's tragedy, to the clear implication in Goethe "that Mephisto is indeed Faust's grosser alter ego" as John Williams puts it (Williams 165), to the point made in the anonymous introduction to the *Analysis* of the play read by Byron and Shelley, that "the easiest clue to the moral part of this didactic fiction is, to consider Faust and Mephistopheles as *one* person, represented symbolically, only in a two-fold shape" (Anon. 2), to the creative-cum-intellectual projection of the Devil that Adrian Leverkühn experiences at Palestrina in 1912.

The Deformed Transformed

The Deformed Transformed (*DT*) inserts itself effortlessly into this set of variations on the Faust theme. Marlowe's and Goethe's Fausts are introduced to us as powerfully dissatisfied intellectuals, isolated by choice, like Manfred; Byron's Arnold is more like Caliban and Frankenstein's Monster, with "no home, no kin, / No kind" (*DT* 1.2.35-6), driven away as an abject cripple by his mother to gather firewood. But all three heroes are suicidal: Faustus talks of dispatching himself by one of any number of means (Marlowe *Doctor Faustus*, 2.3.667-74), Faust has a deadly potion to hand, "dark and brown" (Goethe *Faust* 1 l. 733), and Arnold is ready to throw himself on an upturned knife when Byron's "Stranger" appears to him in the guise of a black man out of a cloud. In *Cain* the hero really is morally undermined by the equivalent of *zersetzende Kritik* rather than the hurly-burly of life; but he, like Manfred, Arnold, and all the other Fausts, is intellectually aspirational. "If thou dost long for knowledge", Lucifer tells him, "I can satiate / That thirst" (*Cain* 1.1.558-9), "upon one condition": "That / Thou dost fall down and worship me – thy Lord" (*Cain* 1.1.302-03). In *The Deformed Transformed* the Mephistophelean relation is more egalitarian: the Stranger is the "ironic scold" from Goethe (Goethe *Faust* 1 l. 339), aristocratic but congenial, and a dealer in "fiendish sarcasm", as Arnold puts it, only up to a point (*DT* 1.1.118). His sarcasm mostly falls on deaf ears, as in Goethe. He calls himself Arnold's "servitor" (*DT* 1.1.518), and calls Arnold "my young charge" (*DT* 2.1.170) and "my hero" (*DT* 2.2.1). Arnold conjures up his Mephistopheles, sure enough, as Faustus did his: "Oh … that the devil, to whom they liken me, / Would aid his likeness!" (*DT* 1.1.40-41). The Stranger duly descends, and allows Arnold to leave his old body behind and choose a new form: "The brightest which the world e'er bore" (*DT* 1.1.138). "On what condition?" Arnold insists: "But name your compact: / Must it be signed in blood?" "Not in your own", The Stranger replies: a remark that suggests that Arnold's ultimate crime will be murder – and Byron's marginal note to the fragmentary third part of the drama indicates that the murderee will be Olimpia, married to Arnold/Achilles but attracted to "his former figure," Caesar (Byron *CPW* 6:574).[7] No

---

7   Robinson remains an important study, though in arguing that Byron's drama "is a central document for a literary motif transcending continents and centuries" (Robinson 177) it is the double he has in mind rather than Faust. On the basis of the many intertextual elements converging on the poem (particularly Calderon via Shelley) Robinson is able to speculate that it would end with Arnold's murder of Olimpia out of jealousy: Arnold "would assume

wonder The Stranger tells him, "You shall have no bond / But your own will, no contract save your deeds" (*DT* 1.1.150-51). Once the double transfiguration is complete – Arnold to Achilles, The Stranger to Arnold, now named Caesar – the world of *Lust und Taten* opens up. "But come, pronounce", Caesar asks; "Where shall we now be errant?" "Where the world / Is thickest", Arnold replies, "that I may behold it in / Its workings" – that is, Caesar suggests, "where there is War / And Woman in activity' (*DT* 1.1.492-96). This time the Mephistophelean chaperon has a new role: rather than the "servant" (Goethe *Faust* 1 l. 1648) or "companion" for Faust, he shall be "Yourself for ever by you, as your shadow" (*DT* 1.1.458). "I would be spared this", Arnold protests, but it is all too late. "To horse! to horse!". Caesar commands (in words incongruously taken from Walter Scott's "War Song of the Edinburgh Light Dragoons"): "From the Alps to the Caucasus, ride we, or fly! / For we'll leave them behind in the glance of an eye" (*DT* 1.1.567-68).

"Byron may not … have read Marlowe's *Doctor Faustus* at the time he wrote *Manfred*", Anne Barton writes: "He certainly read it afterwards" (Barton 217). She gave no support for this conclusion – though Byron's naming the heroically suicidal heroine of *The Deformed Transformed* Olimpia suggests that he knew *Tamburlaine*. Perhaps the best piece of evidence for the statement is straightforward: that the world of *Lust und Taten* to which Caesar takes Arnold is nowhere else but the "bright resplendent Rome" that Faustus visits (Marlowe *Doctor Faustus* 3.1.866), as per the *Faust Book* and Reformation anti-Catholicism. There is no Roman episode in Goethe, where the scenario is German throughout; Byron's dramatic decision suggests that, like Thomas Mann, he stood with one foot in the sixteenth century.

The Rome of Marlowe's 1616 Quarto is unabashedly unhistorical, with twelfth-century and sixteenth-century events sharing the stage. "The reader should not, however", Clifford Davidson writes, "be offended at Marlowe's use of anachronism; undoubtedly he was deliberately telescoping Adrian IV and Alexander III with Adrian VI, a Pope who reigned during the life-time of the historical Faustus …. There was no reason why Marlowe should not present a character put together from hints and snatches of history" (Davidson 236). But Byron's procedures are a world away from Marlowe in this regard. The Rome he carries Arnold to is the reverse of bright and resplendent and is as unambiguously historical as could be, focusing on the sack of the city of 1527. The choice returns us to Faust's century of origin, but it serves a wider set of purposes than that. The sack of Rome has often been regarded as a watershed in European history. It marks both the end of the Renaissance – "The Sapienza, Rome's famous university, was completely ruined" (Hook 178); "The school of Raphael, famous throughout Europe, was completely broken up" (Hook 179) – and the beginning of the Counter-Reformation. The

---

the spiritual depravity of Caesar just as Caesar had assumed Arnold's physical deformities" (Robinson 194). Anne Barton agrees: "Byron must have intended Arnold, in a jealous fury, to kill Olimpia and then follow this act of violence with another in which, by striking down his mocking doppelgänger, he would in effect commit suicide, and be damned forever" (Barton 216).

closer liaison between the papacy and the Holy Roman Empire, and the expansion of Spanish interests in the peninsula at large, both engineered by Charles V in the aftermath of 1527, had the effect of both stifling early forms of *Italianità* until the Risorgimento and (since Charles was Katharine of Aragon's nephew) of driving Henry VIII towards the disestablishment of the Church in England. Yet for an event of this magnitude, the sack's origins are peculiarly murky. "The 'fortuitous' act or event", André Chastel suggests,

> like the notion of fate, does not impress the historian until it is given meaning and dimension by the collective conscience. This holds true for the sack of Rome. The decline that within a few short years plunged the capital of Christendom into an abyss was caused by an accumulation of circumstances; the precise details were unforeseeable, but one can clearly see the irreparable consequences of each small mistake. (Chastel 9)

It was an "accumulation of circumstances" that Byron studied with care in the available historiography (see Byron *CPW* 6:732). Charles, Duke of Bourbon had been appointed Constable of France by Francis I in 1515, but eight years later had been driven from the country as a traitor. Having fought for Charles V at the Battle of Pavia in 1525, at which Francis was defeated and imprisoned, Bourbon was sent by the Emperor on a punitive raid against Pope Clement, Francis's ally, as commander of a profoundly mutinous army made up of German Lutherans, Spanish Catholics, and Italian mercenaries. Unsupplied and unpaid, Bourbon could keep this force together only with the promise of the wealth of Rome – and Pope Clement had meanwhile settled his issues with Charles, so making the entire enterprise futile anyway. Now pursued by the anti-imperial forces left or reassembled after Pavia in the League of Cognac, Bourbon abandoned his artillery and sought entry to the apparently impregnable city via siege ladders within a day of his arrival on 5 May, only to be shot dead by Cellini, according to the sculptor's own account (Cellini 60). Bourbon's death removed the last restraint on an army that had already pillaged numerous northern Italian cities and now transformed Rome into what Cellini called (Cellini 66) a "cruel, hellish place". The expression was not unwarranted. "What Goths, what Vandals, what Turks were ever like this army of the emperor in the sacrilege they have committed?" one witness asked:

> Volumes would be needed to describe but one of their misdeeds. They strewed on the ground the sacred body of Christ, took away the cup, and trod under foot the relics of the saints to spoil their ornaments. No church or monastery was spared. They violated nuns amid the cries of their mothers, burnt the most magnificent buildings, turned churches into stables, made use of crucifixes and other images as marks for their harquebuses. It is no longer Rome but Rome's grave. (Chastel 106)

"It seems to me", Cardinal Francesco Gonzaga wrote, "that the whole world has been turned topsy-turvy" (Hook 285). A semblance of order was returned to the city only in February 1528.

Byron was a past master at siege literature, as *The Siege of Corinth* and the seventh and eighth cantos of *Don Juan* (drafted at much the same time as *The Deformed Transformed*) demonstrate. But Anne Barton is surely right to suggest that the Roman event "was bound to register as a horror and desecration greater than the previous two, and not only because of the atrocities Byron found recorded in his sources. His own visit to Rome, in 1817, had provided him with one of the most intense imaginative experiences of his entire life" (Barton 210) – reflected in climactic visions in both *Childe Harold's Pilgrimage* (*CHP*) 4, and *Manfred*. In those earlier visions Rome stood for the palimpsest of history ("Rome is as the desert, where we steer / Stumbling o'er recollections" [*CHP* 4.726-27]; "Ivy usurps the laurel's place of growth" [*Manfred* 3.4.26], and so on). Now it stood for *Lust und Taten* to the ultimate degree. The only purpose of Bourbon's army was to maintain itself by violence; the only military significance of Rome was to provide a military object. The sack is historically absurd: an accumulation of circumstances like the notion of fate.

Thus, there is nothing random about Byron's choice of the sack of Rome. He is following out the Mephistophelean mission to bring about damnation by raw experience and a "shining *want* of thought". When the drama arrives at Rome on 5 May 1527 it is clear that Caesar and Arnold have accompanied Bourbon throughout his grotesque campaign. Arnold feels he has been "lured ... / Through scenes of blood and lust", and his "path / Hath been over carcases" (*DT* I.2.19-20, 1-2) – like the "life's wastes" Mephistopheles plans to drag Goethe's Faust through ("every kind / Of meaningless banality"; Goethe *Faust* 1 ll. 1860-61). But for every Mephistopheles there is always a *primum mobile*, a "fixed Necessity" that his Faust (despite appearances and assurances) must obey (*DT* 1.2.31-32):

> From the star
> To the winding worm, all life is motion; and
> In life *commotion* is the extremest point
> Of life. (*DT* 1.2.23-25)

Like *Faust*, *The Deformed Transformed* is a drama of perspectives, only without a Prologue in Heaven setting them proleptically in order. Caesar's perspective here is something like Lucifer's in *Cain*, quintessentially diabolical: "The planet wheels", he says, "till it becomes / A comet, and destroying as it sweeps / The stars, goes out" (*DT* 1.2.25-27). Rome has been a "never-ceasing scene of slaughter / For ages" (*DT* 1.2.89-90):

> They are gone,
> And others come: so flows the wave on wave
> Of what these creatures call eternity,
> Deeming themselves the breakers of the ocean,
> While they are but the bubbles, ignorant
> That foam is their foundation. (*DT* 2.2.52-57)

"I must play with these poor puppets", accordingly, Caesar reflects (*DT* 1.2.320). Bourbon, on the other hand, is the *victim* of this delusion, and that is his perspective. The "mighty spirits" of "imperious Rome" warn him to retreat (*DT* 1.2.188-94), but the historical succession encourages him to attack:

> Civilized, Barbarian,
> Or Saintly, still the walls of Romulus
> Have been the Circus of an Empire. Well!
> 'Twas their turn – now 'tis ours ... (*DT* 1.2.280-83)

No wonder he comes to grief with comic inevitability. "Now boys! On! on!" he shouts, with his foot on the ladder. "And off!" Caesar adds with black relish, as the heroic commander is immediately shot (*DT* 2.1.126). "Oh these immortal men! and their great motives!" (*DT* 2.1.169) is basically a comment from the first perspective on the futility of the second. Finally, Arnold's perspective is strikingly like Faust's, as John Williams describes it: "superior to Mephisto's in that … he is aware of and believes in his higher spiritual urge" (Williams 89), which is love. His mother rejects him as "a monstrous sport of nature" at the beginning of the drama (*DT* 1.1.15) when all he needs is a kind word from her; his, he later insists, is "a heart all love", which she has broken (*DT* 1.1.339); he is tempted to transform into Antony, "who lost / The ancient world for love" (*DT* 1.1.236-37); and he chooses Achilles in order to compel affection in those "of whom I / Would be beloved" (*DT* 1.1.360-61). "I love and I shall be beloved! Oh life! / At last I feel thee!" is his ecstatic reaction to his transformation (*DT* 1.1.420-21). For him love *is* life. But as Charles Robinson and Anne Barton have shown, Arnold is doomed to disappointment. Like every other Faust "his life will be cold", like Leverkühn's; Olimpia will ironically gravitate towards Arnold's shadow, the identity he was so eager to abandon at the play's opening, and so he will become jealous of himself.

If military heroism and love are both snuffed out in "the wave on wave" of time and history – and if the tantalizing figure of Cellini, with whom Byron could surely have done more (contrasting the artist with the man of action, for example), only "disappears through the portico" after three lines (*DT* 2.2.43) – is there anything left in "life's wastes"? Is Arnold's "superior perspective" just another illusion? Not entirely, because unfinished as it is *The Deformed Transformed* is still a work of art, able to comprehend things its protagonists cannot. The Tower of Babel, for example, is alluded to by Caesar appropriately enough, given the "varied nations" (*DT* 2.1.57) of Bourbon's army; but on each occasion the cultural and historical relativism the legend symbolizes is subjected to dramatic criticism. When Caesar first alludes to Babel Arnold simply tells him to "Be silent" and listen to the besieging soldiers' singing, "Softened by distance to a hymn-like cadence" (*DT* 1.2.118-19): suggesting that military violence can itself be subject to a higher, "softening" perspective. On its second outing a Lutheran is shot by one of the Pope's Swiss Guards on the point of assassinating the Pope; but Clement lives to fight another day, despite Caesar's reductive comments about the "comic pantomime" of history (*DT* 2.3.32).

An image more deeply integrated in the drama, given its Faustian obsession with the double and the alter ego, is that of *twins*: Arnold and Caesar, their two horses Huon and Memnon, War and Woman, blood and lust, Francis and Bourbon ("our leader from France is", sing the besieging troops, "Who warred with his brother"; *DT* 1.2.165-66), Lutherans and Catholics, "the mild twins – Gore and Glory" (*DT* 2.2.12), and Olimpia and Penthesilea, but above all Romulus and Remus – rescued from their she-wolf wet nurse, the story says, by a shepherd named Faustulus. Romulus's murder of Remus brings the pattern to a murderous focus. "Roma's sire forgot his mother", according to the Chorus of Spirits at the beginning of the drama's second part, "When he slew his gallant twin, / With inexpiable sin":

> See the giant Shadow stride
> O'er the ramparts high and wide!
> When he first overleapt thy wall,
> Its foundation mourned his fall.
> Now, though towering like a Babel,
> Who to stop his steps are able?
> Stalking o'er thy highest dome,
> Remus claims his vengeance, Rome! (*DT* 2.1.74-84)

The story from Plutarch that Romulus killed Remus in anger for jumping over the fortifications of his preferred site for what would become Rome attaches itself not just to the sack overall ("Christians war against Christ's shrine"; *DT* 2.1.39), but to Bourbon specifically as Remus reincarnate, killed re-ascending the battlements of Rome but unleashing a terrible revenge even in death on its citizens, "the great robber sons of Fratricide" (*DT* 1.2.88). The ironical perspective of history, which Byron employed in so many of his major works from *Childe Harold* onwards, does not tell the whole truth. "Deformity is daring", Arnold tells The Stranger: "It is its essence to o'ertake mankind" (*DT* 1.1313-14). Like Marlowe's Faustus he will try his brains to gain a deity (Marlowe *Doctor Faustus* 1.1.93); but like Goethe's Faust he is ultimately "The unhoused, the fugitive, / The aimless, restless reprobate" (Goethe *Faust* 1 ll. 3348-49) caught up in historical patterns, but also intermittently capable of comprehending and even transforming them.

The Faust Syndrome: A Philosophical Perspective

But to insert Lord Byron into the history of Anglo-Germanic Faustianism is to insert him into what, exactly? What are the origins of "Faustianism" that it should have persisted for 400 years in Western culture? No discussion of this length could answer that question, but perhaps some light can be shed on it from a philosophical point of view, especially as the myth (like those of Robinson Crusoe and Frankenstein) is so manifestly a product of *modern* thought.

"We would like to know what, as moral agents", Iris Murdoch writes, "we have got to do because of logic, what we have got to do because of human nature, and what we can choose to do" (Murdoch 2). This is a set of distinctions fundamental to modern philosophy, and *The Sovereignty of Good* pits itself against what Murdoch sees as a fundamentally reductive psychological reading of them – "a Luciferian philosophy" (Murdoch 48) – under the terms of which "goodness is not an object of insight or knowledge, it is a function of the will" (Murdoch 4). That philosophical tradition, with its "inflated and yet empty conception of the will" (Murdoch 76), invariably prioritizes agency over contemplation, and movement over vision. ("All life is motion", as Caesar tells Achilles/ Arnold.) For it, "actions are, roughly, instances of moving things about in the public world"; "Our personal being is the movement of our overtly choosing will"; and "Immense care is taken to picture the will as isolated" from other mental perspectives such as belief, reason, and feeling (Murdoch 5, 8).

Whether Murdoch's characterization of this tradition (which she associates with the likes of A. J. Ayer, Stuart Hampshire, Richard Hare, Wittgenstein, and, ultimately Heidegger: possibly "Lucifer in person"; Murdoch 72) is accurate hardly matters in this context. It is an image of humanity that she has in mind:

> It is behaviourist in its connection of the meaning and being of action with the publicly observable, it is existentialist in its elimination of the substantial self and its emphasis on the solitary omnipotent will, and it is utilitarian in its assumption that morality is and can only be concerned with public acts. (Murdoch 9)

That image is the one embodied in Faust, from the Renaissance to the twentieth century. Under its terms, "What I am 'objectively' is not under my control; logic and observers decide that. What I am 'subjectively' is a foot-loose, solitary, substanceless will" (Murdoch 16). "Here I stand alone, in total responsibility and freedom, and can only properly and responsibly do what is intelligible to me, what I can do with a clear intention" (Murdoch 30). But it is very much part of Murdoch's case – of profound relevance to the Faust myth – that existentialism has its dark side as well as its (apparently) light and lucid one: a turn "towards determinism, towards fatalism, towards regarding freedom as a complete illusion", that she associates with Dostoevsky and Sartre. "When I deliberate the die is already cast. Forces within me which are dark to me have already made the decision" (Murdoch 36). The perspective of the (delusory) "clear intention", one might say, is Faust's; the perspective of determinism and fatalism is that of Mephistopheles; and the dramas are tragic because the first perspective is brought to rack and ruin by the second. Every time Doctor Faustus reaches up to Christ's blood in the firmament, despair brings him down. Faust is therefore the embodiment of *Angst*, which is, Murdoch argues, "a disease or addiction of those who are passionately convinced that personality resides solely in the conscious omnipotent will," and who cannot bear or even comprehend the notion that "moral change and moral achievement are slow", beyond the reach of the kinds of revolutionary change that Faust anticipates (Murdoch 39).

What we learn from art like that of Marlowe, Goethe, Byron, and Thomas Mann, by contrast – art *about* the behaviourist, existentialist, and utilitarian Faustian condition – "is something about the real quality of human nature when it is envisaged, in the artist's just and compassionate vision, with a clarity which does not belong to the self-centred rush of ordinary life" (Murdoch 65). The self-centred rush, the resplendent or brutal world of *Lust und Taten*, and the choice of motion over vision and agency over contemplation are lures the Faust-writers lay before us, Byron included.

Works Cited

Anon. *An Analysis of Goethe's Tragedy of Faust, in Illustration of Retsch's Series of Outlines, Engraved from the Originals by Henry Moses*. London: Boosey and Sons, 1820.

Barton, Anne. "*Don Juan* Transformed". *Byron: Augustan and Romantic*. Ed. Andrew Rutherford. Basingstoke: Macmillan, 1990. 199-220.

Burwick, Frederick and James A. McCusick, eds. *Faustus from the German of Goethe Translated by Samuel Taylor Coleridge*. Oxford: Oxford UP, 2007.

Byron, Lord [George Gordon]. *Complete Poetical Works*. Ed. Jerome J. McGann. 7 vols. Oxford: Oxford UP, 1980-93.

Byron's Letters and Journals. Ed. Leslie A. Marchand. 12 vols. London: John Murray, 1973-82.

Cellini, Benvenuto. *My Life*. Trans. Julia Conaway Bondanella and Peter Bondanella. Oxford: Oxford UP, 2002.

Chastel, André. *The Sack of Rome, 1527*. Trans. Beth Archer. Princeton: Princeton UP, 1983.

Davidson, Clifford. "Doctor Faustus at Rome". *Studies in English Literature, 1500-1900* 9.2 (1969): 231-39.

Goethe, Johann Wolfgang von. *Faust: Part One*. Trans. David Luke. Oxford: Oxford UP, 1987.

Hazlitt, William. *Complete Works*. Ed. P. P. Howe. 21 vols. London: Dent, 1931-34.

Hook, Judith. *The Sack of Rome, 1527*. London: Macmillan, 1972.

Jones, Frederick L., ed. *The Letters of Percy Bysshe Shelley*. 2 vols. London: Oxford UP, 1964.

Lovell, Ernest J., ed. *His Very Self and Voice: Collected Conversations of Lord Byron*. New York: Macmillan, 1954.

Mann, Klaus. *Mephisto*. Trans. Robin Smyth. London: Penguin, 1995.

Mann, Thomas. *Doctor Faustus*. Trans. John E. Woods. New York: Knopf, 1997.

---. *Thomas Mann's Addresses Delivered at the Library of Congress 1942-1949*. Washington: Library of Congress, 1963.

---. *The Genesis of a Novel*. Trans. Richard and Clara Winston. London: Secker and Warburg, 1961.

Marlowe, Christopher. *Doctor Faustus* with *The English Faust Book*. Ed. David Wootton. Indianapolis: Hackett, 2005.

Mason, Eudo C. *Goethe's* Faust: *Its Genesis and Purport*. Berkeley: University of California Press, 1967.

Medwin, Thomas. *Conversations of Lord Byron*. Ed. Ernest J. Lovell, Jr. Princeton: Princeton UP, 1966.

Murdoch, Iris. *The Sovereignty of Good*. London: Routledge and Kegan Paul, 1970.

Robinson, Charles E. "The Devil as Doppelgänger in *The Deformed Transformed*: The Sources and Meaning of Byron's Unfinished Drama". *Bulletin of the New York Public Library* 74 (1970): 177-202.

Shelley, Percy Bysshe. *Complete Poetical Works*. Ed. Thomas Hutchinson. London: Oxford UP, 1914.

Swales, Martin. *Thomas Mann: A Study*. London: Heinemann, 1980.

Williams, John R. *Goethe's Faust*. London: Allen and Unwin, 1987.

Diego Saglia

Of Flesh and Boundaries: Transgressing Gaps and Orifices in Romantic Orientalism

It is hardly a contentious point to make that the Romantic-period imagination is criss-crossed by boundaries and borders inviting countless forms of negotiation and trans-gression. If "[a]ll limits call for a crossing", as Bertrand Westphal puts it (Westphal 41), Jeffrey Cass emphasizes how recent Romantic studies tend to focus on the "proliferation of crossings" of the multiple lines and borders marking the period's geographical, his-torical, and cultural environment and imagination (Cass 11). Tracing a progressively expansive geo-cultural panorama, Cass notes that, even "within the lone context of Brit-ish romanticism, the boundaries (if they exist at all) are not only unstable, they actually riot outward from Greenwich to the ends of the earth and back again" (Cass 2). This nexus of borders, boundaries, and crossings produces literature that is intrinsically "het-erotopian – the gateway to elsewhere – to remote and previously inaccessible otherness" (Cass 10).

With this complexity in mind, in the following pages I concentrate on what was arguably one of the most intricate and pervasive sites of boundaries and crossings in the Romantic period – the line between East and West. Mobile and unstable, since single representa-tions place them in widely divergent locations, from the South of Spain to China, the evanescent borders of the Orient were constantly reinvented and utterly ubiquitous in Romantic-era literature.

A text that speaks of this multiplication and dispersal in emblematic form is Felicia Hemans's lyric "Casabianca" (1826) about the boy "on the burning deck" of the French flagship *L'Orient*, which had transported Napoleon on his expedition to Egypt in 1798 and was destroyed by the British under Horatio Nelson at the Battle of Aboukir. Caught up in the explosion, the body of young Giacomo Casabianca, the son of the ship's com-mander, is torn to pieces and scattered across the scene together with the ship's splintered mast and planks: "There came a burst of thunder sound – / The boy – oh! where was he? / Ask of the winds that far around / With fragments strewed the sea! –" ("Casabianca" ll. 33-36). Climaxing on the fate of the noble and loyal boy, Hemans's lines dramatically locate his fragments on the restless surface of the sea through expressions of place ("where", "far around", "the sea") that repeatedly point to the poem's setting – Aboukir Bay, where one of the mouths of the Nile flows into the Mediterranean, and where the French fleet was anchored on Napoleon's orders. In light of this locative emphasis, the poem reads also as a powerfully allusive orientalist text. Besides referring to a place and an event inextricably bound up with Western control of an oriental area, it refers to the pervasiveness of the East in Romantic-era literature: just as the Orient enshrined in the ship's name blows up and covers the sea around with fragments, so traces of the Orient are dispersed throughout Romantic-period culture. And these traces reach all the way to distant outposts like the Highlands in William Wordsworth's "The Solitary Reaper" (1807), where a Gaelic song transmutes into a melody wafting in "some shady haunt, / Among Arabian sands" (ll. 11-12, Wordsworth 1:657), so that the Orient functions as a medium for translating and making familiar the impenetrable words and exotic sounds intoned by the titular character.

Hemans's scene of fragmentation and dispersal also posits the Romantic Orient as the site of iterated processes of *mise en abîme* based on the recycling and re-envisioning of heterogeneous materials. Confronting the Romantics' "'infinitely diversified' Asia" and the "shifting parameters" of the period's "collective imaginary of the East", critical approaches to Romantic orientalism have given rise to an endless fugue of interpretations both in dialogue with, and diverging from, Saidian perspectives (Watt 8, 3). Within this frayed picture, a recurrent feature of the Romantic Orient is its tendency to translate into writing centred on liminalities to be crossed and, in turn, transgressed. As Andrew Warren argues, second-generation orientalism can be envisaged as a collective text informed by repeated negotiations of the "porous border between self and other, autonomy and influence, action and reflection" (Warren 22). More broadly, the Orient and its boundaries are a Romantic master trope condensing questions of otherness and what David Simpson terms the pivotal "question of the stranger" in Romanticism – an inherently fissured trope, given the instability of an East/West border that is both material and intangible, a *limes* (the frontier or boundary, a mark of enclosure) and a *limen* (a threshold) – the former, when transgressed, mutating into the latter, a site of access to another zone, a place of opening, transition, and transformation (Simpson 11).[1]

These premisses take us back to some familiar questions: where does the East end and the West begin? Where do the archaic and the modern, the barbaric and the civilized, clearly diverge? Overlaps are patent in Romantic representations of a contact zone such as the South of Spain, that fuzzy border with Africa and the Orient emblematically located at one of Europe's westernmost points, as is visible in Byron's portrait of Donna Julia in the first canto of *Don Juan* (*DJ*):

> The darkness of her oriental eye
> Accorded with her Moorish origin;
> (Her blood was not all Spanish, by the by;
> In Spain, you know, this is a sort of sin.)
> When proud Grenada fell, and, forced to fly,
> Boabdil wept, of Donna Julia's kin
> Some went to Africa, some staid in Spain,
> Her great great grandmamma chose to remain. (*DJ* 1.56)

The divide between East and West, Spain and Africa, Islam and Christianity lies in, as well as on, Julia's body. It is in her blood and visible in her physical appearance. Histori-

---

1   On the difference between *limen* and *limes*, see Westphal 98. More generally, see also Tally.

cally, it is bound up with the fall of Granada and the end of the last Muslim kingdom in Western Europe in 1492, as well as the expulsions of the Moors beginning in the same year, which saw another line being crossed, that between the Old and the New World, and the opening up of dizzying transatlantic vistas. By the same token, though, this divide is also conspicuously transgressed by Julia's "not all Spanish" blood. Thus, straddling the multiple boundaries she embodies, Juan's first sexual transgression is also racially, culturally, and historically connoted. His family boasts *pureza de sangre* (purity of blood), his father being described as "[a] true Hidalgo, free from every stain / Of Moor or Hebrew blood, he traced his source / Through the most Gothic gentlemen of Spain" (*DJ* 1.9.2-4). This heritage collides with Julia's impurity, a fact that heightens the explosively transgressive nature of her sexual relationship with Juan. As Caroline Franklin remarks, "Julia's heredity identifies her with paganism and Southern passion", making her a personification of that subversive, second-generation "Cult of the South" opposing the conservative-led cultural climate of the immediate post-Waterloo years (Franklin 125; Butler 1981, 121-37; see also Lew 174). Envisaging Julia also as partly Oriental illuminates her sexual acts with Juan as expressions of another outstanding feature of the East-West border – its many holes and gaps, those apertures that, by making the dividing line passable, invite the transgressor in. With a nod to Deleuze and Guattari's contrast between smooth and striated space, Westphal considers such imbrications of the geographical, the spatial, and the bodily as evidence that "[t]ransgression is not just crossing porous boundary lines" but also "assumes a closed and striated space and a will to penetrate" (Westphal 42).

This dynamic of blockage and transit is central to a foundational but seldom examined work in the Romantic orientalist canon: Thomas Beddoes's *Alexander's Expedition down the Hydaspes and the Indus to the Indian Ocean* (1792). Originating from the radical milieu of late-eighteenth Bristol, this is a poem simultaneously about and against empire. A doctor based in the West Country port and known for his use of laughing gas (Coleridge and Southey famously took part in his experiments), Beddoes was a fervent democrat and supporter of French revolutionary ideals, as well as an active critic of Britain's commercial and military overseas expansionism and slave-based colonial economy. Written in blank verse and heavily laden with notes and appendices, his poem addresses these concerns by charting the protagonist's eastward progress and evaluating his Asian exploits.

In *Alexander's Expedition* Beddoes portrays the ancient hero as a model of Enlightenment, while also refraining from celebrating him as a forerunner of Britain's present-day expansionistic ambitions. Instead, he harnesses the initial success and eventual failure of Alexander's Indian campaign to criticize contemporary imperialism, its mythology of commerce, and attendant constructions of India as an inexhaustible storehouse of commodities and goods (see Saglia 2019, 163-81). The poem traces an ideology of "radical imperialism" and, as Nigel Leask observes, while castigating both India's caste system and Britain's conquest monopoly, it announces that these evils will be dispelled by the onset of "free trade and its inevitable concomitant social modernization" (Leask 92-93).

Accordingly, both poetic text and notes are threaded through with forms of liminality and transgression, and the protagonist is depicted as a figure in transit from the outset:

> Now the new Lord of Persia's wide domain
> Down the fierce Hydaspes seeks the Indian Main;
> High on the leading prow the Conqueror stands,
> Eyes purer skies, and marks diverging strands. (*Alexander's Expedition* 1-2)

Transgression of the *limes* is inscribed in the references to Alexander's push towards India's "purer skies" and across the boundary of the Hydaspes, and reappears in the narrator's address to the Indian natives:

> … You, mild tenants of the peaceful shore,
> Which ne'er Invader's step profaned before,
> Who bask secure mid your sunny glades,
> Or ply the loom beneath your scented shades,
> How throbbed each gentle breast with wild alarms,
> As o'er you burst the startling blaze of arms? (*Alexander's Expedition* 10-12)

The boundary returns in aptly mutable forms as Alexander's army advances:

> And now the Hosts, on India's sultry verge,
> See smooth-spread shores receive the sailing Surge;
> Hoarse round his sinuous sweep of marshy bounds
> Hear Ocean murmur storm-portending sounds,
> Or roar, impatient, from his wave-worn cells,
> Loud o'er the lands, where listening Plenty dwells. (*Alexander's Expedition* 27)

Representing an invasion that crosses multiple geographical lines, Beddoes challenges expectations by casting it as a potentially beneficial event inspired by Alexander's "originality" of genius, the "enlargement of his conceptions", and "equity of his mind" (*Alexander's Expedition* 25). He extols the conqueror's "liberal policy in the treatment of his conquered subjects" in contrast to present-day "West-India planters" and their allies in power (*Alexander's Expedition* 25). And the body once again reinforces this interpretation, as the narrative of Alexander's eastward march is scattered with references to his physical presence: his invasion of India is effected by his armies as well as through the projection of his superhuman physique over Asia. Towering over the opening line ("High on the leading prow the Conqueror stands"), Alexander's body as a conduit for East/West transgression resurfaces in the following imperial apotheosis:

> Around the soul-wrapt Chief – in crowded rings
> His kindling warriors press – the destined Kings,
> Of mighty states – They catch the monarch's fire:
> Their gestures, soon, the train remote inspire;
> From soul to soul triumphant ardours run,
> And all partake the bliss of Philip's son (*Alexander's Expedition* 26)

Alexander's central position in this circular picture bodies forth a desire for triumph and power that clashes with the humane principles of peace and prosperity motivating the Indian campaign. Even though he has to stop his advance, the conqueror's westbound journey is not presented as a retreat, but as a "Triumphant March" back, and Beddoes ultimately declares him to be "encouraged and confirmed in his great commercial scheme" (*Alexander's Expedition* viii). From start to finish, Alexander's progress beyond the *limes* stands in an ambivalent relation to the processes of subjugation and liberation, altruism and the will to power, that ground the poem's intriguingly enigmatic textuality.

A few years after the publication of *Alexander's Expedition*, Walter Savage Landor composed an epic about another eastbound conqueror, a transgressor and unusual imperialist driven by a hunger for conquest but also deeply conflicted about it (and one who eventually meets with a much worse fate than Beddoes's Alexander). *Gebir* (1798) brought Landor to critical attention, receiving high praise from some quarters – Southey wrote enthusiastically about it in the *Critical Review* for September 1799 – though it was also widely accused of excessive obscurity or even utter incomprehensibility.[2] An epic in seven cantos reworking a prose tale from Clara Reeve's *The Progress of Romance* (1785), *Gebir* centres on the eponymous Iberian king's attempted conquest of Queen Charoba's Egypt. Its narrative follows the dual movements of Gebir's invasion and the Egyptians' resistance. A terrified Charoba consults her nurse and advisor, Dalica, who suggests that she placate the conqueror by feigning interest in him; however, the queen genuinely falls in love. Gebir decides to rebuild the ruined city of Sidad, originally founded by one of his ancestors, but its reconstruction by day is undone by magic at night. As conquest is delayed indefinitely, he visits the underworld to gain useful knowledge for its fulfilment. Eventually, the queen and the Western invader's wedding-day approaches, and Dalica, who believes Charoba to be pretending, obtains a poisoned shirt from her sister, the sorceress Myrthyr. During the festivities, Dalica places it around Gebir's shoulders and, as the poison spreads, he dies a slow and painful death. A heartbroken Charoba is left to mourn, and the Iberian conquest of Egypt is averted.

Mapped on familiar epic *topoi*, the poem's opening puts invasion and transgression firmly centre stage:

> I sing the fates of Gebir! ...
> ... incens'd
> By meditating on primeval wrongs,
> He blew his battle-horn, at which uprose
> Whole nations: how, ten thousand, mightiest men,
> He call'd aloud; and soon Charoba saw
> His dark helm hover o'er the land of Nile. (*Gebir* 1.12-21)

This opening vision of darkness looming over Egypt is reinforced by Dalica's later condemnation of Gebir's territorial encroachment: "with lust of power inflamed / The western winds have landed [him] on our coast" (*Gebir* 5.136-37). Blending sexual desire and desire for power, this couplet foreshadows the interlinking of Gebir's eastward transit with the theme of the body – desiring and desired, the hero's and the queen's – through

---

2   Incidentally, Landor first drafted some sections in Latin, which he then translated into English. In 1803 he published a full Latin version of the poem, *Gebirus*. See Tucker 82.

which the poem works out the tension between Western transgression and Eastern resistance. The trespassing of the boundary is present in Gebir's desire for the conquest of
Egypt, which, through the clichéd equation of woman and country, becomes desire for
Charoba, who in turn develops feelings for her antagonist ("He pity'd me: he lov'd me,
he obey'd; / He was a conqueror, still am I a queen" *Gebir* 4.148-49).

Centred on transgressive desires destined to implode, Landor's poem reaches one of its
climaxes in the disintegration of Gebir's body on his wedding day (a second, more aus-
picious plotline concludes with the union of Gebir's brother Tamar and a nymph of the
Nile, whose progeny will bring enlightenment and freedom to humanity). In the scene
of the hero's gruesome death, modelled on that of Hercules caused by the poisoned shirt
of Nessus in Sophocles' *Women of Trachis*, Landor carefully orchestrates the hero's and
the queen's actions and reactions through keywords related to the physical:

> She [Charoba] hung upon his bosom, prest his lips,
> Breath'd, and would feign it his that she resorbed;
> She chafed the feathery softness of his veins,
> That swell'd out black, like tendrils round their vase
> After libation: lo! he moves! he groans!
> He seems to struggle from the grasp of death. (*Gebir* 7.236-41)

As Gebir's blood blackens and his veins thicken and freeze, his body becomes a reticulation of dark lines ("tendrils") that bespeak his thirst for power ("libation") and are
allusive of the lines on a map. A chart of borders and boundaries, his dying body is also
inscribed with a blackness that intimates the racial implications in the East/West and
Europe/Africa binarism. These features complicate further the political import of a poem
suffused with Francophilia, and the publication of which happened to coincide with
France's expedition to Egypt in 1798. Since *Gebir* simultaneously incriminates and extols imperial expansionism, James Watt perceptively envisages it as a "complex fable of
liberty and empire", which demonizes *ancien régime* despotism and endorses "liberal
imperialism" while also subscribing to a radical Enlightenment discourse of "Islamic
republicanism" (Watt 158). Providing a key to these intricacies, Herbert Tucker notes
that, as a product of the 1790s, the poem reads "like a young British Jacobin poet's un-
repentant belatedness within that rightward-veering decade" (Tucker 80). These disso-
nances are keyed into a poem that, as Adam Roberts argues, thrives on "misunderstand-
ing, the instability of interpretation, and the tendency of intense emotion to overwhelm
clean comprehension" (Roberts 92). *Gebir*'s negotiation of boundaries illuminates further these formal and ideological fluctuations, which are inseparable from its geo-cultural transitions and transgressions, and from the contradictory flows of desire that
power them.

Landor's poem made a substantial contribution to the Romantics' protracted and fraught
engagements with epos. It offered an alluring reinterpretation of neoclassical aesthetics
through what Tucker calls its "arresting vignette descriptions of scene and action, struck
off in clean fresh lines of blank verse" (Tucker 80), while its re-invention of classical
epic doubles as a reworking of romance and its quest narrative based on repeated

crossings of visible and invisible demarcations. Indeed, it is also because of its statutory deployment of spaces to be entered and negotiated that romance is central to Romantic representations of the East as a geography of unauthorized, perilous transitions – most visibly in William Beckford's paradigmatic orientalist fantasia *Vathek* (1786). In Fred Botting's terms, this novella is an exemplary script of excess pervaded by the "fascination with transgression" that informs the Gothic aesthetic and its countervailing tendency to the "reconstitution of limits and boundaries" (Botting 2, 8).[3] In its labyrinthine transcription of unlawful longings writ large (or small), desire and its dangers are inscribed in the minuscule characters carved into the magic sabre the caliph purchases from a mysterious foreigner, the monstrous-looking "giaour". Tantalizingly unreadable and endlessly metamorphic, these characters excite Vathek's desire beyond all rational control: "Agitated with so much anxiety, Vathek entirely lost all firmness; a fever seized him, and his appetite failed. Instead of being one of the greatest eaters, he became as distinguished for drinking. So insatiable was the thirst which tormented him, that his mouth, like a funnel, was always open to receive the various liquors that might be poured into it, and especially cold water, which calmed him more than every other" (*Vathek* 12).

Goaded to a madness of desire, Vathek is subsequently tempted by the giaour to acquire power on a global scale. The demonic stranger urges the caliph on his accursed, blasphemous quest with patently transgressive words:

> adore … the terrestrial influences, and abjure Mahomet … On these conditions I will bring thee to the Palace of Subterranean Fire. There shalt thou behold, in immense depositories, the treasures which the stars have promised thee … the talismans that control the world. (*Vathek* 22)

There follows a journey into "dark spaces and unexplored geographical areas", which, as Massimiliano Demata remarks, outlines a space organized around the "bordering of the known with the unknown" (Demata 19). During their doomed quest, Vathek and his retinue cross a number of boundaries, the most formidable of which is the vast desert separating them from their goal, the underground city of Istakhar. Guarded by the giaour, the city's gates are the final line awaiting transgression:

> "Ye are welcome!" said he to them, with a ghastly smile, "in spite of Mahomet, and all his dependents. I will now admit you into that palace, where you have so highly merited a place."

> Whilst he was uttering these words, he touched the enameled lock with his key; and the doors, at once, flew open with a noise still louder than the thunder of the dog days, and as suddenly recoiled, the moment they had entered. (*Vathek* 109)

The gate opens on to the terrifying vista of the palace of subterranean fire, a cavernous space enveloped in Miltonic darkness visible and the endpoint of a narrative threaded through with multiple dangerous desires – for forbidden knowledge, power, treasures, pleasure, and bodies.

---

3   On transgression in *Vathek*, see also Chow 53-76.

To be sure, the lines crossed by Vathek are not East/West boundaries, as Beckford's tale is wholly comprised within an Oriental cultural and geographic perimeter. Yet the Western dimension re-emerges in the extensive annotations to the text drawn from a variety of works in French and English, at the time the two major cultures and languages of orientalist scholarship. The notes are a counter-text channelling the Orient into Western epistemological paradigms, though also producing a convergence of oriental and Western knowledge, so that, as Demata notes, "[t]he movement from the text to its note brings about a reversal and confusion of the West-East opposition" (Demata 18). If we read the fictional narrative *with* the annotations, the line between Europe and Asia mutates into a porous *limen* between a knowing subject and a known object, which informs Beckford's representational strategies and determines the narrative and thematic-ideological structure of *Vathek*.

The epic in Beddoes's and Landor's poems and the romance in Beckford's prose narrative converge in Southey's twelve-book *The Curse of Kehama* (1810), a hybrid poem expanding on the author's earlier generic experiments in *Thalaba the Destroyer* (1801). Tellingly dedicated to Landor, it centres on the eponymous Hindu rajah, a tyrannical and ambitious figure akin to Beckford's overreaching caliph. In the preface, Southey illustrates the cultural premises of the tale and clarifies its primarily transgressive impulse:

> In the religion of the Hindoos, which of all false religions is the most monstrous in its fables, and the most fatal in its effects, there is one remarkable peculiarity. Prayers, penances, and sacrifices, are supposed to possess an inherent and actual value, in no degree depending upon the disposition or motive of the person who performs them. They are drafts upon Heaven, for which the Gods cannot refuse payment. The worst men, bent upon the worst designs, have in this manner obtained power which has made them formidable to the Supreme Deities themselves, and rendered an *Avatar*, or Incarnation of Veeshnoo the Preserver, necessary. (*Curse* 3)

A "poetic figuring of Napoleon" from a Tory perspective, unlike Landor's Gebir, Kehama is unfalteringly and irredeemably evil (Butler 1994, 417). His goal is to gain the power of the gods in order to oust and replace them, as declared in the opening of Book 8, "The Sacrifice":

> Dost thou tremble, O Indra, O God of the Sky,
> Why slumber those Thunders of thine
> Dost thou tremble on high, ...
> Wilt thou tamely the Swerga resign, ...
> Art thou smitten, O Indra, with dread?
> Or seest thou not, seest thou not, Monarch divine,
> How many a day to Seeva's shrine
> Kehama his victim hath led? (*Curse* 8.1-8)

The danger is temporarily averted when the low-caste hero Ladurlad trespasses into the sacred compound where Kehama is about to complete the rites for the invasion of the Hindu heaven. The peasant's providential transgression hinders Kehama's blasphemous one, though only briefly. In Book 12, "The Sacrifice Completed", the climax of the rajah's violation of the line between human and divine is announced as the moment "When Indra's heavenly sphere / Must own the Tyrant of the World below" (*Curse* 12.11-12). At "the inevitable hour", Kehama acquires superhuman power "over Earth and Heaven" and the outcome is cosmic chaos:

> Heaven trembles with the thunder-drowning sound;
> Back starts affrighted Ocean from the shore,
> And the adamantine vaults, and brazen floor
> Of Hell, are shaken with the roar.
> Up rose the Rajah through the conquer'd sky,
> To seize the Swerga for his proud abode;
> Myriads of evil Genii round him fly,
> As royally, on wings of winds, he rode,
> And scal'd high Heaven, triumphant like a God. (*Curse* 12.123-31)

A new chapter of accidents opens for Kehama's antagonists, Ladurlad and his daughter Kailyal, who undergo further misery and pain, whereas the seemingly invincible rajah eventually attains the magic cup Amreeta, which grants immortality to those who drink from it. However, in keeping with the blackness of his soul, the cup only bestows an immortality of torment on Kehama, who is eventually defeated by Shiva, the destroyer god who removes evil from the world. With this literal *deus ex machina* intervention, the poem's finale neutralizes all transgressions and reinstitutes appropriate divisions and separations (though, in fact, Shiva finally transforms the persecuted Kailyal into a divine being, giving her eternal life with her supernatural beloved, Ereenia).

Southey's heavily Gothicized Eastern verse tales left a mark on Byron's narrative poems – either specifically, as in the reference to vampirism in *The Giaour* (1813) taken from *Thalaba*, or, more generally, his placing of an Oriental female body at the centre of struggles for power and related transgressions, a pattern anticipated by *Kehama*'s Kailyal. With its sustained reworking of earlier models and sources (Southey's and Beckford's in particular), Byron's orientalist output is suffused with dividing lines, their crossings and trespassings. By the same token, as Warren highlights, it presents us with "a far more vexed and porous border between East and West" than earlier texts (Warren 108), one that translates into fraught confrontations, as conveyed by the words a Muslim fisherman addresses to the protagonist of *The Giaour*: "I know thee not, I loathe thy race", "Right well I view thee, and deem thee one / Whom Othman's sons should slay or shun" (*Giaour* ll. 198-99). Such verbal hostility raises a barrier between the Western adventurer and the Turks, and against the former's trespassing into the East or, more precisely, into Emir Hassan's harem for love of the slave-girl Leila. Thus, on one hand, Byron's first Eastern tale foregrounds what Westphal terms the inbuilt tendency of transgression to rebel against the "geometrical figures of policed space" (Westphal 43). Yet, on the other, the poem explicitly reduces the transgressive act to an ellipsis:

> The hour is past, the Giaour is gone;
> And did he fly or fall alone?
> Woe to that hour he came or went,
> The curse for Hassan's sin was sent

To turn a palace to a tomb;
He came, he went, like the Simoom,
That harbinger of fate and gloom. (*Giaour* ll. 277-83)

The Giaour's crossing into the harem is a narrative blank. The only traces of his transgression are the death of Hassan and the ruinous state of his stronghold: "The steed is
vanished from the stall, / No serf is seen in Hassan's hall; / ... / The Bat builds in his
Haram bower; / And in the fortress of his power / The Owl usurps the beacon-tower"
(*Giaour* ll. 288-94). The transgression of bodies remains implicit, too. Just as there are
no references to the Giaour's penetration into the harem, so there are none to Leila's
body as an object of transgression.

However, if we turn to the vampiric curse aimed at the protagonist, physical transgression reappears in suitably resonant, labyrinthine forms:

... on earth as Vampire sent,
Thy corse shall from its tomb be rent;
Then ghastly haunt thy native place,
And suck the blood of all thy race,
There from thy daughter, sister, wife,
At midnight drain the stream of life (*Giaour* ll. 755-60)

The curse is directed at the Giaour's body as well as his soul, and is meant to punish him
for his invasion of Eastern spaces and bodies. The unspoken vampiric suction points offer
a *mise en abîme* representation of the bodily orifices linked to his transgressions: Leila's
sex and the wounds in Hassan's corpse. In other words, Byron conjures up an intricate
semantic concatenation around vampiric suction as an oriental(ized) incision in the Western body (the Giaour's prospective victims are primarily his closest relations), which
however stems from a Western trespassing into Eastern land- and bodyscapes. Warren
correctly notes that Byron's early poetic career, "from *Childe Harold i and ii* to *The
Corsair*, is built upon transgressing the border between East and West", which constitutes "an imagined, fantasmatic boundary" (Warren 114-15). While this is beyond doubt
since, after all, boundaries are in some degree imagined and intangible, *The Giaour*'s
peculiarity lies in its emphasizing their physical and body-related features.

This figurative pattern underwent several mutations in Byron's subsequent orientalist
ventures, perhaps most conspicuously in *The Bride of Abydos* (1813) and *The Corsair*
(1814), and in works that reprised and revised them such as Thomas Moore's *Lalla
Rookh* (1817) and Felicia Hemans's *The Abencerrage* (1819) (see Saglia forthcoming).
Byron also produced a markedly ironic reimagining of the Western transgression of an
Eastern border in *Don Juan* 5, the first of the poem's "Ottoman cantos", written in late
1820. As the fate-buffeted protagonist is smuggled into the Sultan's harem at Istanbul
disguised as a female slave (Juanna) to satisfy the Sultana Gulbeyaz's carnal desires, a
series of variations on the lexis of East/West transgression is set in train – variations that
are largely comedic yet carry considerable tragic potential. The first line the protagonist
crosses is the outside gate of the palace and, subsequently, that into the harem, a process
Byron represents in amusingly monumental terms:

This massy portal stood at the wide close
Of a huge hall, and on its either side
Two little dwarfs, the least you could suppose,
Were sate, like ugly imps, as if allied
In mockery to the enormous gate which rose
O'er them in almost pyramidic pride:
The gate so splendid was in all its *features*,
You never thought about those little creatures (*DJ* 5.87)

A possible reference to Beckford's Fonthill Abbey, where a dwarf was employed to open the main doors (thus increasing the sense of scale of the entrance hall), the harem dwarves also re-echo the physical *grotesquerie* in *Vathek*, from the Caliph's overwhelming physical presence and instincts to the giaour's monstrous appearance. Finally, Juan's ritualized, gradual approach brings him face to face with Gulbeyaz's spectacularized body: "In this imperial hall, at distance lay / Under a canopy, and there reclined / Quite in a confidential queenly way, / A lady" (*DJ* 5.95.1-4). The unconventional sultana takes on a masculine prerogative by asking him "'Christian, can'st thou love?'" (*DJ* 5.116.7), thus halting his transgressive progress. But the protagonist's unauthorized entrance into the unauthorized space of the East does not culminate in his access to Gulbeyaz's body. Instead, it takes a detour, leading to his (possible) penetration of the harem girl Dudù's sexual dreams, if not her body outright, for the text leaves things tantalizingly ambiguous. When, at night, Juan/na is instructed to share a bed with Dudù, the latter has a disturbing dream from which she awakens with a sudden scream, "agitated, flushed and frightened, / Her eye dilated and her colour heightened" (*DJ* 6.72.7-8). In Canto 7, an irate Gulbeyaz orders Juan and Dudù to be executed, a sentence from which they escape by leaving the palace through another passage in its porous walls.

The narrative and symbolic development of Juan's adventure in Istanbul centres on bodily orifices linked to apertures in a forbidden building: the secret watergate to the palace, the many thresholds crossed by Juan and his guide, the imposing entrance to the sultana's apartment, the door into the harem itself and, finally, the gate through which Juan and Dudù are to be smuggled out of the palace and sent to their deaths on the sultana's orders: "Let the boat / Be ready by the secret portal's side" (*DJ* 6.113.2-3). In addition, the episode is set in a frame of geo-political shifts and commercial traffic, pivoting on the piratical acquisition and trading of bodies on the slave markets dotting the inland sea in the early nineteenth-century (see Colley). Byron adapts this historical context to investigate a range of questions associated with power relations, as well as employing it to titillate his readers in ways that are reminiscent of contemporary orientalist pornographic fare.[4]

Emblematic in this respect is the anonymous *The Lustful Turk* (1828), an epistolary pornographic novel published by John Benjamin Brookes as part of a series of seraglio

---

4   Colette Colligan sees *Don Juan* as a major episode within a nineteenth-century development of "obscenity" in relation to "reprographic media, popular consumption, and orientalism" (Colligan 26).

fiction, and one with conspicuous literary ambitions since it revises Byron's "explorations of male experiences in the harem" in a plot based on "the dynamics of male despotism and female enslavement, evoking the mood and themes of licentious Gothic novels like *The Monk*" (Colligan 48). Mainly composed of letters from Emily Barlow to her friend Sylvia Carey, the novel opens with Emily leaving England for India, where her mercenary parents expect her to find a rich husband, having removed her from Sylvia's brother, Henry, whom she loves. Emily and her companion Eliza Gibbs set out in June 1814, as the narrator significantly specifies, but their ship is attacked by Barbary pirates who take them to Algiers, where their captain donates them to the local ruler, the Dey. The latter proceeds to deflower Emily, who initially resists but then yields to his attacks, and several more such experiences follow. In the meantime, she meets some of the other women of the harem – the Italian Honoria Grimaldi (kidnapped off Corsica), the Greek Adianti, and a French lady – whose stories constitute as many inset narratives. Eventually, Emily's correspondent Sylvia is also captured and ends up in the Dey's harem, where she undergoes the usual treatment. As in pornography generally, the novel's structure is predicated on endless repetition with some degree of variation.

From a geo-political perspective, *The Lustful Turk* is a pan-Mediterranean tale: ships travel across the inner sea, known in Arabic as *al-Baḥr [al-Abyaḍ] al-Mutawassiṭ* or "the [White] Middle Sea"; the harem is a multilingual, multicultural collection of women; and the Dey speaks Italian, Greek, French, Turkish, and English (and, implicitly, Arabic). Once again, and not unlike the more demure works examined so far, the narrative is inwoven with boundaries, crossings, and acts of transgression – of places and, here much more conspicuously, bodies. Emily makes this clear from the outset, as she records her passing through "the watergate of the Dey's harem" at "about half-past six o'clock in the evening of the 12th of this month" (*Lustful Turk* 15). She then becomes the object of his attentions with predictable consequences: "whilst his lips were as it were glued to mine, he forced his tongue into my mouth"; while "his lascivious proceedings, convey[ed] his kisses, brutal as they were, to the inmost recesses of my heart", "an unknown fire rushed through every part of me" (*Lustful Turk* 16); "I felt his hand rapidly divide my thighs, and quickly one of his fingers penetrated that place which, God knows, no male hand had ever before touched" (*Lustful Turk* 17), and with his "terrible instrument" (*Lustful Turk* 19) "forc[ed] his way into me" (*Lustful Turk* 25). The vocabulary of penetration and transgression shifts from location (the watergate) to the female body, a process that gradually intensifies as the Dey explores and enters Emily's every orifice. The ultimate, most dramatic transgression is anal penetration, which she resists with all her might before eventually giving in to this "second undoing" (*Lustful Turk* 62).

On becoming one of the Dey's possessions, Emily's name changes to Zulima, a transformation hinting at a whole series of crossings of linguistic and cultural boundaries linked to the exchanges and transits made possible by ships. If Emily rather conventionally styles the Dey's penis an "instrument", an "engine" (*Lustful Turk* 32), and a "machine" (*Lustful Turk* 34), these terms point to a mechanical and technological dimension that, in line with the novel's geo-political and economic context, alludes to the crafts crisscrossing the Mediterranean in all directions during the narrative. Scored by the mercantile routes along which goods and bodies are stolen and sold, traded and gifted, the "Middle Sea" is also at the centre of an intricate map made up of countless toponyms and other geographical terms. Emily is attacked by "Moorish pirates" (*Lustful Turk* 13) and ends up in the hands of "barbarous Turks" (*Lustful Turk* 12), whose captain, an "Algerine corsair" (*Lustful Turk* 14), takes them past Gibraltar to Algiers. The Dey of Algiers recounts his sexual deeds in letters to Muzra, the Bey of Tunis. Corsairs are repeatedly instrumental in securing slaves for the Dey, like the "African corsair" (*Lustful Turk* 41) that brings him the Italian woman who, together with the French and the Greek (*Lustful Turk* 38), forms a Mediterranean triad in his harem (while the English Emily and Sylvia are indexes of Britain's status as a Mediterranean power). A host of minor figures compounds this picture of intercultural contacts: various apostates, such as the first pirate captain, an English renegade (*Lustful Turk* 14); "missionaries arrived … from the South of France" to ransom French prisoners from the Barbary states (*Lustful Turk* 97); an "English Jew diamond merchant" disguised as an "English priest" (*Lustful Turk* 135); Father Angelo, a Catholic clergyman and also a letter-writer, who helps Abdallah, another pirate in the Dey's service, "secure" Sylvia for the latter (*Lustful Turk* 123); and Father Angelo's Spanish correspondent, Pedro "Abbot of St Francis" (*Lustful Turk* 100), whose letters introduce further lewd narratives based on the Gothic topos of monastic imprisonment.

Two places unify this variegated geography – the harem and the slave market, the latter described as a "system" where "captives are exposed, naked, and left unreservedly to the sight and feel of whoever chooses to bid for them" (*Lustful Turk* 126). In other words, the novel reprises and literalizes what Byron's *Don Juan* intimates, depicting a zone of traffic and transit where piratical activities transgress the principles of legal navigation, the acquisition and trading of goods is inseparable from that of bodies, and women's bodies in particular are repeatedly violated within a web of exchanges, conquests, competition, and influence woven by Christians and Muslims, merchants and priests, pirates and rulers. Fittingly, in accordance with this intersection of lines and boundaries, *The Lustful Turk* concludes with the tracing of a line: the Dey receives a new Greek girl from one of his captains, but, as a fiery anti-Muslim independentist, she does not submit to anal deflowering. At the earliest opportunity, she seizes a knife and emasculates him, thus putting an end to the tale. The conclusion is castrating in two senses: literally, of the male character, and, symbolically, of the fantasies he embodies, which Steven Marcus defines as expressions of "a sexuality of domination … in which the aggressive and sadistic components almost exclusively prevail" – a symbolism with obvious valences, not least of a geo-political type (Marcus 211).

The textual corpus analyzed in this chapter confirms the centrality of *limina* and *limites* to the Romantic-era orientalist imaginary, which conjures up a polysemic space of transit "located 'between/among' things – one which, by creating contact, separates, or possibly, by separating creates contact among people, things, cultures, identities, different spaces" (Zanini xiv, my translation). This is a location "where all the identities present in it are equally constitutive and representative, and where each identity exists precisely because it is confirmed by the others" (Zanini xvi). If viewing the boundary as an area of simultaneous contact and friction is a familiar move, these theoretical pointers usefully indicate the inherently *located* and, therefore, site- and context-specific nature of the textual renditions of *limina* and *limites*.

In the works examined here, the Romantic East is a reticulation of boundaries and thresholds that imply and invoke transgression, an act that has repercussions on the transgressor and the transgressed alike. And these repercussions do not only affect individual characters, as in the tragic destinies of Gebir, Vathek, or the Dey of Algiers. In view of the status of the boundary as a Romantic master trope, the effects of its crossing concern, more broadly, the notion of the Orient as a space to be conquered, controlled, and used, yet also one with which a more or less fruitful exchange can be established (see Watt 6-8). As Westphal reminds us, transgression is "coextensive with mobility" and "encompasses all border crossings", resulting in a "state of transgressivity", that is, a textual regime composed of different forms of transgression that, as in the analyses offered here, are only partly related to the spatial or geographic sphere (Westphal 45, 41).

Romantic orientalist transgressions of the boundary represent movement towards a goal, or a series of goals, and as such they are bound up with progress and progression. But they are also inextricable from regression and degeneration, as appears from the gradual withering of Gebir's dying body or the objectification of the women in the Dey's harem. In various ways, by imagining a passage to the East, these works also speak of a transition to regressive physical conditions and cultural contexts. Their intertwined forms of transgression, progression, and regression are intrinsic to a Romantic orientalist imaginary concerned with armies and ships, war and trade, things and human flesh. In this fictional universe placed along the line of East and West, apertures, gaps, and orifices are repeatedly probed and mapped through an endlessly recursive journey beyond the border and back again.

Works Cited

Anon. *The Lustful Turk or Scenes in the Harem of an Eastern Potentate*. Ware: Wordsworth, 1997.

Beckford, William. *Vathek*. Ed. Roger Lonsdale. Oxford: Oxford UP, 1970.

Beddoes, Thomas. *Alexander's Expedition down the Hydaspes and the Indus to the Indian Ocean*. London: John Murray, 1792.

Botting, Fred. *Gothic*. London and New York: Routledge, 1995.

Butler, Marilyn. *Romantics, Rebels and Reactionaries: English Literature and Its Background, 1760-1830*. Oxford: Oxford UP, 1981.

---. "Orientalism". *The Penguin History of Literature*, vol. 5: *The Romantic Period*. Ed. David B. Pirie. London: Penguin, 1994. 395-447.

Byron, Lord [George Gordon]. *The Complete Poetical Works.* Ed. Jerome J. McGann. 7 vols. Oxford: Clarendon Press, 1980-93.

Cass, Jeffrey. "Introduction: Heterotopia and Romantic Border Crossings". *Romantic Border Crossings.* Ed. Jeffrey Cass and Larry Peer. Aldershot: Ashgate, 2008. 1-23.

Chow, Jeremy. "Go to Hell: William Beckford's Skewed Heaven and Hell." *Trans-Gothic in Literature and Culture.* Ed. Jolene Zigarovich. New York and Abingdon: Routledge, 2018. 53-76.

Colley, Linda. *Captives: Britain, Empire and the World 1600-1850.* London: Jonathan Cape, 2002.

Colligan, Colette. *The Traffic in Obscenity from Byron to Beardsley: Sexuality and Exoticism in Nineteenth-Century Print Culture.* Basingstoke: Palgrave Macmillan, 2006.

Demata, Massimiliano. "Discovering Eastern Horrors: Beckford, Maturin, and the Discourse of Travel Literature". *Empire and the Gothic: The Politics of Genre.* Ed. Andrew Smith and William Hughes. Basingstoke: Palgrave Macmillan, 2010. 13-34.

Franklin, Caroline. *Byron's Heroines.* Oxford: Clarendon Press, 1992.

Hemans, Felicia. "Casabianca". *Selected Poems, Letters, Reception Materials.* Ed. Susan J. Wolfson. Princeton and Oxford: Princeton UP, 2000. 428-30.

Landor, Walter Savage. *Poems.* Ed. Geoffrey Grigson. London: Centaur, 1964.

Leask, Nigel. *British Romantic Writers and the East: Anxieties of Empire.* Cambridge: Cambridge UP, 1992.

Lew, Joseph. "The Necessary Orientalist? The Giaour and Nineteenth-Century Imperialist Misogyny". *Romanticism, Race and Imperial Culture, 1780-1834.* Ed. Alan Richardson and Sonia Hofkosh. Bloomington: Indiana UP, 1996. 173-202.

Marcus, Steven. *The Other Victorians: A Study of Sexuality and Pornography in Mid-Nineteenth-Century England.* London and New York: Routledge, 2017.

Porter, Roy. *Doctor of Society: Thomas Beddoes and the Sick Trade in Late Enlightenment England.* London: Routledge, 1992.

Roberts, Adam. *Landor's Cleanness: A Study of Walter Savage Landor.* Oxford: Oxford UP, 2014.

Saglia, Diego. "'A Mart for Everything': Commercial Empire and India as Bazaar in Long Eighteenth-Century Literature". *Eastern Resonances in Early Modern England: Receptions and Transformations from the Renaissance to the Romantic Period.* Ed. Claire Gallien and Ladan Niayesh. Cham: Palgrave Macmillan, 2019. 163-81.

---. "Broken, Wild, Untold Tales: Byron's Orientalist Poetry and Romantic-Period Narrative Verse". *Byron Among the English Poets: Literary Tradition and Poetic Legacy.* Ed. Clare Bucknell and Matthew Ward. Cambridge: Cambridge UP, forthcoming.

Simpson, David. *Romanticism and the Question of the Stranger.* Chicago and London: University of Chicago Press, 2013.

Southey, Robert. *Poetical Works 1793-1810.* Ed. Lynda Pratt. 5 vols. London: Pickering and Chatto, 2004.

Tally, Robert T., Jr. *Topophrenia: Space, Narrative, and the Spatial Imagination.* Bloomington: Indiana UP, 2019.

Tucker, Herbert. *Epic: Britain's Heroic Muse, 1790-1910.* Oxford and New York: Oxford UP, 2008.

Warren, Andrew. *The Orient and the Young Romantics.* Cambridge: Cambridge UP, 2014.

Watt, James. *British Orientalisms, 1759-1835.* Cambridge: Cambridge UP, 2019.

Westphal, Bertrand. *Geocriticism: Real and Fictional Space.* Trans. Robert T. Tally Jr. Basingstoke: Palgrave Macmillan, 2011.

Wordsworth, William. *The Poems: Volume One.* Ed. John O. Hayden. London: Penguin, 1977. 657-58.

Zanini, Piero. *Significati del confine: i limiti naturali, storici, mentali.* Milan: Bruno Mondadori, 1997.

Marvin Reimann

Byron's *The Giaour*: Dismantling the Boundaries between Orient and Occident through Romantic Irony

Introduction

Every practice of orientalist discourse, Edward Said argues, aims at establishing an "in-eradicable distinction between Western superiority and Oriental inferiority" (Said 42). It is thus essentially based on the construction of binary oppositions. East and West are clearly demarcated as they stand in a reciprocal relation in which the one is always de-fined as the exact opposite of the other and vice versa (Ashcroft et al. 19). Since the orientalist discourse constitutes a decidedly Western discipline, the power relations in representing Orient and Occident remain primarily unilateral and hence unbalanced. By distinguishing itself from a projected Eastern alterity, the West is able to construct its own identity and so exercises its hegemonic power over the Orient as the silent, passive, and subaltern other. This Orient/Occident dichotomy perpetuates itself and gains more political strength via the ongoing production of discursive formations, further defining the Orient as a supposedly inferior because less enlightened entity. The cultural hegem-ony established through the permanent generation of such discursive formations there-fore acquires its presumed legitimacy from "an enormous system or inter-textual net-work of rules and procedures which regulate anything that may be thought, written or imagined about the Orient" (Gandhi 76). Here, also literary texts play a substantial role for they naturally participate in the process of producing cultural knowledge and thereby help to consolidate the category of the oriental other (Said 94; see also Gandhi 77).

In light of these complex mechanisms, one might claim that Byron's narrative poem *The Giaour* could be integrated into this orientalist pattern, too, because it depicts a violent conflict between East and West: the Circassian Leila has an affair with the Venetian Giaour and is therefore drowned by her oppressive husband, the Turkish ruler Hassan. In order to avenge his beloved, the Giaour kills Hassan and thereby, one could surmise, corroborates the West's hegemonic position towards the East – or at least the traditional opposition between these two constructed entities.[1] A closer look into the intricate struc-ture of the poem, however, reveals that Byron actually deconstructs this rigid Orient/Occident dichotomy.[2] By foregrounding the poem's multiperspectival and fragmentary

---

1   Such a view is taken by Nigel Leask, for instance, who claims that Byron, even though he condemns the ideologies empowering European imperialism, remains nonetheless caught in this binary opposition (Leask 24).

2   As a matter of fact, many scholars have already voiced their doubts with regard to the assumption that Byron's *The Giaour* really conforms to Said's rigid categorization of ori-entalist discourse. Jan Alber, for example, asserts that the poem rather "represents an am-bivalent or hesitant type of Romantic Orientalism" (Alber 107).

character, Byron continually transgresses and thereby blurs the threshold that allegedly separates these two artificial constructs. As a manifestation of Romantic Irony as outlined by the German Romantic Friedrich Schlegel, I will argue, the poem is aware of its own constructedness and inherent limitations in both form and content. It is thus able to subtly undermine the binary opposition between East and West it seems to establish on the surface.

German Romanticism, the Fragment, and Romantic Irony

In fact, the reader is made aware of the poem's self-reflexive nature before it even begins. Not only does its subtitle describe it as the "Fragment of a Turkish Tale" which has been told to the author by a Turkish citizen; its brief advertisement, moreover, adds that this tale merely consists of "disjointed fragments" (*Giaour* 123). By explicitly identifying itself as a fragment, *The Giaour* already provides the reader with a plethora of implied meanings carried by this concept. It is indeed the poem's awareness of its fragmentary structure which proffers a first hint towards its subversive character because it immediately evokes an inquiry into the relation between fragment and whole. The fragment, as Lucien Dällenbach and Christiaan L. Hart Nibbrig elucidate, cannot be thought without also considering the idea of the whole as its natural counterpart because they dialectically define each other. The fragment could not be a fragment if it coexisted with the whole at the same time and as one of its integrated parts. It must therefore be envisaged as severed from this wholeness – either from an archaeological perspective as a present remainder dissociated from its unity lost in the past, or from an eschatological one as the present seed of an anticipated unity (Dällenbach and Nibbrig 7-15). In both cases, the presence of the fragment always implicitly points at the totality to which it belonged or will belong and which can therefore solely be present as that which is absent.

The ontological and epistemological import of the fragment has been elaborated by Romantic thinkers such as Schelling, Novalis, and Schlegel, whose ideas can indeed be employed as a philosophical basis for the analysis of the transgressive fragmentariness of *The Giaour*. According to them, Manfred Frank explains, the whole that is truly one, total and all-encompassing, i.e. the Absolute, can neither be thought nor even exist. This assumption is based on the simple fact that something can only exist as something determinate – as that what it actually is – by differing from everything that it is not. The distinction between one existing entity and another one automatically establishes a negative and mutually defining relation between them (Frank 1984, 214). Every existing entity is thus merely a fraction of the world's universal web of interrelations and mutual exclusions (Gabriel 82-83). And so is every act of thinking or knowing because they are essentially defined by mediacy, that is, the relationality and reflexivity between the thinking subject and the object that is being thought. The Absolute as the true whole, however, is literally absolute, that is, cut off from all relationality as well as differentiation and therefore entirely unconditioned and infinite. It would no longer be an all-embracing whole but a fragment itself if it simply existed or was made an object of thought since both circumstances would paradoxically involve relations to an entity outside this wholeness. Nonetheless, this absolute totality must be presupposed for it enables relationality and hence existence as well as thought in the first place. Something can relate to something else and thus be determined only because both entities – metaphorically speaking – stand in front of the Absolute as the colourless and contrastless background foil through which they receive their basic contours (Hogrebe 165). This absolute wholeness, according to the Romantics, is both everything and nothing at the same time, for it constitutes the fundamental potentiality for every entity to exist even though it does not exist in itself. Due to this inherently ambiguous nature, it is entirely ungraspable.[3]

Frank continues that from these ideas necessarily follows that absolute truth, unconditioned by anything else and valid simply in itself, does not exists either. In the world's web of relationality, the plurality of coexisting truths and falsities already indicates that they mutually relativize and condition each other. Every judgement which raises a claim to validity must be grounded on an external fact or another judgement and so forth *ad infinitum* – their claims to validity are hence merely hypothetical. If, however, a judgement was absolutely true, it would be grounded on no further principle and therefore be non-existent (Frank 1996, 414-16). In a sense, Hegel's formula that the true is the whole is also valid for the Romantics. But, as Franziska Schmitt clarifies, the essential difference between them is that the latter deny the attainment of absolute truth and, instead, hold the view that truth is infinitely processual and evolves as an ever-growing network of manifold and interdependent relations (Schmitt 45-47; see also Behler 136).

Despite these complexities, Frank elucidates, this absolute and infinite totality fulfils the function of a regulative idea in the Kantian sense. It is an ideal which can never be attained but only be approximated in this existing world which continually evolves through time and must therefore be regarded as a dynamic process of perpetual creation (Frank 2015, 288-89). This world is not a being but a becoming, a constant and fragmentary work-in-progress which can never be completed because this would mean to transcend time and reach the ideal, the infinite, through a temporal movement (Gabriel 31-32).[4] Hence, Schlegel calls the world an *infinite abundance* or *chaos* for its dynamic

---

3   In his *Freedom Essay [Philosophische Untersuchungen über das Wesen der menschlichen Freiheit und die damit zusammenhängenden Gegenstände]* from 1809, Schelling therefore describes the Absolute as the *Ungrund* which "precedes all opposites" and can thus "only be described as the absolute *indifference [Indifferenz]*" which allows opposites to arise in the first place (Schelling 68). Hence also Schlegel's laconic note on this topic: "*Erkennen* bedeutet schon ein *bedingtes* Wissen. Die Nichterkennbarkeit des Absoluten ist also eine identische Trivialität" ["*Knowing* already denotes a *conditioned* knowledge. The unknowability of the Absolute is therefore an identical triviality"; translation mine] (Schlegel *KA* XVIII 511, No. 64).

4   This idea is made explicit by Schlegel himself: "[G]ibt es kein *Sein*, sondern nur *Werden*, so ist das Endliche, wenn auch extensiv begrenzt, doch intensiv durch die unendliche Mannigfaltigkeit und Veränderlichkeit immer *unendlich*. ... Ein werdendes Unendliches aber ist gleichsam ein Unendliches, das noch nicht fertig, und insofern endlich ist" ["If there is no *being* but only *becoming*, the finite, although limited extensively, is nonethe-

processuality naturally involves that the composition of its finite parts incessantly changes as well.[5] Every part that is generated in this process is always set into relation to all other parts whose constellation alters with every new component (Mellor 4-7). This potential multitude must be exhausted to its utmost degree in order to at least approximate the Absolute as closely as possible. With regard to the ideal of absolute truth, this means that a vast plurality of relative truths and perspectives must constantly be produced and expanded in a process of perpetual reflection (Frank 1996, 419-20).[6]

These ontological and epistemological suppositions have a considerable impact on the aesthetics of German Romanticism. Every work of art that is produced inevitably becomes a part of the world's fertile abundance and is integrated into its universal web of relations. Due to its mere existence, the work of art is always already finite, conditioned and relative. It is, by definition, unable to constitute or illustrate what the Romantics call absolute totality. If a work of art presumed to have attained its ideal of depicting this totality, of being utterly complete in itself, however, it would immediately reduce the infinite to the finite, the absolute to the relative. Furthermore, it would falsely posit itself as the only and unconditioned absolute truth, thus elevating itself above the existing plurality of relative truths. In consequence, it would abolish both itself and the whole (Schmitt 38-42). From these assumptions follows that every finite work of art can merely constitute a fragment and – more importantly – must acknowledge as well as reveal itself as such in both form and content. By being externally incomplete or scattered into incoherent pieces, the Romantic work of art reflects its inherent fragmentariness and thus evinces a certain self-awareness. Similar to the perpetually evolving world, the fertile abundance of which it is a mere part, the work of art is a project or work-in-progress indicating through its fragmentary structure that it must always remain incomplete, that is, open for additions and growth (Lacoue-Labarthe and Nancy 48).[7] Hence, Anne K. Mellor correctly states that "[t]he artist cannot merely impose a man-made form or system upon this chaos: that would distort motion into stasis" (Mellor 4-5). And this is what Schlegel calls the fragment's *chaotic universality*: the plurality of inchoate fractions it

---

less always *infinite* intensively due to its unending manifoldness and mutability. ... An evolving infinite, however, is an infinite that is still unfinished and hence finite"; translation mine] (Schlegel *KA* XII 334-35).

5   "Es giebt *zweierlei Arten des Unendlichen*; unendliche Einheit und unendliche Fülle" ["There are *two kinds of the infinite*; infinite oneness and infinite abundance"; translation mine] (Schlegel *KA* XIX 89, No. 67).

6   Again Friedrich Schlegel: "Aber denke dir alle menschliche Gedanken als ein Ganzes, so leuchtet ein, daß die Wahrheit, die vollendete Einheit das notwendige obschon *nie* erreichbare Ziel alles Denkens ist" ["But think of all human thoughts as one whole, then you will see that truth, the perfect unity, constitutes the necessary albeit *never* attainable goal of all thinking"; translation mine] (Friedrich Schlegel to A.W. Schlegel *KA* XXIII 129-30).

7   The idea of the fragment as an interminable project is further elucidated by Helmut Schanze (Schanze 31).

contains and openly exhibits mirrors its awareness that solely a perpetual aggregation but no complete synthesis or absolute oneness of these parts can be achieved (Frank 2015, 296; see also Schmitt 48). It knows that it can never be whole or portray absolute totality and so it relates to itself in an essentially ironic way. Mellor continues that this idea of Romantic Irony consists in a process of "simultaneous creation and de-creation: a fictional world must be both sincerely presented and sincerely undermined, either by showing its falsities or limitations" (Mellor 14). Romantic Irony therefore involves self-negation and self-relativization: on the surface, the text presents itself as a fixed and static creation but simultaneously provides a commentary on itself, an implicit meta-text shining through its fragmentary form, which subtly questions, undermines and hence deconstructs what is being explicitly stated through the text (Frank 2015, 311; see also Schmitt 53-54). On the level of content, moreover, this means that the fragmentary work of art must dispense with an absolute central view and, instead, provide a manifold of subjective perspectives which continuously negate and relativize one another (Frank 2015, 296). This reciprocal interplay can also be regarded, following Philippe Lacoue-Labarthe and Jean-Luc Nancy, as an instance of "infinite reflexivity" (Lacoue-Labarthe and Nancy 86). The self-reflexive nature of the Romantic work of art emphasizes the fact that it is not so much concerned with the "reflection of the world it represents" but rather, as Christopher Strathman states, with "the very nature of representation, the nature of the work of art, itself" (Strathman 19).

The Fragmentariness of *The Giaour* as an Instance of Romantic Irony

On the basis of these considerations, it can now be examined in how far Byron's *The Giaour* operates in exact accordance with these criteria.[8] The poem's fragmentation occurs in both form and content for every single one of its disjointed fragments presents the reader with a shift from one point of view to another. These include the view of a Western poet, a Levantine coffeehouse storyteller, a Muslim fisherman, the Giaour himself and a Christian friar. This continuous oscillation receives its incoherence from the fact that the poem does not provide any explicit indications as to whose perspective is currently given. As a result, the reader is forced to construe them according to the idiosyncrasies of each voice and their relations to the unfolding story. In this regard, Robert Gleckner employs an apt comparison when he maintains that the story can be viewed as

---

8   Here, however, it must be noted that, in contrast to the German Romantics, Byron nowhere propounds the idea of an Absolute as the all-embracing and total oneness which must necessarily be presupposed as a regulative idea and is to be approximated through a continuous creation of more and more relative truths as well as perspectives. Instead, Byron foregrounds relativity and variety for their own sake. Notwithstanding the difference between these thinkers – and here I disagree with Marjorie Levinson (11) – the German Romantics' ideas can still be employed as a basis for an interpretation of Byron's poem since they provide it with an ontological and epistemological framework that clarifies the inevitability of its fragmentariness and multiperspectivity.

"a piece of sculpture surrounded by a number of viewers, each of whom sees it and interprets it in his own light" (Gleckner 97). Indeed, every subject invests a particular set of cultural, moral and religious values in the act of perception in order to adequately understand what they are confronted with, thus enhancing the poem's heterogeneity.[9] This fragmentation is even further complicated by the fact that this manifold of perspectives transcends spatio-temporal boundaries. Almost every observer is situated in a different geographical location and some of their accounts serve as either prolepses or analepses. In consequence of this seemingly arbitrary back and forth, the reader is withheld a linear and coherent story development that could be grasped immediately. In the words of Christoph Bode, *The Giaour* engenders "a multi-dimensional space that cannot be paraphrased in a uni-linear way, but that can only be disclosed and traced in its narrative technique and in its dynamism" (Bode 12). The poem's narrative technique, its fragmented multiperspectivity, compels the reader to permanently reflect on its content, to establish relations between its various narrative elements and to immediately call them into question again.[10] As soon as a new perspective emerges, its relation to the ones preceding it and to the unfolding whole must be renegotiated. This infinite reflexivity or, as Marjorie Levinson calls it, "narrative relativity" (Levinson 115) illustrates the poem's dialectical process of creation and de-creation, for it does not represent a ready-made work with a single and static meaning. As a result, it can be stipulated that its fragmentary structure emphasizes relativity, diversity and doubt instead of absoluteness, totality and certainty – typical features of Byron's sceptical attitude as Richard Cardwell highlights (Cardwell 9).

The Giaour, it can thus be said, presents itself in an ironic twilight as it reveals its very own constructedness and incompleteness through this "experiment in perception" (Shilstone 97). This has a significant impact on the Orient/Occident dichotomy it seems to perpetuate, for the validity of this binary opposition is tacitly undermined through the poem's fragmented multiperspectivity. Neither does it present a so-called "imperial gaze" as its central and absolutely valid perspective (Ashcroft et al. 207) nor does it appoint any cultural hegemony or predominant value-system. Both East and West are equally endowed with a perspective and allowed to speak, but merely as disjunct fragments caught in a web of infinite reflexivity. As soon as one perspective emerges and creates a reality by giving a voice to its subjective view on the world, it is immediately de-created and relativized by those perspectives surrounding it in the poem's fertile abundance. Neither of them can be total or presume to be unconditionally valid due to their inherent limitations as mere fractions. This fragmentary juxtaposition of disparate per-

---

9   Vera and Ansgar Nünning, for instance, explain that the juxtaposition of various perspectives in a text evokes an experience of reality which is inherently defined through complexity, manifoldness, and contrariness (Nünning and Nünning 12). Even though they explicitly refer to the heterogenous multiperspectivity of prose texts, I would argue that their findings can be applied to *The Giaour* as well due to its narrative structure.

10   Scott Simkins further emphasizes the reader's role in attempting to reorganize the poem's fragmented reports into a synthetic whole (Simkins 93).

spectives demonstrates that neither Orient nor Occident can provide an objective and complete grasp of an essentially chaotic world. There exists no absolute truth; rather, every reality is subjectively constructed (Nünning and Nünning 9). Hence, these limited points of view amalgamate in an intersubjective interplay which is entirely ironic and sceptical.[11] One can therefore agree with Andrew Warren's assertion that Byron's "treatment of the Orient becomes – because it is nearly always self-conscious and ironic – itself a critique of ... Orientalism" (Warren 3).

The formal structure of *The Giaour*, however, evinces only one side of the coin that is its transgressive and subversive fragmentariness. It would only be half as suggestive if it did not go hand in hand with the poem's content. As a matter of fact, both dimensions of *The Giaour* continuously mirror and thereby reinforce each other in their thematization of its incompleteness. On numerous occasions, the reader is confronted with the depiction of crumbled ruins, cleaved bodies and conflicting religious positions, all of them enhancing the idea of creation and simultaneous de-creation.[12] Before the actual story begins, for example, the European poet offers a retrospective depiction of Greece, starting with its past glory and ending with its present decay under Ottoman rule. Later in the poem – when Hassan has already been murdered by the Giaour – a similarly constructed account is given but from the perspective of the Turkish fisherman, who describes the current disintegration of Hassan's palace compared to its former splendour. Both accounts reveal a parallel pattern in their dialectics between wholeness and decay as Peter Cochran states: "an occidental (of sorts) ruins an oriental paradise, and an oriental ruins an occidental paradise" (Cochran 52). In the poem's first passage, the European poet illustrates the harmonious and innocent union between human beings and nature as Greece's "blessed isles" are said to "make glad the heart that hails the sight. / And lend to loneliness delight" (*Giaour* ll. 8-11). This positive impact of the unity between the spectator and his surroundings is underscored by the sight/delight rhyme intricately connecting perception and emotion. Moreover, several natural phenomena mirror human qualities as indicated through the personifications "Ocean's cheek" and "laughing tides" (*Giaour* ll. 12-14). These examples of an idyllic wholeness culminate in "a portrait of ideal love in a prelapsarian world" (Gleckner 105) as the following lines illustrate:

> For there – the Rose o'er crag or vale,
> Sultana of the Nightingale,
> The maid for whom his melody –
> His thousand songs are heard on high,
> Blooms blushing to her lover's tale;

---

11   Here, Schmitt arrives at a similar conclusion when she explains that, for Byron, the impossibility to achieve objectivity and to get beyond the subjective conditions of cognition can only be remedied through intersubjectivity (Schmitt 273).

12   The close connection between the literary fragment and the ruin is also addressed by Thomas McFarland in his insightful study *Romanticism and the Forms of Ruin* in which he advances his idea of the "diasparactive trio" of "incompleteness, fragmentation, and ruin" as a definition of "the fragmentary" (McFarland 4).

His queen, the garden queen, his Rose,
Unbent by winds, unchill'd by snows,
Far from the winters of the west,
By every breeze and season blest,
Returns the sweets by nature given
In softest incense back to heaven;
And grateful yields that smiling sky
Her fairest hue and fragrant sigh. (*Giaour* ll. 21-33)

In a footnote to this passage, Byron himself explains that the nightingale singing to the rose is an allusion to "a well-known Persian fable" (footnote to line 22), which is corroborated by Abdur R. Kidwai who elucidates that the nightingale "is generally associated in the Orient with love and melodious song" (Kidwai 90). The poet deconstructs the Orient/Occident dichotomy by merging elements of both entities in his description of Greece's splendour and, in doing so, generates a heightened sense of its vividness and fertility (Sharafuddin 233). The fundamental harmony implied through the nightingale's song is further underlined by the consistent metre of the lines evoking an impression of perfect integrity. In addition to the visual sense focused on before, the bird's song and the flower's odour open up two further dimensions of sensual experience so that the unity between humankind and nature becomes palpable on a multisensory level. Moreover, the last lines of this quote personify the rose by highlighting its reaction to what it receives from the skies, thus illustrating the whole as "a relation of reciprocity and symmetry harmonious in its completeness of gesture and response" (Garber 45).

Notwithstanding these idyllic images of wholeness, the poet is forced to turn from Greece's former glory to its present and portrays the destruction of nature by the intrusion of men who "mar it into wilderness" and "trample, brute-like, o'er each flower" (*Giaour* ll. 51-52). Thus, the rose, which before denoted a harmonious synthesis, is turned into a symbol of Greece's collapse. This perversion of ideal love into its extreme opposite is further stressed as the poet claims that "passion riots in her pride, / And lust and rapine wildly reign" (*Giaour* ll. 59-60). The enumeration of negatively connoted nouns starts with "passion", increases with "lust" and finds its climax in "rapine" – all personified and thus viewed as essentially human actions. This change from the paradisiac into the satanic can also be observed with respect to the poet identifying these intruders as "fiends", "freed inheritors of hell" and "tyrants" (*Giaour* ll. 62-67). The portrayal of Greece's devastation culminates in a gloomy but also captivating metaphor when it is compared to a recently deceased woman with a "sad shrouded eye, / That fires not – wins not – weeps not – now –" (*Giaour* ll. 78-79). Decay and incompleteness are emphasized through the frequent use of dashes as well as "multiple negations ... ripping apart the syntax" and "finally breaking off into [the] silence" of the fragmentary present (Strathman 72).

Similar to the Western poet lamenting the decline of current Greece, the Eastern fisherman bewails the deterioration of Hassan's palace after he has been killed by the Giaour (*Giaour* ll. 288-98). The prevailing dreariness and darkness of this place are not only underscored by the absence of any human being but also by the presence of nocturnal animals which, as presented through a decidedly political imagery, have reconquered their territory and thus reclaimed sovereignty. This place is now reigned by an eerie silence sometimes disrupted by the cacophony of the wild-dog's onomatopoetic howls. The riverbed is now desiccated – a sign not only of vegetative decay but of sexual sterility, too, since Hassan will have no future progeny. The material deterioration of his house is furthermore accompanied by a moral loss "for Courtesy and Pity died / With Hassan" so that these ruins will no longer offer "refuge unto men" (*Giaour* ll. 346-48). All these examples prove that an Ottoman ruler as Hassan cannot be stereotypically defined as a cruel and irrational despot. Rather, hospitality and benevolence are inherent characteristics of every Turkish ruler who respects his people's traditions and values (Kidwai 89). In order to highlight the discrepancy between creation and de-creation, the fisherman subsequently indulges in reminiscences of the palace's peaceful and idyllic past:

> And oft had Hassan's Childhood play'd
> Around the verge of that cascade;
> And oft upon his mother's breast
> That sound had harmonized his rest;
> And oft had Hassan's Youth along
> Its bank been soothed by Beauty's song;
> And softer seem'd each melting tone
> Of Music mingled with its own. – (*Giaour* ll. 308-15)

Due to the fact that the Turkish ruler is portrayed as a child, an apparent emphasis is placed on purity and innocence in contrast to despotism and cruelty. Unlike the Gothic silence mingled with the cacophonous howls of the dogs mentioned above, the atmosphere is now explicitly characterized in terms of harmonious completeness. These originate in the evenly flowing movement of the stream, the musicality of which is reflected in the anaphoric structure of the lines and the constant use of alliterations and 's'-sounds creating the impression of an idyllic haven. Similar to the past Greece, Hassan's palace is described in terms of harmony and euphony. Moreover, the stream symbolizes vegetative as well as sexual fertility, which is underscored by the image of his mother's breast signifying their close unity which has been shattered by the Giaour. As a result, one can indeed argue that both cultures are equally lamentable in so far as both have suffered the deterioration from complete unity into fragmentary ruin due to the intrusion of an other. What each perspective portrays thus reflects the fragmentary nature of each viewpoint itself. Even though the Western and the Eastern perspective remain culturally dissimilar and focus on different places, they are set into a dynamic interplay of constant mirroring so that the boundary created between them is, at the same time, transgressed. The Occident/Orient dichotomy is thereby undermined and none of these fragments is shown to inhere a hegemonic position or a higher truth because every reality depends on the perspective one adopts.

The deconstruction of this binary opposition through reflexive identification can also be observed with regard to the fragmentation of belief systems. Already the title suggests this idea, for the Muslim term 'Giaour' translates into 'infidel' or 'non-believer' and hence introduces the poem's protagonist, whose real name is never given, from a Muslim perspective. Here, Christopher Strathman argues that the poem's title immediately "forces the reader to experience the events of the poem through the eyes of a poet-narrator who sees in Christianity, not Islam, a heterodox persuasion and an outlaw worldview" (Strathman 70).[13] The Western reader's regular set of religious values is subtly replaced by a different religious framework, which engenders a complex entanglement and thereby deconstructs the traditional boundaries between these two perspectives. This ironic inversion through the title mirrors the reflexive interplay of perspectives which constitutes the poem as an unfolding whole. It thus compels the Western reader to reflect on their culturally biased viewpoint and thereby realize the constructedness and arbitrary interchangeability of religious beliefs in general. They are all subjective and relative since they can only grasp a mere fragment of the whole so that neither can claim to be superior or absolutely valid. In this respect, Philip Martin rightly asserts that the poem is "far from setting one religion as more enlightened than another" (Martin 92).

The ironic interchangeability of religious creeds implied through the title pervades the whole poem.[14] After the account of Hassan's death is given, the Turkish fisherman contrastingly depicts the Ottoman's entrance into paradise and the Giaour's damnation. The former is impatiently awaited by the houris, the virgins in heaven, for he has bravely fought against an unbeliever. The Giaour, on the other hand, is cursed by the fisherman in a litany of abundant superstitions since he, an infidel, has murdered a fellow Muslim. He is condemned to suffer the tortures imposed on him by Monkir and Eblis, which will result in an ineffable because internal hell. As if this was not enough, the Giaour will also be doomed to suffer a kind of life-in-death in the form of a vampire forced to plague his fellow Europeans (*Giaour* ll. 747-58). In a spatio-temporal shift, the perspective changes from that of the Turk to that of the Christian friar in whose monastery the Giaour has been living and grieving for the last six years. In view of the Giaour's partial responsibility for Leila's death and his murder of Hassan, this location first of all suggests repentance and piety to the reader. Eric Meyer even suggests that the last scene taking place in the monastery reasserts "the ideological centrality of Western culture" (Meyer 680). Far from reinforcing Western ideology, Byron satirizes it and undermines the

---

13   Gerard Cohen-Vrignaud also claims that "the title undercuts from the start the idea of a true and catholic creed" (Cohen-Vrignaud 191). Byron's critique of Christianity becomes more apparent in Marilyn Butler's essay "Byron and the Empire in the East", in which she analyses the poem's representation of monotheistic religions with reference to its historical context. In doing so, she claims that Byron challenges the anti-liberal Evangelical campaign to enforce Christian proselytism in Britain's Eastern colonies that started around 1810. Thus, she argues, *The Giaour* functions as a contrasting answer to those literary works in favour of these political projects as, for example, Southey's *The Curse of Kehama* from 1810 (Butler 70-74).

14   Bode similarly argues that Byron here foregrounds specific deficits of both religions and, in doing so, reveals "their deep affinities and similarities" (Bode 13).

reader's expectations by pointing out the hypocrisies and insufficiencies of Christianity. Trying to make any sense of the stranger's personality, the monk describes the Giaour as an "evil angel" whose "looks are not of earth nor heaven" and therefore considers him to be "the wrath divine / Made manifest by awful sign" (*Giaour* ll. 910-11). Comparing this depiction to that of the Turkish fisherman, one can clearly see that they do not differ from one another substantially as they both rely on superstitious elements. Hence, Nigel Leask asserts that "Islamic and Christian religion are debased to superstition and the violence of the 'curse' levelled by both the fisherman and the monk usurps the place of a moral agency proper to religion" (Leask 30). This aspect is emphasized when the friar reveals his fear of and aversion to the Giaour. He would prefer to no longer "brook such stranger's further stay" (*Giaour* l. 819) which, in fact, opposes the basic virtues of his creed, such as *caritas*, *benevolentia* and *patientia*. Because of this violation of religious virtues and the Giaour's isolation in which he painfully suffers, Marilyn Butler rightly states that "there is not even a sense of brotherhood in the monastery" (Butler 74). Although the Giaour has been allowed to stay there for six years, this has not been an act of the monks' compassion. Instead, the friar reveals, the Giaour has brought "great largess to these walls" and thus bought "the abbot's favour" (*Giaour* ll. 816-17), which exposes their hypocrisy and the cardinal sin opposed to *caritas*, namely *avaritia*. As these examples elucidate, the Giaour occupies a liminal position between these two belief systems, for he is welcomed by neither of them. Thus, he constitutes the central point at which both perspectives enter into a reflexive interplay, the point at which they mirror each other and thereby expose themselves as merely relative fragments betraying their moral insufficiencies.

In response to the monk's condescending remarks, the last part of the poem consists in a pseudo-confession in which "the Giaour persistently taunts the priest listening to him and repeatedly declines to utter the regret needed for God's pardon" (Cohen-Vrignaud 196):

> But talk no more of penitence,
> Thou see'st I soon shall part from hence –
> And if thy holy tale were true –
> The deed that's done canst *thou* undo?
> Think me not thankless – but this grief
> Looks not to priesthood for relief. (*Giaour* ll. 1202-07)

Despite the fact that he is on the verge of dying, the Giaour keeps on mocking Christianity by questioning its presumptuous claims to truth. This is implied through his use of a conditional clause which is itself fragmented because unfinished, thus not only suggesting the improbability of redemption but also and essentially the limitations of any belief system. Through the following rhetorical question and the true/undo rhyme, he further underscores the naivety of any religious creed because no bestowed mercy can reverse the crimes that have been committed. Hence, the Giaour demonstrates the tension between moral responsibility and religious faith. More importantly, however, Byron himself assumes a meta-textual position at this point as he provides an insightful footnote to these lines: "The monk's sermon is omitted. It seems to have had so little effect on the patient, that it could have no hopes from the reader. It may be sufficient to say, that it was of customary length ... and was delivered in the usual tone of all orthodox preachers" (footnote to line 1207). Byron blatantly avails himself of his poem's fragmentary structure and reinforces its ironic effect, for the footnote enables him to ridicule Christianity's presumptuous claim to preach absolute truths. This ellipsis and especially its reflexive self-thematization not only underscore the banality and futility of religious preaching but also foreground the constructedness and incompleteness of the poem in general – including every perspective presented therein. By demonstrating that he as the author can randomly create and de-create his text, Byron stresses the idea that not a single perspective is entirely indispensable as they always present merely one limited aspect of the whole despite their hubristic claims to absoluteness.

This deliberate fragmentation of the text through the omission of certain voices is most evident with respect to the complete absence of Leila's perspective even though her death constitutes the core of the poem's tragedy. In consequence, Caroline Franklin argues that "the autonomous feminine voice is totally suppressed in *The Giaour*. The heroine's story has to be reconstructed by the reader from various male viewpoints" (Franklin 39). The past Leila who once lived can hence be interpreted as a metaphor for the Romantic conception of totality, the Absolute, which does not exist and can only be present in its absence. The present Leila who is now dead or, rather, that which is left of her as a textual reconstruction, in contrast, epitomizes the poem's unavoidably fragmentary structure. She is now merely a silent construct which consists in the accumulation of various scattered perceptions of her without ever engendering a complete and intact synthesis.[15] The Giaour's and Hassan's fatal struggle over the possession of her can therefore be read as a conflict between two claims to totality – futile attempts to gain control over the Absolute. Leila's mute position thus also reveals that the two representatives of Occident and Orient share a decidedly patriarchal standpoint concerning the perception of gender relations. Both establish their selves by generating "the feminine Other" (Franklin 38), which indicates that Leila merely functions as a passive means in the creation of male identity. Neither Hassan nor the Giaour perceive her as a human being worthy in herself but simply project their desires and hopes of self-fulfilment on her.

One of the fragmentary accounts of Leila is provided by the Levantine storyteller who attempts to reconstruct her unparalleled beauty through an explicitly natural imagery. The colour of her cheeks is compared to the "young pomegranate's blossoms", her hair has a "hyacinthine flow" and her feet are "whiter than the mountain sleet" (*Giaour* ll. 494-501). However, one could likewise argue that, through this beauty catalogue, the storyteller intends to highlight her erotic sensuality in order to further expose her as an

---

15   Here, Laura Mulvey's concept of the "male gaze" can be applied as well because Leila's objectification in the eyes of the male characters renders her bereft of any agency and hence merely subaltern (Mulvey 837).

unfaithful and sinful seductress. Notwithstanding this ambiguity, this oriental stereotype – as Naji Oueijan views it (7-25) – is contrasted with a special emphasis placed on the purity of her soul:

> But Soul beam'd forth in every spark
> That darted from beneath the lid,
> Bright as the jewel of Giamschid.
> Yea, *Soul*, and should our prophet say
> That form was nought but breathing clay,
> By Alla! I would answer nay;
> [...]
> Oh! who young Leila's glance could read
> And keep that portion of his creed
> Which saith that woman is but dust,
> A soulless toy for tyrant's lust? (*Giaour* ll. 477-90)

This passage is particularly striking since the storyteller's male gaze on the beauty of Leila forces him to a critical self-reflection regarding his religious beliefs. One could argue that his gaze is reflected in the mirror of her eyes and creates an oppositional gaze that fixes himself in a subsequent act of self-questioning. This mirroring is underscored by a simile in which her eyes are compared to a jewel through which beams of light can be reflected. As he clearly perceives Leila's soul through her eyes, the storyteller challenges the view supposedly propagated by the prophet Mohammed that women are merely corporeal beings and therefore not allowed to enter paradise. Through a rhetorical question at the end he implies that no Muslim would approve of this assumption when being confronted with Leila. Shortly before the passage ends, the storyteller states that, "arm'd with beauty", Leila would prevent "intrusion's glance, till Folly's gaze / Shrunk from the charms it meant to praise" (*Giaour* ll. 513-15). The observer's projection of sensuality and desire through the male gaze finally elevates her to a position superior to the gazing subject trying to objectify her so that she is able to defy subjugation. In contrast to Caroline Franklin's claim that the description of Leila exclusively corroborates the patriarchal structures of the Orient and constructs her as merely sinful, one could therefore argue that it remains rather ambiguous (Franklin 42-44). In consequence, this instance highlights Leila's function as a metaphor for the poem's fragmentary structure itself. Both offer a fertile abundance of contradictory ideas and notions which can never be exhausted and thus stimulates the reader/spectator to continuously question their own perspective. In doing so, the reader/spectator is forced to set their view into an ironic interplay of perspectives which negate, relativize and complement each other.

The deconstruction of the Orient/Occident dichotomy through the depiction of Leila finds its most striking manifestation in the reflexive identification of Hassan and the Giaour as the latter speaks the following lines:

> Yet did he but what I had done
> Had she been false to more than one;
> Faithless to him – he gave the blow,

> But true to me – I laid him low;
> Howe'er deserved her doom might be,
> Her treachery was truth to me; (*Giaour* ll. 1062-67)

Since they both deem death the correct punishment for her, Elizabeth A. Bohls aptly points out that both males share "an uncompromising attitude to female infidelity" (Bohls 158). Like Hassan, who feels himself forced to assert his male authority in order to no longer suffer degradation, also the Giaour would egoistically secure his male dominance by killing her. "The power relations of gender", as Nigel Leask states, "transcend cultural difference" (Leask 29). Their similarity is further emphasized as the Giaour himself thematizes the poem's fragmented multiperspectivity in a reflexive interplay of opposed viewpoints (Bode 16): while Leila's affair signifies loyalty to him ("true to me"), it concurrently means disloyalty to Hassan ("Faithless to him"). The parallelistic structure of these two lines pointedly mirrors the fragmentation of absolute truth into juxtaposed and ambivalent interpretations. In addition, the two dashes which formally separate but content-wise link her (dis-)loyalty to Hassan's and the Giaour's deeds, establish a causal connection which holds true in both cases and thus renders the two males' actions basically equal. The last line quoted here enhances this idea by explicitly stating the interchangeability as well as identity of truth and falsity. These two categories are thereby pointed out to be depending on one's highly subjective and hence merely relative viewpoint, which suggests that all perspectives, since they can solely grasp fragments of the whole, necessarily demand an ironic and sceptical revision.

Conclusion

Having closely examined various aspects of Byron's *The Giaour*, it has been illumined that the poem persistently denies being forced into the static framework of oriental discourse as defined by Edward Said. Rather, it remains highly ambiguous in its representations of Orient and Occident, thereby pointing out their constructedness and how this, in turn, depends on the specific viewpoint one adopts. It has been argued that the deconstruction of the Occident/Orient dichotomy mainly stems from the poem's multiperspectivity and fragmentation, both resulting in Romantic Irony – a dynamic interplay of infinite reflexivity. Thus, Byron stresses the relativity of every perspective as each is limited in its subjectivity and therefore unable to presume absolute truth. Through an accumulation of views, every culture is enabled to speak for itself and construe its counterpart in its own gaze. These different perspectives, however, have been shown to also mirror each other so that the clear-cut distinction and hierarchy between the Western Self and the Eastern Other are blurred and subverted.

Works Cited

Alber, Jan. "The Specific Orientalism of Lord Byron's Poetry". *AAA: Arbeiten aus Anglistik und Amerikanistik* 38.2 (2013): 107-27.

Ashcroft, Bill et al. *Post-Colonial Studies: The Key Concepts*. London: Routledge, 2007.

Behler, Ernst. "Das Fragment". *Prosakunst ohne Erzählen: Die Gattungen der nichtfiktionalen Kunstprosa*. Ed. Klaus Weissenberger. Tübingen: Max Niemeyer Verlag, 1985. 125-43.

Bode, Christoph. "Byron's Dis-Orientations: *The Giaour*, for Example". *Romantik: Journal for the Study of Romanticisms* 4 (2015): 9-25.

Bohls, Elizabeth A. *Romantic Literature and Postcolonial Studies*. Edinburgh: Edinburgh UP, 2013.

Butler, Marilyn. "Byron and the Empire in the East". *Byron: Augustan and Romantic*. Ed. Andrew Rutherford. London: Macmillan, 1990. 63-81.

Byron, Lord [George Gordon]. *Byron's Poetry and Prose*. Ed. Alice Levine. New York: W. W. Norton, 2010. 121-56.

Cardwell, Richard A. "Byron: Text and Counter-Text". *Renaissance and Modern Studies* 32 (1988): 6-23.

Cochran, Peter. "Introduction: Byron's Orientalism". *Byron and Orientalism*. Ed. Peter Cochran. Newcastle: Cambridge Scholars Publishing, 2006. 1-154.

Cohen-Vrignaud, Gerard. *Radical Orientalism: Rights, Reform, and Romanticism*. Cambridge: Cambridge UP, 2015.

Dällenbach, Lucien and Christiaan L. Hart Nibbrig. "Fragmentarisches Vorwort". *Fragment und Totalität*. Ed. Lucien Dällenbach and Christiaan L. Hart Nibbrig. Frankfurt am Main: Suhrkamp, 1984. 7-17.

Frank, Manfred. "Das 'fragmentarische Universum' der Romantik". *Fragment und Totalität*. Ed. Lucien Dällenbach and Christiaan L. Hart Nibbrig. Frankfurt am Main: Suhrkamp, 1984. 212-24.

---. "'Alle Wahrheit ist relativ, alles Wissen symbolisch': Motive der Grundsatz-Skepsis in der frühen Jenaer Romantik (1796)". *Revue Internationale de Philosophie* 50.3 (1996): 403-36.

---. *Einführung in die Frühromantische Ästhetik: Vorlesungen*. Frankfurt am Main: Suhrkamp, 2015.

Franklin, Caroline. *Byron's Heroines*. Oxford: Clarendon Press, 1992.

Gabriel, Markus. *Das Absolute und die Welt in Schellings 'Freiheitsschrift'*. Göttingen: Bonn UP, 2006.

Gandhi, Leela. *Postcolonial Theory: A Critical Introduction*. Edinburgh: Edinburgh UP, 1998.

Garber, Frederick. *Self, Text, and Romantic Irony: The Example of Byron*. Princeton: Princeton UP, 1988.

Gleckner, Robert F. *Byron and the Ruins of Paradise*. Baltimore: Johns Hopkins Press, 1967.

Hogrebe, Wolfram. *Echo des Nichtwissens*. Berlin: Akademie Verlag, 2006.

Kidwai, Abdur R. "'Samples of the Finest Orientalism': A Study of the Orient in Lord Byron's 'Turkish Tales'". University of Leicester, Dissertation, 1993. https://hdl.handle.net/2381/34865.

Lacoue-Labarthe, Philippe and Jean-Luc Nancy. *The Literary Absolute: The Theory of Literature in German Romanticism*. Albany: SUNY Press, 1988.

Leask, Nigel. *British Romantic Writers and the East: Anxieties of Empire*. Cambridge: Cambridge UP, 1992.

Levinson, Marjorie. *The Romantic Fragment Poem: A Critique of a Form*. Chapel Hill and London: University of North Carolina Press, 1986.

Martin, Philip W. "Heroism and History: Childe Harold I and II and the Tales". *The Cambridge Companion to Byron*. Ed. Drummond Bone. Cambridge: Cambridge UP, 2004. 77-98.

McFarland, Thomas. *Romanticism and the Forms of Ruin: Wordsworth, Coleridge, the Modalities of Fragmentation*. Princeton: Princeton UP, 1981.

Mellor, Anne K. *English Romantic Irony*. Cambridge, MA: Harvard UP, 1980.

Meyer, Eric. "'I Know Thee not, I Loathe Thy Race': Romantic Orientalism in the Eye of the Other". *ELH* 58.3 (1991): 657-699.

Mulvey, Laura. "Visual Pleasure and Narrative Cinema". *Film Theory and Criticism: Introductory Readings*. Ed. Leo Braudy and Marshall Cohen. Oxford: Oxford UP, 1999. 833-44.

Nünning, Vera and Ansgar Nünning. "Von 'der' Erzählperspektive zur Perspektiven-struktur narrativer Texte: Überlegungen zur Definition, Konzeptualisierung und Untersuchbarkeit von Multiperspektivität". *Multiperspektivisches Erzählen: Zur Theorie und Geschichte der Perspektivenstruktur im englischen Roman des 18. bis 20. Jahrhunderts*. Ed. Vera Nünning and Ansgar Nünning. Trier: WVT, 2000. 3-38.

Oueijan, Naji. "Sexualizing the Orient". *Essays in Romanticism* 14.1 (2006): 7-25.

Said, Edward W. *Orientalism*. London: Penguin Books, 2003.

Schanze, Helmut. "Das romantische Fragment zwischen Chamfort und Friedrich Nietz-sche". *Über das Fragment / Du fragment*. Ed. Arlette Camion et al. Heidelberg: Winter, 1999. 30-37.

Schelling, Friedrich Wilhelm Joseph. *Philosophical Investigations into the Essence of Human Freedom*. Trans. Jeff Love and Johannes Schmidt. Albany: SUNY Press, 2006.

Schlegel, Friedrich. *Kritische Ausgabe*. Ed. Ernst Behler. Paderborn: Schöningh, 1958-79.

Schmitt, Franziska. *'Method in the Fragments': Fragmentarische Strategien in der englischen und deutschen Romantik.* Trier: WVT, 2005.

Sharafuddin, Mohammed. *Islam and Romantic Orientalism: Literary Encounters with the Orient.* London: I.B. Tauris Publishers, 1994.

Shilstone, Frederick W. "Byron's *The Giaour*: Narrative Tradition and Romantic Cognitive Theory". *Research Studies* 48 (1980): 94-104.

Simkins, Scott. "*The Giaour*: The Infidelity of the Romantic Fragment". *Approaches to Teaching Byron's Poetry.* Ed. Frederick W. Shilstone. New York: MLA, 1991. 89-93.

Strathman, Christopher A. *Romantic Poetry and the Fragmentary Imperative: Schlegel, Byron, Joyce, Blanchot.* Albany: SUNY Press, 2006.

Warren, Andrew. *The Orient and the Young Romantics.* Cambridge: Cambridge UP, 2014.

Sophia Möllers

The Historian Turned Anatomist of the Soul:
Tracing Transgressive Psychology in William Godwin's *Mandeville*

> Early I learned to be dissatisfied with myself, and to despise myself. Disappointment cowered with its depressing and heavy wings over my cradle; and mortification hung round my childish steps, and waylaid me in my path.
>
> Godwin, *Mandeville*

With these heavy words, reeking of melancholia and vapours, the eponymous narrator of William Godwin's *Mandeville: A Tale of the Seventeenth Century in England* illustrates his deficient character in the search for answers as to why control over his own agency seems to have escaped his trembling hands. In this novel, published in 1817 and thereby preceding his daughter Mary Shelley's masterpiece *Frankenstein; or, The Modern Prometheus* in 1818, Godwin confronts his readers with a narrator whose psyche is corroded by envy, shame and severe depression. While the story revolves around the emotional downfall of the angst-ridden narrator who explicitly states that his intention is not to write an account of national history (*Mandeville* 1:11), the novel undoubtedly transgresses clear boundaries of genre in its fusion of autobiographical character study and national history. In fact, multifaceted transgressions are precisely what lie at the core of this work. For not only does this text transcend the boundaries of genre conventions, but it also performs stark transgressions as it traces the emotional rupture of its protagonist-as-narrator. Shaped by the tumultuous events of the French Revolution, commonly viewed as the decisive historical momentum of the long nineteenth century, many Romantic writers challenged hegemonic power structures and intervened in dominant representations of marginalized individuals. A deliberate transgression of artificially erected boundaries can easily be perceived in key texts of writers of the period who employed their texts to criticize societies shaped by a proto-capitalist devaluation of individuals deviating from the norm and inspire socio-economic change.

Unlike William Wordsworth, William Blake, or even his son-in-law Percy Bysshe Shelley, William Godwin is frequently excluded from the discussion of British Romantic texts by reducing his literary œuvre to the philosophical and proto-anarchist *Enquiry Concerning Political Justice and its Influence on Morals and Happiness* (1793) and its literary counterpart *Things as They Are; or The Adventures of Caleb Williams* (1794). The major impact of those two works served to frame Godwin as a political writer indebted to the sober tradition of anarchist thought, which in turn often implicitly excluded him from prominently featuring in the discussion of Romanticism's counter-reaction to a scientific empiricism that negated individual imagination. These rather misleading notions must, however, be opposed as William Godwin was one of the first thoroughly psychological novelists who investigated the nature of man in scrutiny of his innermost desires. In consequence, he should be reframed as a distinctly Romantic writer who discussed how external influences shape characters and minutely considered the overall intersections of socio-economic realities and individual psyches. His 1817 novel *Mandeville: A Tale of the Seventeenth Century in England* will serve to exemplify this claim. This essay argues that the main character Mandeville's complex processing of trauma transgresses the socially acceptable and thereby facilitates an understanding of the intersection of psychology and socio-political history. The emotional downfall of Mandeville offers striking psychological insight into how individuals are determined by their personal histories, which in turn can generate an understanding of the complex interplay of history and society.

As many Godwinian scholars have already taken up their metaphorical dissecting knives and traced the "pressures of politics and history on the individual" (Clemit 96) in *Mandeville* or established the novel as "a case history of its protagonist's failure to become a historical figure" (Rajan 174), this chapter draws attention to the novel's transgressive psychologizing in its construction of empty nostalgia as both chronic illness and source of the narrator's pathological fantasies. In its representation of a relationship that borders on incest, the novel considers how the lack of personal history contributes to a transgression of socially appropriate sibling relationships. Finally, the proto-psychological character history of Mandeville and his obsession with his sister, caused by an empty nostalgia for a non-existent past, will also allow for a reflection on Godwinian constructions of historical narratives.

In *Mandeville*, the reader is thrown into the eponymous protagonist's narration of his life story, from his birth in the North of Ireland (Ulster) in 1638 to his metaphorical death as he is scarred for life, both physically and psychologically, in a duel with his main antagonist Clifford. Born into a Presbyterian family, the young boy Mandeville is immediately confronted with the violent outbreaks following the onset of the Irish Rebellion of 1641. His parents are brutally murdered by the Catholics in the course of the Rebellion and Mandeville states that while he was only three years of age at the time, the scene "will live in [his] memory as long as [his] pulses continue to beat" (*Mandeville* 1:33). Fortunately, Mandeville is saved by his Irish maid and, via a stopover with the rigorous anti-Papist Reverend Bradford, who once more tears him from the hands of his beloved, brought to presumed safety with his melancholic uncle Audley in England. Suffering from forbidden love and profound loneliness, Audley is described as "the shadow of a man only" (*Mandeville* 1:101) and does not provide the appropriate emotional model for Mandeville to develop a stable personality. The only other relation, Mandeville's sister Henrietta, is placed with their mother's family and soon grows to become the focal point of Mandeville's emotions. As the only connection to his native soil and most personal history, Mandeville idealizes his sister and develops an obsession for her, which challenges the boundaries of the socially acceptable. He expresses that "[he] had never loved but one thing, and that was Henrietta. [He] found, or fancied in her, every perfection. She was [his] teraphim[1], [his] idol; and before her semblance [he] prostrated [himself] every day in worship" (*Mandeville* 3:310). While their encounters are never explicitly sexual, it is certain that Henrietta embodies her brother's desires and as she falls for the charming and universally adored Clifford, Mandeville's emotional stability is disrupted, and he tumbles down a dark mental abyss. Sparked by an unfortunate incident during the young men's shared time at college, which disgraces Mandeville and turns him into a misanthrope, the royalist Clifford becomes "an obstacle interposed in [his] path that must be removed" (*Mandeville* 1:302). From thereon, their lives are intertwined in what seems to Mandeville an endless struggle for dominance, culminating in Clifford's engagement to Henrietta, which causes him to vow "inextinguishable vengeance" on them (*Mandeville* 3:323). This passionate eruption illustrates that Mandeville's emotional well-being is tied to his self-perception as the heir to an important house as well as to the sensual availability of his sister as the last remnant of his native identity. His lack of personal history creates an uprooted identity, which finds its only outlet in the manic emotional idealization of his sister. Godwin thereby portrays how an unfulfillable, transgressive longing for an idealized past, personified by Henrietta as his last remaining family, breeds misanthropy, mania and psychological turmoil.

When Johannes Hofer wrote his dissertation on nostalgia and its accompanying symptoms in 1688, the illness had been "explained by many of the doctors, [but, according to the author,] deserved to be described and expounded more fully" (Hofer qtd. in Anspach 380). Until the publication of Hofer's account, nostalgia lacked a proper name in medicine and was simply referred to by its German or French equivalents *Heimweh* or *la Maladie du Pays* (Hofer qtd. in Anspach 380). A disease particularly affecting young Swiss soldiers sent on foreign missions, nostalgia is generated, so Hofer claimed, by "arousing especially the uncommon and ever-present idea of the recalled native land in the mind" (Hofer qtd. in Anspach 381) and is typically accompanied by "continued sadness, … decrease of strength, hunger, thirst, senses diminished, and cares or even palpitations of the heart, frequent sighs, [and] also stupidity of the mind" (Hofer qtd. in Anspach 386). The only possible cure for this disease is to return the patient to his homeland. Should it be impossible to thus satisfy the patient's burning desire, the disease will prove most dangerous if not "incurable and fatal" (Hofer qtd. in Anspach 388). While Hofer's description of nostalgia may today simply be called a state of anxiety or traumatic depression, nostalgia was later "perceived as a critical problem in France during the Revolutionary and Napoleonic Wars" (O'Sullivan 627). Particularly "young rural, normally illiterate, conscripts" felt unable to perform their duties because it was believed that when recreating images of the homeland, the soldiers' "reconstruction of these lost homes became so engrossing and overwhelming that the energy needed by the body for normal functioning was diverted" (O'Sullivan 628). For the French government, this sentiment was problematic as it furthered rural attachment amongst those young soldiers

---

1   Hebrew: תרפים, "[s]tatues of household gods; legal as well as religious importance was attached to possessing them" ("teraphim").

who were urgently needed to transport the much-desired patriotism of a unified France (O'Sullivan 629). It thus becomes clear how the concept of sickly[2] nostalgia was still of importance in Godwin's times and how it contributed to an understanding of the interconnectedness not only of place and identity but also of body and mind. According to Margaret E. Farrar, nostalgia precisely embodies what one may refer to as body memory as in emotional responses to geographical spaces, "places become written on the body, wired into memory" (Farrar 725). In imagination's ability to overpower bodily functions by idealizing a lost past, the mind became a locus of interest for medical writers, which can be read as symptomatic of the much-discussed subjective turn in Romanticism, as well as the emerging desire for national identities in the early nineteenth century.

In Godwin's psychological novel, Mandeville displays a severe case of nostalgia-as-illness. Surely, this line of argumentation can be countered by stating that the protagonist was only three years old when he was taken from his homeland – so what could he possibly be longing for? Nothing, one would answer, and this precisely is at issue. What can be traced in Mandeville is not nostalgia-as-illness *per se*, but it is in fact an *empty nostalgia*. His traumatic childhood experience of having to witness the violent murder of his parents and subsequently being torn away from his native land has severely uprooted his entire existence, body and mind. Not only is in this fatal action disrupted what developmental psychologist Erik H. Erikson would come to call a basic trust in his core family,[3] essential for a child's healthy development, but the means of identifying with his native soil is also violently taken away from him. His is, thus, an empty nostalgia, as it signifies a longing for something that he has never consciously known and, in fact, should not be able to rationally long for. It is an all-encompassing emptiness which cannot be filled. The only means of veiling this void is Mandeville's relationship to his sister Henrietta, who symbolizes his only remaining family tie and thereby embodies the sole connection to his pre-traumatic life. In consequence, Mandeville idealizes Henrietta as holding "the master-string, that alone could wake the soul of harmony in [his] rugged bosom" (*Mandeville* 2:315). She becomes an *idée fixe*[4] for him, a medical term com-

---

2   The term "sickly" is used here in preference to "pathological", as the latter was first mentioned by Jeremy Bentham to describe mental diseases in his *Introduction to the Principles of Morals and Legislation* in 1789 and is therefore less suitable to describe the type of nostalgia illustrated by Hofer in the seventeenth century.

3   Basic trust = German *Urvertrauen*, first mentioned by Erikson in 1950 in *Childhood and Society*. Erikson describes eight stages of childhood, the first being the stage of "Trust vs. Basic Mistrust" (Erikson 219-22), covering the period from 0-18 months. From 1-3 years, the child is in the stage of "Autonomy vs. Shame and Doubt" (Erikson 222-24), with shame occurring when the child feels incompetent to complete tasks and survive. Self-control without a loss of self-esteem will not be achieved. In early childhood, Erikson stresses the importance of contact with peers to facilitate a healthy personality and form knowledge of the world, instead of experiencing guilt and lack of purpose (Erikson 224-26).

4   An *idée fixe* is "a single pathology of the intellect" based on "a single compelling idea or from an emotional excess" (Shapiro 100). The victim of the *idée fixe* is usually unaware of the unreality of their frame of mind. Due to its close connection to the pathologizing

monly used in the early nineteenth century to discuss forms of neurosis in monomaniacs,[5] as he develops an amorous fixation on his sister. Since Clifford is not only Mandeville's nemesis in terms of social acceptance, political and historical importance, or religion, but also in terms of romantic rivalry for his dear sister, the celebrated hero becomes the target of Mandeville's hatred. The protagonist's wrath centres solely on Clifford and as he develops pathological fantasies of romance and violence, it becomes clear that his need to fill the void created by empty nostalgia has fabricated severe monomania in an incestuous transgression of emotional boundaries.

Alan Richardson has pointed out that fictional violations of the incest taboo "broach the fundamental laws of human society and raise the question of a shared human nature" (Richardson 553-54), as incest is a much-represented phenomenon in different historical periods and cultures. According to Richardson, it is striking that the incest taboo is recognized as universal by creative artists as well as scientists seeking to demonstrate similarities among different cultures, since the depiction of incestuous desires is omnipresent across national and historical momenta (Richardson 553-54). This idea of a shared human nature or identity lies at the core of Romanticism and is also central in Godwinian thought concerning his discussion of mental perfectibility and universal benevolence as prerequisites for social progress.[6] The form of incest which is of special importance in Romantic writing is the incest between siblings. Portrayed by Percy Bysshe Shelley as a form of idealized love[7] and "like many other *incorrect* things a very poetical circumstance" (Shelley *Letters* 749),[8] the incestuous relationship between brother and sister

---

of ideas, the term appeared in treatises on criminal law in the nineteenth century and was also employed to reframe criminal acts as "disorders of the will" (Berrios 355).

5   The term "monomaniac" was first defined by Jean-Étienne Dominique Esquirol, a student of the celebrated Philippe Pinel at the Salpêtrière, in the *Dictionaire des sciences médicales* in 1819, but had been in use since the early 1810s in French medical discourses (cf. Goldstein 160-61).

6   "However, Godwin's endorsement of both the principle of utility as the sole guide to moral duty and the principle of private judgment as a block on the interference of others, is not without tensions. His consistent doctrine is a combination of these two principles: that it is each individual's duty to produce as much happiness in the world as he is able, and that each person must be guided in acting by the exercise of his private judgment, albeit informed by public discussion. If the resulting doctrine is utilitarian it is a highly distinctive form: it is act-utilitarian in that it discounts reliance on rules; it is ideal, in that it acknowledges major qualitative differences in the pleasures; and it is indirect, in that we can only promote over-all utility by improving the understanding of our fellow human beings." (Philp n.p.)

7   Cf. Shelley, Percy Bysshe. *Rosalind and Helen, A Modern Eclogue*. 1819. Rosalind and her brother have an incestuous relationship.

8   "Incest is, like many other incorrect things, a very poetical circumstance. It may be the excess of love or hate. It may be the defiance of everything for the sake of another, which clothes itself in the glory of the highest heroism; or it may be that cynical rage which, confounding the good and the bad in existing opinions, breaks through them for the purpose of rioting in selfishness and antipathy." Shelley writes this to his and his wife's friend

harbours poetical potential as the purity of its love remains outside of and thus un-
distorted by social norms and boundaries. To Shelley, as much as to Byron, who also
frequently employs the image of incestuous sibling love in his poetry,[9] only a blood
relation, ideally a thoroughly pure and innocent woman, can truly understand the emotional turmoil of the sensitive Romantic hero. Familial ties between brother and sister,
therefore, are understood as an alternative to sexualized relationships between man and
woman which are strongly regulated by the social conventions of patriarchal societies.
Whereas this love between siblings usually remains platonic since it is not necessarily
sparked by sexual desire (cf. Richardson 554), the intense emotional connection exemplified by many sibling quasi-couples in Romantic texts sheds light on the immense
pressure exerted over individuals in their negotiation of *nature versus nurture* at a time
of all-encompassing turmoil. In Godwin's novel, the relationship between Mandeville
and his sister Henrietta can be understood as embodying and even transgressing the Romantic incestuous relationship between siblings.

While Godwin employs a deeply emotional protagonist and equips him with a morally
pure and innocent sister as sensitive guide and focal point of the protagonist's only af-
fections, the image of idealized purity is harshly disrupted. For in this novel, the protagonist is not a sensitive Romantic hero, as portrayed in Shelley's and Byron's poetry, but
a deeply troubled individual whose manic fixation on his sister highlights his inability
to think and act rationally. Their connectedness is, as in other Romantic texts, never
perverted, but it becomes clear that it creates an emotional infertility on the part of the
highly fixated Mandeville, who seems unable to live without the constant attendance of
his sister. The narrator-as-protagonist describes their relationship as electric, resembling
ideas promoted by Franz Anton Mesmer regarding animal magnetism, and enabling
them to "partake by anticipation, of the prophetic spirit and the unearthly vision that
characterize the state of saints above" (*Mandeville* 1:178). In their brotherly and sisterly
love, they "seemed to understand, what ordinary mortals do not understand" (*Mandeville*
1:178), indicating that their closeness is superior to the ties formed in commonplace
relationships between men and women. Mandeville frequently expresses that Henrietta
is "the whole world to [him]" (*Mandeville* 1:213) and his emotional attachment to her is
made especially clear as she seems to be the only person able to calm him after his
numerous mental breakdowns. These are usually triggered by events disgracing him and
questioning his position in the world, which ultimately unleash the traumatic experiences of his parents' death yet again as the "scenes of atrocious massacre … presented
themselves in original freshness" (*Mandeville* 2:113). Her soothing voice, however, is

---

Maria Gisborne in Florence on November 16, 1819, shortly after the completion of the
manuscript for his *The Cenci, A Tragedy, in Five Acts* (1819), which makes frequent use
of the incest theme (see Shelley, Percy Bysshe. "Letter to Maria Gisborne, November 16,
1819.").

9   Cf. Byron's *The Bride of Abydos*, *Parisina*, *Manfred*, *Cain* and his alleged incestuous
relationship with his half-sister Augusta Leigh (rumoured to have fathered one of her children, his "perverse passion").

to him like "the song of the Sirens" (*Mandeville* 2:131) and as he comes to reject other human contact, pleasing her and envisioning their life together becomes the one thing seemingly preventing relapses into trauma. Framing Henrietta's attempts to calm her brother's nerves as similar to the songs of the Sirens as Muses of the Underworld in Greek mythology, enchanting sailors and thus luring them into their wet grave, implies that her influence over Mandeville might prove disastrous.

This intense connection, prominently felt in its enchanting power and manically idealized by Mandeville, is depicted as a direct result of his childhood trauma and the void created by the consequential empty nostalgia-as-illness, which he desperately tries to fill by clinging onto his only blood relation in an emotionally transgressive manner. While Mandeville never precisely refers to his illness in terms of "trauma", his statements concerning the brutal murder of his parents and the all-encompassing coldness of Mandeville House reveal the traumatic impact of these experiences, for they, as he informs the reader, inhibited him from becoming a happy human creature and part of a peaceful community (*Mandeville* 1:209-10). In another instance, as the result of a fit of madness, his parents' death presents itself to him in feverish dreams rife with "scenes of unspeakable distress" and the protagonist relays how "[t]hese visions ate into [his] inmost soul, and exhausted [his] strength in misguided and empty exertions" (*Mandeville* 2:114). To Mandeville, who was forced to endure such terrifying scenes at a very young age and in consequence "had neither father, nor mother, nor brother ... Henrietta was father, and mother, and every thing [sic] to [him] in one" (*Mandeville* 1:168). Following Richardson's line of thought, it is a shared feature of Romantic sibling relationships that their "mutual isolation – from the rest of the family and from the world – ... only intensifies the effect of a shared history" (Richardson 556), yet in *Mandeville*, this idea is distorted. The common image of sibling relationships is transgressed, for while Henrietta and Mandeville have both been violently uprooted in early childhood, Henrietta is universally loved for her "naiveté and grace" (*Mandeville* 1:167) due to her thoughtful upbringing in Beaulieu Cottage, where "every thing [sic] was soothing and agreeable, and strikingly addressed itself to the better and more beneficent passions of the soul" (*Mandeville* 1:208). In the constant confrontation with his angelic sister, Mandeville cannot help but emotionally fixate on her as she displays his innermost longing for social acceptance and distinction.

Henrietta, on the other hand, is not nearly as fixated on her brother. She most often rather transgresses her role as sister to act upon Mandeville as an amateur psychologist. In a manner resembling a fusion of Philippe Pinel's *traitement moral* and what will later be known as 'the talking cure', first mentioned in Josef Breuer and Sigmund Freud's *Studies on Hysteria* (1895), Henrietta draws "a bewitching portrait of an obscure and rural life" for in peaceful tranquillity, the individual "hears nothing of kings, and ministers, and the intrigues of a court, ... and is never told of the factions and wars to the right hand and the left, in which men tear one another to pieces with a thousand barbarities" (*Mandeville* 2:129). This idyllic framing of domestic happiness as supportive to the restoration of the madman's faculties of course strongly draws on late eighteenth-century insights regarding the necessity to remove mental patients from those surroundings which gave rise to psychological illness in the first place (cf. Sedlmayr 69-73). As she continuously encourages Mandeville to speak about his inner turmoil, Henrietta's enquiry into her brother's psyche to improve his emotional condition resembles the techniques of *moral management*, an approach most famously employed by William Tuke and his grandson Samuel at the York Retreat. Similar to the Tukes' idea of surrounding the mentally ill with people who share their values and can thus create a familiar atmosphere for the psychologically challenged,[10] Henrietta reminds him of his personal worth and refers to the Earl of Shaftesbury's influential *Characteristics of Men, Manners, Opinions, Times* (1711) to stress that people are "formed for mutual sympathy, and cannot refrain from understanding each other's joys and sorrows" (*Mandeville* 1:140). It could be argued that her attempts to save Mandeville are selfless and precede insightful developments in modern psychoanalysis, but there lies a danger in their implicit roles as patient and quasi-psychotherapist. The hierarchical imbalance of their sibling-relationship is increased and not only does Henrietta thereby transgress her role as sister, but she also potentially violates personal boundaries and harms Mandeville's psyche even more seriously. In attempting to cure his disease, Henrietta presses Mandeville to give her the joy of seeing him happy and stresses how important it is for her to be proud of him, for "[he is] the only creature in the world, to whom [she] intimately, and by the closest ties, belong[s]" (*Mandeville* 2:146). In her subtle yet constant appeal to Mandeville to let go of his hatred for Clifford and to finally be happy again, Henrietta becomes to her brother the "empress of [his] fate, [his] only consolation on earth, that better part of [his] soul, for whom and by whom only [he] live[s]" (*Mandeville* 2:177). Instead of working through his trauma and its triggers, Mandeville attempts to conceal his illness for the sake of Henrietta's happiness. This is mainly achieved by perceiving the expected conciliation with Clifford as "a part to act upon [that] mortal stage", which he must perform to be rewarded with a closer relationship with his sister (*Mandeville* 2:177). In consequence, while Mandeville expresses his attempt to become personified magnanimity, which is, to him, "the crown of a man, ... the befitting ornament of a gentleman" (*Mandeville* 2:177), it becomes clear that his intentions are hardly altruistic, as they are but a means to redeem possession of Henrietta.

It is of little surprise that her somewhat naïve attempts to thus cure her brother prove infertile and instead contribute to his emotional distress. While Mandeville still fantasizes about a glorious future with his sister, he does not realize that her heart already belongs to his ultimate rival Clifford. As mentioned before, in terms of the fictional depiction of incestuous relationships between siblings, the impossibility of their unity follows an established literary pattern in Romanticism. Challenging social norms, Romantic writers often do portray sexual attachment between siblings, but the love depicted is hardly ever consummated – perhaps to avoid public scandal and diminished sales. Mary Shelley's *Frankenstein* expands this idea in her novel, for Frankenstein's

---

10   For further references cf. Sedlmayr.

bride and first cousin Elizabeth (1818 version) is murdered on their wedding night, in-hibiting any sort of sexual encounter between the two. While in the case of *Franken-stein*'s 1831 rewrite, there is no blood relation between Victor and Elizabeth, their pre-vented sexual encounter illustrates that even "adopted siblings ... tend to have the same valence in Romantic narratives as do siblings by blood" (Richardson 554). In *Mande-ville*, the protagonist may not be violently murdered and thereby hindered from his lov-ing unification with Henrietta, but his final defeat by Clifford is certainly manifested as a form of psychological death. The fact that Mandeville and Henrietta have not shared a significant amount of their childhood arguably contributes to their erotic attachment, for according to the Finnish anthropologist Edward Westermarck, erotic feelings be-tween people living together are often remarkably absent (cf. Westermarck 2:192, qtd. in Richardson 558). Consumed by manic hatred for his rival, who has – in most cases unknowingly – served as a source for his degradation and rendered his attempts for am-bition and glory impotent, Mandeville's pathological anger is released as he hears of the impending union between his sister and Clifford. Not only does their marriage symbol-ize Mandeville's final defeat in terms of the struggle for his sister's love, but it also met-aphorically cuts all ties with their shared history yet again. Clifford is a firm Papist and by that implicitly associates with those who violently murdered their parents. To Mande-ville, the union between his rival and Henrietta therefore means universal shame and disgrace, not only for his sister and remaining family, but also the entirety of England (*Mandeville* 3:330). Tellingly, he deems the union between the Protestant-bred Henrietta and the Papist Clifford "worse than incest" (*Mandeville* 3:330). This statement rather openly alludes to the transgressive sibling relationship depicted in this novel, while at the same time relating the transgression to both the narrative's and the author's historical circumstances.

This comment on England's shame brought upon itself by the union of Presbyterian and Papist believers is precisely what unifies the different points of analysis in this paper. In the character of Mandeville, a deeply traumatized individual suffering from an empty nostalgia-as-illness reflected in his constant idealization of Henrietta as representative of his lost past, Godwin plays out potential options for the future of his contemporary Britain, shaken by social and political unrest.[11] One might be tempted to read reactionary tendencies into the novel, for Mandeville's longing for the past, in which his Presbyterian parents lived harmoniously alongside their Catholic neighbours, seems to create a desir-able image of peaceful serenity, potentially expanding the Godwinian ideal image of domestic attachments in pastoral simplicity, as expressed in *St Leon* (1799). In *Mande-ville*, Godwin certainly chose to present a rather critical image of domestic attachments as potentially contributing to the downfall of the individual. Naturally, attachments are

---

11   1812: Tory Prime Minister Spencer Perceval is assassinated by John Bellingham; 1811-1816: textile workers in Midlands break machines in fear of unemployment (called Lud-dites, referred to themselves as *blanketeers*) and march to London; 1815: Corn Laws raised food prices and costs of living, increasing demands for reform overall, terrible housing conditions, anticipating 1819: Peterloo Massacre in Manchester

not depicted as harmful *per se*, but should manic nostalgia prevail, encroachingly unbalanced relationships can become toxic. In this reading of the novel, Mandeville's manic fixation on his sister has been the focal point of the analysis, but his traumatic past also gives rise to numerous other toxic attachments in the novel, such as to the ill-meaning (and tellingly named) Mallison or the misanthropic Lisle, which all result in mental disruptions, causing the narrator to hide from the world.

On the novel's meta-level, this challenging approach to nostalgia in an individual's character history can be transferred to the author's view of Britain's past and his vision for Britain's future. Answers to questions regarding desirable socio-political developments should not be searched for in the past, as manic attachment to the good old days will only lead to stagnation and decay. In his *Political Justice*, Godwin had already claimed that history has seen gradual progress as people liberated themselves from political subjugation, especially in monarchical and aristocratic governments (Philp n.p.). Modes of government shape people's lives and must be in continuous evaluation regarding their contribution to universal benevolence. As expressed in his much-cited essay "Of History and Romance", Godwin therefore deems it essential to study individual men, as "[h]e who would study the history of nations abstracted from individuals whose passions and peculiarities are interesting to people's minds, will find it a dry and frigid scene. It will supply him with no clear ideas" (Godwin "History and Romance" 361) Instead, he proposes to focus on the individual as *pars pro toto*:

> It will be necessary for us to scrutinise the nature of man, before we can pronounce what it is of which social man is capable. Laying aside the generalities of historical abstraction, we must mark the operation of human passions; must observe the empire of motives whether grovelling or elevated; and must note the influence that one human being exercises over another, and the ascendancy of the daring and the wise over the vulgar multitude. It is thus, and thus only, that we shall be enabled to add, to the knowledge of the past, a sagacity that can penetrate into the depths of futurity. … He that would prove the liberal and spirited benefactor of his species, must connect the two branches of history together, and regard the knowledge of the individual, as that which can alone give energy and utility to the records of our social existence. (Godwin "History and Romance" 362-63)

Only by analyzing individual histories and individual passions can the past thus be understood and give rise to future improvements. While it is still of the utmost importance to also investigate humankind's history in general, Godwin clearly stresses the centrality of character studies and their potential to relay how circumstances shape characters.[12]

---

12   Godwin further proposes that people should look towards the ancient Greeks and Romans for inspiration, instead of analysing modern governments in England or France, as they were men of "a free and undaunted spirit" (Godwin "History and Romance" 365), so often inhibited in oppressive modern modes of government. In the Greek and Roman republics, ideas of men of genius "expanded and fired the soul", prompting others to follow Virgil, Horace, and Cicero, amongst others, in their passionate "exhibition of bold and masculine virtues" (Godwin "History and Romance" 364).

In the mode of a personal case history, Godwin created a multi-layered character portrait traversed by transgressions in the depiction of an individual haunted by empty nostalgia and a quasi-incestuous, manic, yet unfruitful relationship to his sister, which is pioneering in terms of later depictions of individual case histories in psychoanalysis.[13] At the same time, this portrait of nostalgia-as-illness functions as a commentary on the sociopolitical development of Britain in the late 1810s, in which it is clearly expressed how a pathological adherence to the past would only lead to impotent standstill. Since, in *Mandeville*, history as such becomes highly unreliable and complicated, the novel necessarily cannot and does not aim at providing a coherent and precise account of the past and *things as they were*. Godwin's ultimate contribution in his construction of a fruitful future lies in his role as both a writer of romance and of history[14] as he relates how circumstances shape character to shed light on the multi-layered web of power structures operating on individuals and thereby determining human progress.

Works Cited

Anspach, Carolyn Kiser. "Medical Dissertation on Nostalgia by Johannes Hofer, 1688". *Bulletin of the Institute of the History of Medicine* 2 (1934): 376-91.

Bentham, Jeremy. *Introduction to the Principles of Morals and Legislation*. London: T. Payne and Son, 1789.

Berrios, German E. *The History of Mental Symptoms: Descriptive Psychopathology Since the Nineteenth Century*. Cambridge: Cambridge UP, 1996.

Breuer, Joseph and Sigmund Freud. *Studies on Hysteria*. Leipzig and Wien: Franz Deuticke, 1895.

Byron, Lord [George Gordon]. *The Works of Lord Byron*. 12 vols. London: John Murray, 1824.

Clemit, Pamela. *The Godwinian Novel: The Rational Fictions of Godwin, Brockden Brown, Mary Shelley*. Oxford: Clarendon Press, 1993.

Erikson, Erik Homburger. *Childhood and Society*. New York: W. W. Norton, 1950.

Esquirol, Jean-Étienne Dominique. *Dictionnaire des sciences médicales*. Paris: C.-L.-F. Panckoucke, 1819.

Farrar, Margaret E. "Amnesia, Nostalgia, and the Politics of Place Memory". *Political Research Quarterly* 64 (2011): 723-35.

Godwin, William. *Mandeville: A Tale of the Seventeenth Century in England*. Edinburgh: Archibald Constable and Co., 1817.

---

13   See for example the case study of Anna O. (Bertha Pappenheim) in Breuer and Freud's *Studies on Hysteria* (1895).

14   See Godwin "History and Romance" 373.

---. "Of History and Romance". *Caleb Williams*. Ed. Maurice Hindle. London: Penguin, 2005. 359-74.

Goldstein, Jan E. *Console and Classify: The French Psychiatric Profession in the Nineteenth Century*. Chicago: University of Chicago Press, 2001.

O'Sullivan, Lisa. "The Time and Place of Nostalgia: Re-situating a French Disease". *Journal of the History of Medicine and Allied Sciences* 67 (2012): 626-49.

Philp, Mark. "William Godwin". *The Stanford Encyclopedia of Philosophy*. Ed. Edward N. Zalta. https://plato.stanford.edu/archives/sum2017/entries/godwin/ (accessed 19 May 2020).

Pinel, Philippe. *A Treatise on Insanity*. Trans. D. D. Davis. London: W. Todd, 1806.

Rajan, Tilottama. "The Disfiguration of Enlightenment: War, Trauma, and the Historical Novel in Godwin's *Mandeville*". *Godwinian Moments: From the Enlightenment to Romanticism*. Ed. Robert Maniquis and Victoria Myers. Toronto: University of Toronto Press, 2016. 172-93.

Richardson, Alan. "Rethinking Romantic Incest: Human Universals, Literary Representation, and the Biology of Mind". *New Literary History* 31 (2000): 553-72.

Sedlmayr, Gerold. *The Discourse of Madness in Britain, 1790-1815*. Trier: WVT, 2011.

Shapiro, Ann-Louise. *Breaking the Codes: Female Criminality in Fin-de-Siècle Paris*. Stanford: Stanford UP, 1996.

Shelley, Mary. *Frankenstein; or, The Modern Prometheus*. London: Lackington, Hughes, Harding, Mavor & Jones, 1818.

Shelley, Percy Bysshe. *Rosalind and Helen, A Modern Eclogue; With Other Poems*. London: C. and J. Ollier, 1819.

---. *The Letters of Percy Bysshe Shelley*. Ed. Roger Ingpen. Vol. 2. London: G. Bell and Sons, 1914.

"teraphim." *A Dictionary of the Bible*. Ed. W. R. F. Browning. Oxford Biblical Studies Online. http://www.oxfordbiblicalstudies.com/articwilsole/opr/t94/e1881 (accessed 19 May 2020).

Westermarck, Edward. *The History of Human Marriage*. 3 vols. London: Macmillan and Co, 1925.

Alexandra Böhm

Transgressive Encounters: Sympathy with Animals in John Aikin and Anna Laetitia Barbauld's *Evenings at Home* and Samuel Taylor Coleridge's "Rime of the Ancyent Marinere"

Encountering Animals in Romantic Period Writing

This chapter will deal with transgressive human-animal encounters in Romantic period writings. Trans-species encounters in literary texts have the potential of being transgressive, when they violate established frames of perceiving and classifying the world. Texts such as John Aikin and Anna Laetitia Barbauld's *Evenings at Home; Or The Juvenile Budget Opened* (1792-96) or Samuel Taylor Coleridge's "Rime of the Ancyent Marinere" (1797-98) seriously question hierarchic relationships between humans and animals by portraying alternative models of cohabitation, inclusion or resonance, which are grounded in sympathy with the animal other.

Sympathy as a human trait became one of the central virtues of the eighteenth century, most prominently in the writings of the Scottish moral philosophers David Hume and Adam Smith.[1] They assumed that the primary source for society, its sociability and community, is not, as, for instance, Bernard Mandeville argues, the egoistic drive of self-love but sympathy and compassion, i.e. the capacity for feeling and connecting with others.[2] The focus on the passionate instead of the rational human subject has also far-reaching consequences for the relationship between humans and animals. If the capacity to feel becomes a main concern, then the traditional exclusion of animals from the moral community because of their assumed lack of speech and reason becomes problematic. When transferred to non-human animals, sympathy can acquire a transgressive quality, as it questions the line between humans and animals and inverts (God-)given hierarchies, meanings and orders.

Though hardly taken seriously in Romantic scholarship before the so-called 'animal turn', non-human animals abound as subjects of Romantic period writing in almost every genre and with most writers of the period. If we take a short glance at some of the best-known Romantic poems by the 'big six' we come across such canonical texts as John Keats's "Ode to a Nightingale", William Blake's "Tyger" from *The Marriage of Heaven and Hell* and Percy Bysshe Shelley's "To a Skylark". William Wordsworth wrote a pastoral "The Pet-Lamb", and Lord Byron an elegy to his dog Boatswain. The "most famous

---

1   See especially David Hume's *A Treatise of Human Nature* and Adam Smith's *The Theory of Moral Sentiments* for their influential concepts of sympathy.

2   For an extensive discussion of the concept of sympathy and its relation to the cultural and socio-historical discourse of the long eighteenth century, see Jonathan Lamb.

animal poem of the period", as Onno Oerlemans puts it, is perhaps Samuel Taylor Coleridge's "Rime of the Ancyent Marinere" (Oerlemans 51), where the killing of an albatross has disastrous consequences for the mariners. Apart from those widely known poems on animal figures, there is also a large, but lesser-known body of work where non-human animals and their relations to humans are central. In their pivotal studies on animals in British Romantic writings, Tess Cosslett and Christine Kenyon Jones have pointed to the eminent role of animals in the period's children's literature as in Sarah Trimmer's *Fabulous Histories* from 1786 (later edition 1798), Mary Wollstonecraft's *Original Stories from Real Life* from 1788 or Anna Laetitia Barbauld and John Aikin's *Evenings at Home*, written between 1792 and 1796. In addition to children's literature, animals feature prominently in contemporaneous discussions of animal rights.[3] The period around 1800 may rightly count, as Kenyon Jones puts it, as a "sea-change in attitudes to animals" (Kenyon Jones 2009, 137).

The eighteenth-century 'culture of sensibility' contributed significantly to the enduring commitment to the protection of animals as sentient beings from cruelty and pain by clergymen, philosophers, democrats, poets and most notably by educated women of the middle classes (cf. Roscher 124-73). An essential part of the successful struggle for the recognition of animals as sentient beings with their own rights was, as sociologist Rainer Wiedenmann emphasizes, the increase in media distribution, which led to the formation of a civic public (cf. Wiedenmann 398). Literary texts played a crucial role in this process, I argue, as they are able to depict or stage encounters that encourage sympathy with the 'brute creatures'. In the course of the eighteenth century, and especially in Romantic period writing, non-human animals are no longer just symbols of or stand-ins for humans such as in the traditional animal fable with its stereotypical traits, characters and morale (cf. Spencer 54). Animals increasingly act as protagonists in stories, which means that they fully operate as characters on the diegetic level of the text and exceed mere semiotic functions. Encounters between human and non-human animals are generally at the core of an ensuing relationship between both parties.

What is an encounter, though?[4] As primary meaning of the term 'encounter' the *OED* gives "a meeting face to face" that happens mostly "undesignedly or casually". Deriving from the Old French *encontre* or the late Latin *incontrāre*, there is, however, also a confrontational quality inherent in the word. An encounter is also "a meeting (of adversaries or opposing forces) in conflict; hence, a battle, skirmish, duel, etc." The *OED* entry indicates that the term 'encounter' not only denominates a simple meeting between two parties, but that 'encounter' is also a conceptually charged construct (cf. Wilson 451). Donna Haraway, one of the leading Animal Studies scholars, transfers Mary Louise Pratt's concept of encounters between colonizers and colonized, who often act in asym-

---

3   See David Perkins for a detailed account of the development of Animal Rights during the second half of the eighteenth century and the role Romantic writing takes in it.

4   For a comprehensive overview to encounter theory and especially to human-animal encounters in various disciplines see Böhm and Ullrich, eds.

metrical power relations, to human-animal encounters, and envisions positive contact zones. In her influential study *When Species Meet*, she describes encounters between human and non-human animals in the contact zone as "world-making entanglements" (Haraway 4).

For my reading of literary animal encounters in Romantic period writing, I would like to distinguish with the animal ethics philosopher Martin Huth between two different forms of encounters, i.e. 'framed' and 'disruptive' encounters. Huth stresses that each time "one encounters an animal representing a certain species, population, or category, frames of perception and recognition are reproduced" (Huth 49). Framed encounters hence tend to affirm and consolidate given notions about the animal other and thereby reinforce boundaries – such as between human and animal, culture and nature, civilized and wild, morally relevant or irrelevant. Whereas framed encounters reproduce typical definitions and locate animals within ordinary classifications, for example, a cow is an efficient provider of milk or meat, disruptive encounters upset ordinary categorizing and acknowledge the singular situatedness of non-human animals. Disruptive encounters challenge and transgress set boundaries. The notion of encounter as disruption, which challenges and destabilizes conceptual and symbolic orders, is associated with experiences of shock, surprise, rupture and transgression. Rhetorical means or aesthetic figures that can express this experience in literary texts are e.g. epiphanies or the sublime. American political theorist and New Materialist Jane Bennett mentions two different forms of disruptive or, in her term, surprising encounters. For Bennett surprising encounters possess two main features, unexpectedness and overpowerment. Thus, a surprising encounter is "a meeting with something that you did not expect and are not fully prepared to engage". According to her, "[c]ontained within this surprise state are (1) a pleasurable feeling of being charmed by the novel and as yet unprocessed encounter and (2) a more *unheimlich* (uncanny) feeling of being disrupted or torn out of one's default sensory-psychic-intellectual disposition" (Bennett 5). Encounters can act thus as unexpected disruptions of the habitualized frames we use for understanding the world and ourselves. They can further have the power to upset fundamentally taken for granted hierarchies, orders or distinctions. The shifting or destabilizing of established borders and categories is likely to bring about a state of non-sovereignty that the subject experiences as uncanny.

In the following, I will look at sympathetic animal narratives and analyse in which way they are transgressive of the human-animal divide that dominates Western thinking in the Stoicist, Aquinian or Cartesian tradition, and thus present a counter-narrative to hierarchically ordered human-animal relations. I will further ask to what extent protagonists and readers of Aikin and Barbauld's collection *Evenings at Home*, and of Coleridge's Romantic poem "The Rime of the Ancyent Marinere" experience encounters between human and non-human animals as transgressions, as violations of boundaries, and in which way encounters contribute to negotiations of borders. With Donna Haraway, I will also inquire which transformational potential human-animal encounters possess in the contact zone. The interplay between framed and disruptive encounters, I argue, is characteristic for the narratives of Aikin and Barbauld's children's stories as well as Coleridge's poem, which both rather enact an ethics of sympathetic inclusion than reinforce borders and hierarchies that underlie notions of radical alterity.

Sympathetic Animal Encounters in Children's Literature

Recent animal and ecocritical studies in Romanticism like David Perkins's *Romanticism and Animal Rights* or Onno Oerlemans's *Romanticism and the Materiality of Nature* have paid increasing attention to the often ideologically and politically charged cultural discourse of sympathy and its practices, which, as research shows, informed also a substantial part of the period's literary writing.[5] "Art, poetry, and prose during the period are full of sympathetic animals", as Lucinda Cole puts it with a view to the later part of the eighteenth century (Cole 5). However, many scholars come to the conclusion that "most who wrote in favour of humane treatment of animals did so with the explicit premise that humans are far superior to animals, and that cruelty to animals needs to be avoided primarily because it reflects poorly on our moral supremacy" (Oerlemans 53). Children's literature was intended to teach kindness to animals presuming that cruelty to animals furthers cruel behaviour towards humans. This idea already governed for example William Hogarth's famous series of plates *The Four Stages of Cruelty* from 1751, portraying schoolboy Tom Nero's cruelty to animals, which he also continues to practise as an adult. The subsequent plate suggests that this brutality leads to the murder of a pregnant servant he had seduced. Finally, his career ends on a dissection table under the physician's knife with a dog eating his intestines.[6] As John Locke put it: "For the custom of tormenting and killing of beasts will by degrees harden [the children's] minds even towards men, and they who accustom themselves to delight in the suffering and destruction of inferior creatures, will not be apt to be very compassionate or benign to those of their own kind" (Locke 349).

Children's literature, then, had the educational task to generate fellow feelings for animals to teach them morality. A standard rhetorical device that those texts employ is, as Tess Cosslett observes, the reversal of roles as in assuming an animal eye's view (cf. Cosslett 16). The child reader's task is to imaginatively take on the role of the animal and see the world from his or her perspective. This exercise is also fundamental to Adam

---

5   For the political and ideological dimension of the discourse of sympathy in the eighteenth century, see especially Tobias Menely's study *The Animal Claim: Sensibility and the Creaturely Voice* and his account of zoöphilpsychosis – "a nervous disorder by an obsessive sensitivity to animal suffering" – for contemporary critique of sympathy with animals (Menely 199).

6   Kathryn Shevelow points out that Hogarth's plates illustrate the omnipresence and interconnection of violence and cruelty on the level of the individual and the state. She argues that in contrast to anthropocentric positions that are only concerned about the humans when teaching sympathy to animals, Hogarth "maintained that animals genuinely suffer and that inflicting this abuse on them is wrong in itself" (Shevelow 138).

Smith's theory of sympathy, which he developed in *The Theory of Moral Sentiments* in 1759. For the Scottish moral philosopher, sympathy is the ability to project ourselves into the situation of other people by the imagination. Sympathy works as placing ourselves into the position of another and envisioning how we would feel if we were them. Smith is convinced that, "[a]s we have no immediate experience of what other men feel, we can form no idea of the manner in which they are affected, but by conceiving what we ourselves should feel in the like situation" (Smith 11). For Elisa Aaltola this is "still the most common idea of empathy, as children are taught to imagine the experiences of others" in the sense of "'How would you feel?'" (Aaltola 27). Indeed, in Sarah Trimmer's immensely popular book *Fabulous Histories, Designed for the Instruction of Children, Respecting their Treatment of Animals*, later published as *The Story of the Robins*, the instructor of the text, Mrs. Benson, asserts "that it would be a good way to accustom one's self, before one kills any thing, to change situations with it in imagination" (Trimmer 1798, 122). In his influential theory, Smith emphasizes, however, that there is no access to the actual feelings of the object of sympathy. The sympathizer can never know the sensations even of his or her next of kin:

> Though our brother is upon the rack, as long as we ourselves are at our ease, our senses will never inform us of what he suffers. They never did, and never can, carry us beyond our own person, and it is by the imagination only that we can form any conception of what are his sensations. Neither can that faculty help us to this any other way, than by representing to us what would be our own, if we were in his case. It is the impressions of our senses only, not those of his, which our imaginations copy. By the imagination we place ourselves in his situation, we conceive ourselves enduring all the same torments, we enter as it were into his body ... (Smith 11-12)

Smith's theory of sympathy is a self-oriented form of fellow feeling that ultimately keeps a distance between self and other. According to Smith, there is no way of experiencing the pain of the other, as the sympathetic encounter with the other is only available through the imagination. It operates as a projection of the self's feelings onto the other, to the extent that self and other remain distinct. Sympathy in this sense has been critiqued as a selfish principle that is too often guided by the sympathizer's own interests and mental concepts, which can easily lead to misrecognition and appropriation of the other (cf. Aaltola 30).

Research on the period's children's literature by authors such as Christine Kenyon Jones, Tess Cosslett, or more recently Richard De Ritter and Jane Spencer, widely agrees on the notion that the narratives employ sympathy for animals as a means to teach children their place in society and ultimately to reinforce ideas of social and species hierarchy.[7] The texts' appeal for sympathetic identification with animals is accordingly not a sign of equality or moral consideration, but of human superiority and difference. One of the

---

7   See Kenyon Jones on Mary Wollstonecraft's *Original Stories* (Kenyon Jones 2001, 63), Cosslett on Sarah Trimmer's *Fabulous Histories* (41), De Ritter on Barbauld and Aikin's *Evenings at Home* (50-51), and Jane Spencer generally on children's literature of the period (chap. 3).

most popular children's stories that solidifies hierarchical frameworks is Sarah Trimmer's *Fabulous Histories*. Hierarchies in the natural world mirror social hierarchies as well as familial structures: parents have a firm authority over their children and humans over animals, exactly as "the great CREATOR" (Trimmer 1798, 124) has power over human beings. Though the narrative encourages sympathy, consideration and compassion for animals, it is mandatory to draw "a line of distinction" (Trimmer 1803, 304). As the instructress Mrs. Benson points out with regard to the text's eponymous bird family: "It is very true, that we ought not to indulge so great a degree of pity and tenderness for such animals as for those who are more properly our fellow-creatures; I mean men, women, and children; but, as every living creature can feel, we should have a constant regard to those feelings, and strive to give happiness rather than inflict misery" (Trimmer 1798, 33).

By renouncing cruelty to animals, Kenyon Jones emphasizes, "one could not only show one's superior education and sensibility, but could also actively demonstrate how *unlike* the beasts one was" (Kenyon Jones 2009, 148). Sympathizing with animals, in other words, works as a way of reassuring humankind's superiority and exceptionalism. Animal protection serves as a means to protect humans' own brutalization. This view underlines what Immanuel Kant argued for in his *Grundlegung zur Metaphysik der Sitten*, namely, that animals as non-rational beings are only of relative worth and have no intrinsic value (cf. Kant 60). According to Kant, there are no duties to animals. If humans behave kindly to animals, they only perform an indirect duty towards humanity. In agreement with Hogarth's ideas, Kant is convinced that cruel treatment of animals numbs and weakens a natural moral capacity, which is beneficial in relation to other people. In this notion, animals have no worth of their own, but rather a derivative and instrumental one.

In the introduction to Aikin and Barbauld's altogether 97 pieces of *Evenings at Home*, the reader learns that friends and visitors of the Fairborne mansion composed little texts "for promoting the instruction and entertainment of the younger part of the household" (*Evenings* 5). Afterwards the mother kept them in a box until the holidays, when the children drew them randomly out of the box and read them out aloud over a period of thirty evenings. The fictional editor states that because of the interest in those readings by the neighbourhood, they now make the pieces available to the public. The fiction of the introductory note contains already central poetic principles of the text. First, it announces the polyphonic character of the collection. It points to the different voices that are gathered in the collection. They account for the great variety of genres and forms used, such as fable, story, dialogue, natural history lesson, fairy tale or poem. Rather than presenting a "methodical arrangement", the contents are given in "the promiscuous order in which they came to hand" (*Evenings* 6). Apart from this note, no further authorial voice comments on the single pieces. This corresponds with the dialogic character of the collection. There are not only (Socratic) dialogues between parents and children as a form of presentation, but the whole structure of the text is dialogic. The pieces present subjects from different perspectives, which comment on and stand in relation to one another. The reader cannot deduce stable and fixed truths from any one piece, but has to acknowledge their provisional, fragmentary and interdependent character. Like in a mosaic, the whole picture only emerges, when all pieces come together.[8] Consistent with the presentation of multiple perspectives, a central feature of the stories is the technique of defamiliarization, which makes things strange. In this way, the reader perceives them with other eyes and from a new viewpoint that questions assumed habits and opinions. One exceptional example is the story "Traveller's Wonders" in which a father figure tells his children "some curious particulars" of people he had observed during his travels. The story makes extensive use of the traveller's defamiliarizing gaze on actually close and familiar objects, a technique that became famous with Charles de Montesquieu's *Lettres Persanes* (1721). In the end, the father informs the children that he meant to show them "that a foreigner might easily represent everything as equally strange and wonderful among us, as we could do with respect to his country" (*Evenings* 16).

The defamiliarizing stance is also characteristic of "The Young Mouse", where the human world is seen from the perspective of the animal protagonist. The subtitle identifies the piece as belonging to the genre of the fable and accounts for the speaking animal. Animal fables usually work with stereotypical, recognizable character traits. The mouse typically is small, naïve and in need of protection. As such, she is a classical figure for sympathetic identification.

One day the young mouse of the story excitedly reports to her mother about a 'perfect house' she found:

> Mother! Said she, the good people of this family have built me a house to live in; it is in the cupboard: I am sure it is just big enough: covered all over with wires; and I dare say they have made it on purpose to screen me from that terrible cat, which ran after me so often: there is an entrance just big enough for me, but puss cannot follow; and they have been so good as to put in some toasted cheese, which smells so deliciously, that I should have run in directly and taken possession of my new house, but I thought I would tell you first that we might go in together, and both lodge there tonight, for it will hold us both. (*Evenings* 12)

The mother of course warns the young mouse that this house is a trap, and the moral of the fable is not to trust first appearances. "Though man has not so fierce a look as a cat,

---

8   This may be one of the reasons for the quite contrary interpretations of *Evenings at Home*. See Darren Howard, who also emphasizes the importance of multiple perspectives. Some stories, he claims, achieve a new meaning when read in the light of another piece, as for example "The Wasp and the Bee", which seems on its own to propagate servility and industriousness to the human masters. "The Transmigrations of Indur", however, put the human-animal relationship, which the bee praises, in a completely new perspective. Humans, it becomes clear, only care for bees in order to steal their honey, and subsequently smoke them to death when no longer useful (cf. Howard 657). De Ritter, in a recent analysis, however comes to the conclusion that Aikin and Barbauld's *Evenings at Home* reinforce a hierarchical relationship between humans and animals, "suggesting that for children to become fully human they must learn to assert their biblically ordained dominance over animals" (De Ritter 51).

he is as much our enemy, and has still more cunning" (*Evenings* 12). For Cosslett this is an "animal-centered, anti-human moral" (Cosslett 33). It is also, I argue, a meta-reflexive reader instruction. Rather than situated in the world of the fable, the story depicts a widespread violent human-animal relation that results from framed human-animal encounters. The frames of perception by the people of the house who put up the mousetrap are not those of the traditional fable. In their reliance on unquestioned frames, they see the animals as a cumbersome multitude, as transmitters of diseases who greedily help themselves to human storage. Against the background of these habitualized expectations, mice are vermin that need extermination.

Through the anthropomorphic projections in the quoted passage, however, the child learns to see the mouse as something other than a pest. The mouse possesses a voice and with it, a subjectivity that makes her appear as a creature with delight and distress as well as with strong familial bonds. She longs for a secure home, where she can be happy and need not fear the cat. Obviously, the animal creature mirrors the child reader through its age, perspective and longing for untroubled happiness. The similarity between reader and child engenders sympathy and is the catalyst for the disruptive encounter between reader and text that transgresses the frames of the habitualized notion of the mouse.

When paying a closer look at the first part of the fable, the fable discloses its multiple layers. The reader is acquainted with the daily life of the small animal: "A young mouse lived in a cupboard where sweetmeats were kept: she dined every day upon biscuit, marmalade, or fine sugar. Never any little mouse had lived so well" (*Evenings* 11). The description of the third-person narrator suggests an undue and gluttonous behaviour of the animal that trespasses into the world of the human and her property. In the following passage, the semantic of verbs like 'peep at', 'steal down' and 'run to', emphasize the reader's perception of the mouse's conduct as forbidden or transgressive. This reading corresponds with the perception of mice in framed human-animal encounters. At the same time, this pattern of interpretation is juxtaposed with an emotionalization of the mouse's life, her innocent hopes and desires. 'Never had any mouse lived so well', expresses her ambition for a good life. The formulation, she "picked up the crumbs, and nobody had ever hurt her" (*Evenings* 11), stresses her trust and the triviality of her 'theft' to which the humans' reaction is – as implied – rather out of scale. Her ultimate goal to be "quite happy" (*Evenings* 11) is only marred by the existence of the cat. What ethic does the story of the mouse express then other than the fable's simplistic moral?

The child reader's identification with the mouse that rests to a great extent on the perception of similarities between them, necessitates a re-evaluation of the non-human animal and its relationship with humans. Sue Donaldson and Will Kymlicka describe such animals that live in the proximity of humans as "liminal animals, to indicate their in-between status, neither wilderness animals nor domesticated animals" (Donaldson and Kymlicka 210). These animals, they explicate, are mostly unacknowledged and remain invisible. However, this does not lead to indifference from the humans; rather they are often "stigmatized as aliens or invaders who wrongly trespass on human territory"

(Donaldson and Kymlicka 211). Instead of eliminating them from what is conceived as distinctively human space, they argue for "strategies of inclusion and coexistence" (Donaldson and Kymlicka 216). Some of the pieces in *Evenings at Home*, make those liminal creatures visible as humans' neighbours. Another piece in which liminal animals play a role is "On the Martin". There the father praises the birds' sagacity, solidarity and diligence to teach the children consideration and respect. He accounts for his caveat not to destroy their nests or steal their eggs with the martins' trust, who "always build in towns and villages about the houses" (*Evenings* 53). Their leap of faith morally asks for humans' reciprocity, "for as they come such a long way to visit us, and lodge in our houses without fear, we ought to use them kindly" (*Evenings* 54). While the ethic in the fable with the young mouse is a negative one that criticizes human-animal relationships for their failure to consider possibilities of cohabitation, the father in the story of the martins argues positively for inclusion and cohabitation. Humans ought to acknowledge the right of existence of other animals as well as other perspectives on the world.

A critique of the anthropocentric notion that the world is made for man alone is also central to the dialogue "What Animals Are Made For" between Sophia and her father. The child who finds herself pestered by flies asks her father, "pray, what were flies made for?" (*Evenings* 233). The father's answer is tripartite. First, he deconstructs the concept of utility by encouraging her to take the perspective of the fly who is equally "puzzled to find out what men were good for" (*Evenings* 233). Second, he questions humans' anthropocentrism, when he affirms that there is a world independent of humans and their use, a view that according to Keith Thomas "can be fairly regarded as one of the great revolutions in Western thought" (Thomas 166). Many animals, the father claims, are "far from being useful to us", moreover, "there are vast tracts of the earth where few or no men inhabit, which are yet full of beasts, birds, insects, and all living things" (*Evenings* 233). His third argument finally is that each being is "made to be happy" (*Evenings* 234). Although humans may possess some superior qualities, "the Creator equally desires the happiness of all his creatures, and looks down with as much benignity upon these flies that are sporting around us, as upon ourselves" (*Evenings* 234). As Thomas states, this is a view that is common to religious dissent.[9] Special to Aikin and Barbauld's collection is, however, their interpretation of the concept of life. This holds for the life of the individual animal creature that children (and adults) should respect, as life is "all that it possesses" (*Evenings* 234). However, the importance of the individual life – and this is true for human and non-human animals – is counterbalanced by the notion of earth's productive forces that endlessly generate life. "Thou, perhaps, would'st stop the vast machine of the universe to save a fly from being crushed under its wheels; but innumerable flies and men are crushed every day, yet the grand motion goes on" (*Evenings* 326), says the Solitary to the stranger in the story "Shipwreck and Providence". This perspective contrasts with the father's recollection in "What Animals Are Made

---

9   See the chapter "Compassion for the Brute Creation" in Thomas's groundbreaking study
     Man and the Natural World from 1983.

For" of "the old gentleman, that having been a long time plagued with a great fly that buzzed about his face all dinner-time, at length, after many efforts caught it" (*Evenings* 234). Instead of crushing it, he opens the window, saying, "get thee gone, poor creature; I won't hurt a hair of thy head; surely the world is wide enough for thee and me" (*Evenings* 234). To illustrate his point that humans should never abuse animals, the father quotes a famous poetic example from the sentimentalist discourse. The "old gentleman" is of course Uncle Toby from Laurence Sterne's *The Life and Opinions of Tristram Shandy* (1759-67).

While much of the period's children's literature is in its character rather affirmative of hierarchies and clear boundaries, e.g. between children and their parents or between humans and animals, Aikin and Barbauld's *Evenings at Home* is in its dialogic and polyphonous structure essentially anti-hierarchical. The text's trans-species encounters systematically transgress framed perceptions of non-human animals. The organization of the collection resembles the idea of an organism where all parts are independent of each other, in its entirety, though, the parts are kept in balance.[10] *Evenings at Home*, in which humans' relations to animals and the natural world take up an important part, shows humans, as Howard puts it, as "part of an ecosystem" (Howard 665), in which all creatures, human and non-human, equally strive for and have a right to happiness.

Encounters with the Animal Other:
Coleridge's "Rime of the Ancyent Marinere"

Coleridge wrote his ballad about the experiences of a sailor in 1797 and 1798. The poem was published the same year in the first edition of Wordsworth and Coleridge's joint *Lyrical Ballads*. Due to its complexity and the fascination it provokes, the "Rime of the Ancyent Marinere" is perhaps one of the most interpreted Romantic poems. Traditional interpretations incline to read the poems' animals as metaphors, as for instance the albatross came to mean Christ in a tale of the Mariner's sin and redemption. This "disappearing animal trick" is still representative for the handling of animals in literary criticism as Susan McHugh points out. Although "animals abound in literature across all ages and cultures, only in rarefied ways have they been the focal point of systematic literary study" (McHugh 29). Animals, and this is especially true for Romantic poetry, are often

---

10   Although Aikin and Barbauld repeatedly use the metaphor of the machine throughout their pieces, the collection seems closer to the new idea of the organism where single parts possess a greater degree of autonomy and individuality than in the traditional metaphor of the machine. The notion of balancing that is important to *Evenings at Home* (see e.g. "Earth and Her Children") is central to the organism, in which parts and whole interrelate dynamically. A discussion of the question to what extent the organism serves not only as a metaphor for the poetic principle of the text but also characterizes the depiction of the organic world in the collection, and finally reflects – as a model for the state – Aikin and Barbauld's radical political views, would be rewarding, exceeds however the limits of this chapter.

interpreted as metaphors for the poetic imagination or the poet's consciousness. They only seem to gain literary value when they are "metaphorically speaking of and for the human" (McHugh 29). For McHugh, the endeavour to let animals appear as themselves, to take them at their face value, is a challenge to a discipline that only ever interprets animals in literature as "humans-in-animal-suits" (McHugh 29).

As the animal reading of Aikin and Barbauld's fable showed, the mouse is not only a metaphor that transports a human moral but also a diegetic animal that engages the reader in reflecting about human-animal relationships. With regard to Coleridge's poem, there have been several attempts to account for the animals in the poem, especially from an ecocritical perspective. Peter Heymans, for example, dedicates a whole chapter to "The Rime of the Ancyent Marinere" in his study *Animality in British Romanticism*. Heymans's insightful discussion of the poem within an ecocritical frame, however, shows the difficulty of resisting metaphorizing interpretations of animals in literary texts. At the outset, Heymans emphasizes that it "is illustrative of literary criticism's long-standing apathy towards everything non-human that a poem as concerned with animal cruelty and ecological interdependence as Coleridge's 'The Rime of the Ancient Mariner' was, until recently rarely read as an environmentalist text" (Heymans 44). The tendency of what makes Coleridge's poem especially applicable to ecocritical perspectives is, according to Heymans, its "tendency to deploy animals not as mere background puppets against which tragedy unfolds, but as crucial, if persistently vague, characters pushing the plot towards its redemptive conclusion" (Heymans 44). Yet, only one paragraph later, animals and their materiality disappear, in a twist that is characteristic of the discipline. Heymans states that he is not only interested in the moralistic concern of the "touchy-feely animal rights message", but in the "more sophisticated examination of the ways in which nature is aesthetically received and constructed" (Heymans 45). In his analysis, the water-snakes become once more an emblem for the principle of the imagination. The polemical disdain of so-called sentimental animal rights questions and its association with simplistic sentimentality has a long tradition and was used to deride the credibility of the movement.[11] In the following, I propose an animal reading of Coleridge's poem that understands the text as a succession of four distinct animal encounters that start with the Mariner's framed perception of the non-human animals and finally turn into a disruptive experience, which transgresses hierarchical borders. I suggest that a focus on encounters and the sympathetic imagination offers a new focus for the poem's progress that is traditionally read in Christian terms of sin, fall and redemption.

"The Rime of the Ancyent Marinere" is a poem about transgression. Although the Mariner only sparsely informs his listener about the destination and the purpose of the voyage, the "emptiness of reference" as David Simpson calls it (Simpson 156), there are a few indications about the journey. When the Mariner mentions

---

11 See especially Menely's chapter "Sensibilities into Statutes: Animal Rights and the Afterlife of Sensibility" in *The Animal Claim* (Menely 164-201).

> The Sun came up upon the left,
> Out of the Sea came he!
> And he shone bright, and on the right
> Went down into the Sea ("Rime" ll. 29-32)

it is evident that the ship is sailing south. The crew is crossing the equator when the sun is "over the mast at noon" ("Rime" l. 34). From then on, the rhetoric of the Mariner implies that the ship's crew has transgressed a boundary and is reaching into unknown territory. The continuous southward movement of the ship suggests that they are heading towards the *terra australis*, the hidden continent in the Antarctic that James Cook's ship was in search of on his second voyage from 1772 to 1775. This is a likely destination as the Mariner's account stresses the overwhelming experience of the mist and snow and the all-embracing ice ("Rime" ll. 49-62). Coleridge's readers could have recognized the allusion to the *terra australis incognita* from reports by contemporary travellers who were in search of the last unknown land in the south.[12]

Simpson assumes that the poem's refusal to provide the reader with positive facts is part of a strategy of immediacy that arrests and hypnotizes the reader instead of guiding him securely through the story (cf. Simpson 155). The reader is indeed likely to respond to the poem's narrative opacity with puzzlement and disorientation. This poetic strategy reflects the mariners' failure at epistemological control and loss of empowerment in the unsurmountable ice, mist and unfathomable sea. Reassuring identifications collapse in the face of nature's awe-inspiring and overpowering agency.

More and more the frontier narrative with its trope of conquest of the unknown makes way for a narrative of the contact zone where, as Mary Louise Pratt points out, "multiple beings grapple with each other" in meaning-making encounters (Pratt 7). The Mariner and his crew, setting out in an imperial enterprise, meet with a strange and fearsome environment they cannot control or dominate. The rhetoric of the Mariner stresses this loss of control when he anthropomorphizes the devastating wind and ice as howling, growling or roaring (cf. "Rime" ll. 58-59). It is in this setting that the crew first encounters the albatross:

> At length did cross an Albatross,
> Thorough the Fog it came;
> And an it were a Christian Soul,
> We hail'd it in God's name.
>
> The Marineres gave it biscuit-worms,
> And round and round it flew:

---

12   For example Georges-Louis Leclerc, Count de Buffon, commented in his *Natural History* on recent attempts to discover the last unknown land, that "these new voyagers have uniformly met with thick fogs" (Buffon 14). "The thick fog", he assumes, "is produced by the presence or neighbourhood of the ice. This fog consists of minute particles of snow, which are suspended in the air and render it obscure. It often accompanies the great floating masses of ice, and reigns perpetually in frozen regions" (Buffon 14-15).

The Ice did split with a Thunder-fit,
The Helmsman steer'd us thro'.

And a good south wind sprung up behind,
The Albatross did follow;
And every day for food or play
Came to the Marinere's hollo!

In mist or cloud on mast or shroud,
It perch'd for vespers nine,
Whiles all the night thro' fog-smoke white
Glimmer'd the white moon-shine. ("Rime" ll. 61-76)

The mariners first encounter the animal as a reassuring counterpart that is almost human-like. However, as the ice breaks open with the arrival of the albatross so that the ship can pass, they interpret the animal as a symbol or omen. The presence of the albatross thus becomes a projection that is comforting to the human consciousness rather than granting the animal an intrinsic value. The Mariner's repeated use of left and right for East and West, which highlights the assumption of himself as central reference point, further underlines the crew's anthropocentrism ("Rime" ll. 81-84). Although the second encounter represents the pivotal point of the narration, the Mariner recounts it to his listener in only two lines. To the wedding guest's question, "Why look'st thou so?" he simply answers: "with my cross bow / I shot the Albatross" ("Rime" ll. 79-80).

Why does the Mariner shoot the albatross? The killing seems purposeless, as the ship has been doing well since the bird's arrival.[13] The Mariner's seemingly unmotivated, violent act still represents one of the poem's central mysteries. I want to propose an interpretation that relates the Mariner's "hellish" ("Rime" l. 89) deed to the destabilizing of boundaries in disruptive encounters. The albatross appears out of the fog like an epiphany, and the mariners hence hail the bird as a companion – almost as if it were a "Christian Soul". They feed the albatross and play with it, thereby establishing an intimate relationship with the animal. In return, the bird trustingly stays in close distance to the ship and its crew. When the Mariner shoots the Albatross, he returns to the hierarchical notion in the order of being. He corrects the mariners' sympathetic perception of the bird as a fellow creature, which transgresses the human-animal divide. By killing the bird, the Mariner hopes to regain agency and control that he had lost when stuck amidst the ice. By killing the animal other, he reinstates his power over the natural world. Thus, he restores the God-given hierarchy between human, animal, and the natural world, in which he believes. The Mariner's deed consequently results from reverting to a framed perception of the animal as an objectified inferior being that has no other significance than referring to humans' dominion over it, which the Bible assumedly granted.

---

13   Heymans argues that one "sensible explanation for the shooting lies in the Mariner's assumption that the bird is a bad omen, responsible for the 'fog and mist' hampering the ship's progress" (Heymans 47). This is, however, as unconvincing as the assumption that the Mariner is simply acting out of boredom. The crew welcomes the bird as a fellow creature. In the wake of this reassuring encounter, the ice splits and new wind comes up.

After what the ship's crew and the Ancient Mariner himself subsequently interpret as fatal slaughtering of the albatross, they experience a further devastating calm accompanied by tremendous thirst. The Mariner expresses his despair in the third animal encounter, when he exclaims:

> The very deeps did rot: O Christ!
> That ever this should be!
> Yea, slimy things did crawl with legs
> Upon the slimy Sea. ("Rime" ll. 119-22)

Again, the Mariner's subjective needs and desires, here for water, dominate his perception of the external world. In his anthropocentric perspective, the 'rotting' ocean and the 'slimy' water creatures arouse disgust, as they do not fulfil his craving for drinking water. Whereas for Heymans the Mariner's outburst indicates that he "becomes stuck" in "the seeping materiality of nature" (Heymans 50), I rather read the encounter as an attempt at the Mariner's self-preservation. He intends to draw a line of difference, when he stigmatizes the natural world in the frame of the abject so that it appears amorphous, multitudinous and repulsive. At second glance, the construction of a stable boundary, however, proves unreliable, as the slimy things possess legs, a quality that is rather characteristic of human beings than of water creatures. Instead of reaffirming and stabilizing the boundary between human and non-human animals, the Mariner's observation complicates and delinearizes the limit (cf. Derrida 398).

The fourth and final animal encounter is again distinct in its nature. Rather than distancing himself from outward nature as before, the mariner has an immersive experience in the sense that bodily, conscious and pre-conscious states thoroughly intertwine with the world. With the aid of the moon that Robert Penn Warren suggested in his 1946 reading of Coleridge's poem as symbol of the secondary imagination (Warren 405), he has a sudden epiphanic encounter with the water-snakes:

> Beyond the shadow of the ship
> I watch'd the water-snakes:
> They mov'd in tracks of shining white;
> And when they rear'd, the elfish light
> Fell off in hoary flakes.
>
> Within the shadow of the ship
> I watch'd their rich attire:
> Blue, glossy green, and velvet black
> They coil'd and swam; and every track
> Was a flash of golden fire.
>
> O happy living things! no tongue
> Their beauty might declare:
> A spring of love gusht from my heart,
> And I bless'd them unaware!
> Sure my kind saint took pity on me,
> And I bless'd them unaware. ("Rime" ll. 264-79)

In contrast to the sun's light, which, as Warren argues, "shows the familiar as familiar", i.e., it furthers habitualized perceptions, the "elfish light" permits a new insight to the Mariner. The central emotion here is the love he unexpectedly experiences. Through the acknowledgement of the water-snakes' beauty and independent existence that exceeds human knowledge and representation ("no tongue / Their beauty might declare"), he ascribes an inherent value to the non-human beings, whose lives and happiness matter. In this moment of enchantment, the Ancient Mariner achieves a non-anthropocentric perspective. Objectifying appropriation of the non-human other gives way to sympathetic resonance. Instead of making the animals vanish – either by metaphorizing or by killing them – he practises attentiveness to the water creatures and thereby makes them visible as counterpart. In fact, the repetition of the lines, "I watch'd the water-snakes", "I watch'd their rich attire", in two successive stanzas, emphasize the Mariner's act of gazing at the other with wonder and enchantment (cf. Bennett 4).

The sympathy the Mariner experiences with the "water-snakes", however, differs from the type of projective sympathy, which Adam Smith proposed. Coleridge's poem describes an experience of resonance, which recalls David Hume's concept of sympathy as an involuntary communication of affective states from one creature to another (cf. Hume 206). Morality, according to Hume, stems from emotions such as love and sympathy rather than originating in the rational, autonomous self.

The Mariner, however, instantly reframes his transgressive experience in Christian terms, when he assigns the agency to his kind saint who took pity on him and freed him from the curse. The Christian reframing that reconciles moral consideration of animals with a hierarchically ordered Christian universe is also true for the poem's well-known lines, which for many readers possesses a too simplistic moral:

> He prayeth well who loveth well
> Both man and bird and beast.

> He prayeth best who loveth best
> All things both great and small:
> For the dear God, who loveth us
> He made and loveth all. ("Rime" ll. 645-50)[14]

However, the lines' regular iambic meter, the use of repetitions, syndetic construction and alliterations provoke an involuntary response that, in the words of Kenyon Jones, resembles "the form of a refrain" (Kenyon Jones 2001, 71). It mirrors the involuntary communication between the Mariner and the wedding guest who listens to the old man's story against his will:

> He holds him with his glittering eye –
> The wedding guest stood still
> And listens like a three year's child;
> The Marinere hath his will. ("Rime" ll. 17-20)

---

14 For Coleridge's own comment on the poem's moral to Barbauld see Kenyon Jones 2001, 71.

The principle of affective immediacy, which governs the Mariner's disruptive experience with the water-snakes, I suggest, is also the governing poetic principle of the 1798 version of the poem.[15] As David Simpson argues in his Marxist reading of the poem, the hypnotic relation between the Mariner and the wedding guest may also express Coleridge's desire "that he too might have the power of commanding involuntary response" (Simpson 152).

The poem's mesmerizing chant that recalls the ballad tradition also performs an enchantment, which Bennett ascribes to surprising encounters (Bennett 4). For Bennett, to 'enchant' means "to cast a spell with sounds, to make fall under the sway of a magical refrain" (Bennett 6). With reference to Gilles Deleuze's and Felix Guattari's works, she argues that

> the repetition of word sounds not only exaggerates the tempo of an ordinary phrase and not only eventually renders a meaningful phrase nonsense – it can also provoke new ideas, perspectives, and identities. In an enchanting refrain, sense becomes nonsense and then a new sense of things. (Bennett 6)

In this sense, the Mariner's disorienting chant is transformative and provokes new perspectives – a fact, that is underlined by the last lines of the poem that assign a new identity to the wedding-guest:

> He went, like one that hath been stunn'd
> And is of sense forlorn:
> A sadder and a wiser man
> He rose the morrow morn. ("Rime" ll. 655-58)

Romantic period literature offers manifold human-animal encounters that testify to Kenyon Jones's claim that a fundamental change in the attitude towards animals took place in the period. The two literary examples I discussed by Aikin and Barbauld and Coleridge, work towards a transgressive epistemology that probes non-anthropocentric and non-hierarchical perspectives. They also imply a transgressive ethics, as the representation of animals and nature as agents in their own right seriously questions hierarchical notions of humans' exceptionalism. Although both, *Evenings at Home* and "The Rime of the Ancyent Marinere" repeatedly recur to traditional religious conceptions and classifications, their modern and innovative poetics violate, transgress and question these frames.

15　In his later reworking of the original text from the 1798 version of the *Lyrical Ballads*, Coleridge introduced a marginal gloss that comments in prose on the mariner's chant, with which he hypnotizes the listener. The prose additions function as a form of distancing from the poem's immersive 'enchantment' (cf. Bennett 6). The focus on reader impact that is characteristic of the *Lyrical Ballads*, later gives way to an aesthetics of autonomy, which Coleridge valued higher under the impression of his Kantian reading (cf. Menely 200-01). It would be an interesting question, to what extent Coleridge's distancing commentaries in "The Rime of the Ancyent Marinere" parallel his later renouncement of his youthful revolutionary enthusiasm which he expressed e.g. in poems like *To A Young Ass* (cf. Menely 181-82).

Conclusion

Three aspects, I suggest, define transgressive encounters in the literary texts I analysed. First, transgressive encounters in *Evenings at Home* and "The Rime of the Ancyent Marinere" deconstruct epistemological and normative patterns that normally characterize humans' relations to non-human animals. The violation of existing human-animal boundaries in transgressive encounters lies in the awareness of the world-sharing with different species and the acknowledgement of forms of interspecies cohabitation. Second, humans' sympathy with other animals proves to be a central quality for Romantic period literature. It enables alternative approaches of the other by ways of imagination and resonance. Those counter-narratives are in their nature anti-hierarchical and suggest an equality of different ontological modes of being in the world. The third aspect finally relates to the poetic form. The texts resist through their modern poetics the 'vanishing' of the animals – as metaphor, symbol or moral of the fable – and ask for an ethical reassessment of the human-animal relationship.

Works Cited

Aaltola, Elisa. *Varieties of Empathy. Moral Psychology and Animal Ethics*. London and New York: Rowman and Littlefield, 2018.

Aikin, John, and Anna Laetitia Barbauld. *Evenings at Home; Or, The Juvenile Budget Opened: Consisting of A Variety of Miscellaneous Pieces for The Instruction and Amusement of Young Persons*. Edinburgh: William P. Nimmo, 1869.

Bate, Jonathan. *Romantic Ecology: Wordsworth and the Environmental Tradition*. New York and London: Routledge, 1991.

Bennett, Jane. *The Enchantment of Modern Life. Attachments, Crossings and Ethics*. Princeton: Princeton UP, 2001.

Böhm, Alexandra and Jessica Ullrich, eds. *Animal Encounters. Kontakt, Interaktion und Relationalität*. Berlin: Metzler, 2019.

Buffon, Georges-Louis Leclerc Count de. *Natural History, General and Particular*. Transl. William Smellie, vol. 9. London: A. Strahan and T. Cadell, 1791.

Cole, Lucinda. "Animal Studies and the Eighteenth Century: The Nature of the Beast." *Literature Compass* (2019): 1-12.

Coleridge, Samuel Taylor. "The Rime of the Ancyent Marinere, In Seven Parts". *The New Oxford Book of Romantic Period Verse*. Ed. Jerome J. McGann. Oxford: Oxford UP, 1993. 143-61.

Cosslett, Tess. *Talking Animals in British Children's Fiction 1786-1914*. Aldershot: Ashgate, 2006.

De Ritter, Richard. "Rational Souls and Animal Bodies: Race, Religion, and Cross-Species Sympathy in John Aikin and Anna Letitia Barbauld's *Evenings at Home* (1792-96)". *The Lion and the Unicorn* 42.1 (2018): 37-56.

Derrida, Jacques. "The Animal that Therefore I Am (More to Follow)". Transl. David Wills. *Critical Inquiry* 28 (2002): 369-418.

Donaldson, Sue and Will Kymlicka. *Zoopolis. A Political Theory of Animal Rights*. Oxford: Oxford UP, 2011.

Haraway, Donna. *When Species Meet*. Minneapolis and London: University of Minnesota Press, 2008.

Heymans, Peter. *Animality in British Romanticism: The Aesthetics of Species*. New York and London: Routledge, 2012.

Howard, Darren. "Talking Animals and Reading Children: Teaching (Dis)Obedience in John Aikin and Anna Barbauld's *Evenings at Home*". *Studies in Romanticism* 48 (2009): 641-66.

Hume, David. *A Treatise of Human Nature. A Critical Edition*. Ed. David Fate Norton and Mary J. Norton, vol. 1: Texts. Oxford: Oxford UP, 2007.

Huth, Martin. "Framed Encounters, Disruptive Encounters: Encountering Animals Within and Beyond Human-Animal Cultures". Ed. Alexandra Böhm and Jessica Ullrich. *Animal Encounters. Kontakt, Interaktion und Relationalität*. Stuttgart: Metzler, 2019. 43-55.

Kant, Immanuel. *Grundlegung zur Metaphysik der Sitten*. Ed. Wilhelm Weischedel, vol. 6. Darmstadt: WBG, 1956.

Kenyon Jones, Christine. *Kindred Brutes: Animals in Romantic-Period Writing*. Aldershot: Ashgate, 2001.

---. "British Romanticism and Animals". *Literature Compass* 6.1 (2009): 136-52.

Lamb, Jonathan. *The Evolution of Sympathy in the Long Eighteenth Century*. London: Pickering and Chatto, 2009.

Locke, John. *The Educational Writings of John Locke*. Ed. James L. Axtell. Cambridge: Cambridge UP, 1968.

McHugh, Susan. "Coming to Animal Studies". *Animals and Society. An Introduction to Human-Animal Studies*. Ed. Margo DeMello. New York: Columbia UP, 2012. 29-31.

McKusick, James. *Green Writing: Romanticism and Ecology*. Basingstoke: Palgrave Macmillan, 2000.

Menely, Tobias. *The Animal Claim. Sensibility and the Creaturely Voice*. London and Chicago: University of Chicago Press, 2015.

Oerlemans, Onno. *Romanticism and the Materiality of Nature*. Toronto: University of Toronto Press, 2002.

Perkins, David. *Romanticism and Animal Rights*. Cambridge: Cambridge UP, 2003.

Pratt, Mary Louise. *Imperial Eyes: Travel Writing and Transculturation*. London: Routledge, 1992.

Roscher, Mieke. *Ein Königreich für Tiere. Die Geschichte der britischen Tierschutzbewegung*. Marburg: Tectum, 2009.

Shevelow, Kathryn. *For the Love of Animals. The Rise of the Animal Protection Movement*. New York: Henry Holt and Company, 2008.

Simpson, David. "How Marxism Reads 'The Rime of the Ancient Mariner'". *Case Studies in Contemporary Criticism. Samuel Taylor Coleridge: The Rime of the Ancient Mariner. Complete, Authoritative Texts of the 1798 and 1817 Versions with Biographical and Historical Contexts, Critical History, and Essays from Contemporary Critical Perspective*. Boston and New York: Bedford/St. Martin, 1999. 148-67.

Smith, Adam. *The Theory of Moral Sentiments*. Ed. Knud Haakonssen. Cambridge: Cambridge UP, 2002.

Spencer, Jane. *Writing About Animals in the Age of Revolution*. Oxford: Oxford UP, 2020.

Thomas, Keith. *Man and the Natural World. Changing Attitudes in England 1500-1800*. London: Penguin, 1983.

Trimmer, Sarah. *Fabulous Histories. Designed for the Instruction of Children Respecting their Treatment of Animals*. London: Longman, 1798.

---. *The Guardian of Education*. Vol. 1. London: J. Hatchard, 1803.

Warren, Robert Penn. "A Poem of Pure Imagination (Reconsiderations VI)". *The Kenyon Review* 8.3 (1946): 391-427.

Wiedenmann, Rainer E. *Tiere, Moral und Gesellschaft. Elemente und Ebenen humanimalischer Sozialität*. Wiesbaden: VS Verlag für Sozialwissenschaften, 2009.

Wilson, Helen. "On Geography and Encounter". *Progress in Human Geography* 41 (2017): 451-71.

Ian Duncan

Imps of the Perverse: Romantic Fiction and Antinomian Denial

That the ascetic ideal has meant so much to man reveals a basic fact of human will, its *horror vacui; it needs an aim* –, and it prefers to will *nothingness* rather than *not* will.
Nietzsche, *On the Genealogy of Morality*

The Great Refusal

If we were to look for a personification of transgressive Romanticism, we could do worse than point to the protagonist of Byron's dramatic poem *Manfred* (1817). A trafficker in forbidden knowledge, Manfred wanders through the Alps, tormented by the memory of unspeakable deeds. When a posse of demons comes to claim him at the hour of his death, he refuses to acknowledge their jurisdiction. "I am prepared for all things, but deny / The power which summons me", he cries: "I'll die as I have lived – alone" (*Manfred* 3.4.82-83, 90). He stiffens his bravado with a philosophical justification:

> The mind which is immortal makes itself
> Requital for its good or evil thoughts –
> Is its own origin of ill and end –
> And its own place and time – its innate sense,
> When stripp'd of this mortality, derives
> No colour from the fleeting things without,
> But is absorb'd in sufferance or in joy,
> Born from the knowledge of its own desert. (*Manfred* 3.4.129-36)

Manfred refutes the devil by quoting him. We are surely meant to hear the echo of Milton's Satan in *Paradise Lost*:

> Infernal world, and thou, profoundest hell,
> Receive thy new possessor: one who brings
> A mind not to be changed by place or time.
> The mind is its own place, and in itself
> Can make a heav'n of hell, a hell of heav'n. (*Paradise Lost* 1:251-55)

But where Milton steeps Satan's boast in dramatic irony, Byron vindicates his hero, who successfully repels the infernal bailiffs. He alone will determine – he already determines – his own fate. That self-determination transmutes Manfred's suffering, since it is self-imposed, into an ethical redemption, one that is typically modern for its deferral to an open, agnostic horizon. "He's gone – his soul hath ta'en its earthless flight – / Whither? I dread to think – but he is gone", murmurs the Abbot, by way of epitaph (*Manfred* 3.4.152-53).

The end of *Manfred* stages with exemplary clarity one of the representative scenarios of literary Romanticism: the antinomian transvaluation of satanic hubris, the primal rejection of divine law, into a heroic assertion of individual autonomy. In this case the assertion is so pure, so absolute, it must express itself as a negation – a denial of subjection to any order outside the self – as opposed to a positive claim upon an alternative order. Byron's refusal to specify Manfred's original transgression (although it is heavily hinted at throughout the drama) clarifies one of the stakes of his fable, and of some of the other Romantic works I shall be considering in this essay. The hero's, or rather anti-hero's, refusal of subjection posits an ethical state of exception that reinvents for a secular culture the religious idea of sin. In doing so it addresses a central question: After the Enlightenment displacement of theology by philosophy, in a post-metaphysical universe, what might constitute sin, if by 'sin' we are to understand a transgression not simply against man-made laws but against the order of things? The answer, in the present case, is the antinomian claim on the self as the origin and ground of determination, legislating its own destiny in defiance of external codes.

This essay will trace a 'Gothic' genealogy of Romantic antinomianism, in which the denial of external law, in recognizing the law as itself a denial or prohibition ("thou shalt not"), binds a protagonist more tightly to its negative sentence. This Gothic tradition is distinct from the creative recasting of antinomianism, programmatic in the poetry of William Blake and Percy Bysshe Shelley, that we associate with the principled rebellions and resistances of Romantic poetry. Writing from an artisanal and labouring-class tradition of antinomian political as well as religious dissent, Blake scrambles the binary oppositions that premise the act of denial in *The Marriage of Heaven and Hell* (cf. Thompson 19; Mee 1992, 49-60; Mee 1994; Makdisi 70-75). Shelley, in *Prometheus Unbound*, draws upon new scientific resources of Romantic vitalism to convert the satanic anti-hero's negation (his curse on Jupiter) into the form of a Christian ethical affirmation (forgiveness) that transcends its dogmatic substance (cf. Gigante 203-04). In the cases I shall be looking at, however, drawn mainly from prose fiction rather than from poetry, the extreme and arbitrary force of the antinomian refusal – grounding itself on nothing except its own will to negation – voids the possibility of a regenerative or redemptive sequel.

Other Romantic-era scenarios of antinomian denial include Don Giovanni's refusal to repent, struggling in the marble grip of the Commendatore, at the end of the Da Ponte-Mozart opera (cf. Duncan 83-85). Unlike Manfred, Don Giovanni is dragged down to Hell; his defiance, however, diminishes those left in his wake, picking up the pieces of their humdrum lives. In *Faust* Part 1 Goethe converts the satanic speech act to Romantic irony, with Mephistopheles's self-identification as "the spirit that always negates" ("*der Geist der stets verneint*", *Faust* 1 160-61). The spirit of negation is summoned by – it is a dialectical consequence of – Faust's earlier revision of the opening of St John's Gospel, "in the beginning was the Word", to "in the beginning was the Deed". The revision substitutes "das Wort", *Logos*, the word as reason and law, with "die Tat", undetermined and self-determining action (*Faust* 1 152-53). The irony is deepened by Faust's formulation of the Deed as a philosophical, indeed a philological event – an act of translation and revision – before he can contemplate actually doing anything.

Ironical in a different vein is the case of Robert Wringhim, the notably unheroic protagonist of James Hogg's 1824 novel *The Private Memoirs and Confessions of a Justified Sinner*. In common with Manfred, Don Giovanni, and Faust, Wringhim's antinomian claim conjures up a demonic agent of external fatality, his uncanny *doppelgänger* Gil-Martin. Hogg brings the explicitly doctrinal force of Calvinist theology to bear on his character's predicament. Wringhim comes to believe "that I was now a justified person, adopted among the number of God's children – my name written in the Lamb's book of life, and that no bypast transgression, nor any future act of my own, or of other men, could be instrumental in altering the decree" (Hogg 88). This radical freedom to act, premised on a rejection of moral law, entails an absolute annulment of action, since, according to the theology that underwrites it, "works" play no part in salvation. Released (or so he thinks) into the arena of metaphysically inconsequential free action, Wringhim grows increasingly divorced from his own deeds, committing abominable crimes without any memory or consciousness of them. Stripped of his fancied autonomy, he becomes a puppet of the demon who wears his face. In something like a parody of Manfred's last stand, he is himself the devil that damns him.

All of these scenarios of Romantic antinomianism are remarkable for coupling the protagonist's defiance of external law and his claim on a state of ethical exception with the exceptional intervention of a demonic agent from outside the natural order. The violence of the anti-hero's denial provokes a systemic violence – a supernatural recoil of the flouted law. Besides the theological theme, Hogg's treatment is also remarkable for its elaboration of a psychological condition, which occupies the moral vacuum opened by a withdrawal of the traits of heroic virtue. Far from professing the indomitable courage of a Manfred or Don Giovanni, Wringhim is a shameless coward, liar, and worse. Accused of debauching a neighbour's daughter, he protests he has no memory of the deed, but then admits: "Highly as I disapproved of the love of women, and all intimacies and connections with the sex, I felt a sort of indefinite pleasure, an ungracious delight in having a beautiful woman solely at my disposal" (Hogg 136). Later, he is accused of murdering the young woman, along with his own mother: "I cannot tell how it was, but I felt a strange and unwonted delight in viewing this scene, and a certain pride of heart in being supposed the perpetrator of the unnatural crimes laid to my charge" (Hogg 156). Indefinite pleasure, strange and ungracious delight, a murky pride in being charged with unnatural crimes: Hogg attaches a perverse affective and erotic psychology to Wringhim's antinomian pretension. An unacknowledged will to violence goes hand-in-hand with the exterior promptings of a diabolical familiar – who may only be the protagonist's self-projection.

The Spirit of Perverseness

Dissociation from his own will and actions differentiates Robert Wringhim's perverse psychology from the Romantic expressions of perverse eroticism analysed by modern critics, from Mario Praz to Richard C. Sha: the former anatomizing Romantic sexuality's morbid and destructive tendencies, the latter celebrating its dissident, emancipatory potential. Hogg makes the point that Wringhim's erotic drive is low-grade, fitful, a by-product of the stance of antinomian negation, and that this shadowy, second-hand status constitutes its perversity.[1] Twenty years after *Private Memoirs and Confessions of a Justified Sinner*, Edgar Allan Poe names the antinomian imperative "the spirit of PER-VERSENESS" ("Black Cat" 599), in a full-scale internalization and psychologization of its negative drive which decisively severs it from an erotic or pleasure-seeking etiology. Poe's tales give the imperative a forthright definition, stripped of theological cladding, which nevertheless returns it to the formal condition of original sin.

Poe locates the premise of free action or self-determination in "a radical, primitive, irreducible sentiment" ("Imp" 826), "an innate and primitive principle of human action" ("Imp" 827), expressive in the denial of right reason: rewriting Milton's Satan's "evil be thou my good" as the more banal imperative "to do wrong for the wrong's sake" ("Imp" 827). Thus internalized – turned into a primal drive or instinct – the spirit of perverseness no longer needs to be manifest outside the self as a demonic agent. That "paradoxical something, which we may call *perverseness*", Poe writes,

> ... is a *mobile* without motive, a motive not *motivirt*. Through its promptings we act without comprehensible object; or, ... through its promptings we act, for the reason that we should *not*. ... I am not more certain than I breathe, than that the assurance of the wrong or error of any action is often the one unconquerable *force* which impels us, and alone impels us to its prosecution. Nor will this overwhelming tendency to do wrong for the wrong's sake, admit of analysis, or resolution into ulterior elements. It is a radical, a primitive impulse – elementary. ("Imp" 827)

Poe divides this primitive impulse into two expressions which, while complementary, are not identical. One prompts us to an action that reason warns us will result in our harm, like the man on a cliff-edge who feels an irresistible urge to jump. The other prompts us to an action just because it is forbidden, irrespective of a reckoning of consequences, in a purely formal response to a prohibition: "We perpetrate [such deeds] merely because we feel that we should *not*. Beyond or behind this, there is no intelligible principle" ("Imp" 829). The rather sketchy narrative that unfolds in "The Imp of the Perverse" merges both impulses. The spirit of perverseness drives a successful murderer to confess his crime in the public street – *because* he has gotten away with it, because his deed, or so he thinks, has set him free. It is not difficult to recuperate this scenario, and hence a rationale for the perverse, for a conventionally Christian moral fable, according to which it is the prompting of conscience that overrules the baser impulse to self-preservation. What seems perverse, in other words, is the imperative of a higher providence, of grace, misrecognized by the sinner even as he yields to it.

---

1   Compare, in this light, Eve Kosofsky Sedgwick's bravura – if finally unconvincing – diagnosis of "homosexual panic", virulent because unacknowledged in Hogg's novel (Sedgwick 97-117).

Fyodor Dostoevsky – supreme artist of the perverse, master-analyst of the antinomian will – develops this redemptive theme in *Crime and Punishment* (*CP*) (1866), another twenty years later. Dostoevsky couples Raskolnikov's path to repentance, culminating with a confession in the public street (as in "The Imp of the Perverse," but now morally motivated), with the antithetical trajectory of the fantastically perverse anti-anti-hero – we cannot quite call him a villain – Svidrigailov. Entering the novel at its midpoint, Svidrigailov takes over the antinomian impulse that drove Raskolnikov to commit murder at the beginning, and realizes it as an absolute characterological principle in a career of radically undetermined, indeed motiveless acts, which may be generous as well as vicious. In the doubling of Raskolnikov and Svidrigailov we see a variant of the combination of antinomian anti-hero and demonic nemesis in the earlier Romantic treatments. Svidrigailov's career culminates in his suicide. In a sardonic riff on the modern utopia of the antinomian imagination, he calls his act "going to America" (*CP* 520), that westward horizon or blank space (the Pantisocracy of Coleridge and Southey, Robert Owen's New Harmony) where we end up to start over again. Dostoevsky brings the motif to term in his aptly titled later novel *The Devils*, in which the garrulous Nihilist Kirilov shoots himself in a bloody demonstration of suicide as ultimate affirmation of a transcendental human will.

Antinomian Aesthetics

Having sketched a Romantic genealogy of antinomian negation, I turn in the second half of this essay to consider the peculiar status of the aesthetic in the regime of the perverse. In his study of perverse Romanticisms, Sha makes a compelling case for "pleasure without function" as the foundational principle both of queer sexuality, in its detachment from reproductive use, and of aesthetic disinterestedness, Kant's "purposiveness without purpose" (Sha 2). It is tempting, along these lines, to develop an analogy between the antinomian claim on an ethical state of exception and the Romantic autonomy of aesthetic experience. However, the rejection of pleasure in the antinomian gesture – sinking it too in the abyss of negation – opens a different path of inquiry: one that explores the relation between the sensuous apprehension of form and its interpretation, that is, between aesthetic experience and its apperception or resolution into a symbolic order. The two cases I consider track a negative dialectical sequence in which antinomian denial opens the subject to an aesthetic epiphany which, far from sustaining a release from law, in a perpetually self-renewing blaze of *jouissance*, immediately reconstitutes the law as a force of overwhelming, punitive negation.

Before returning to Poe, who gives the sequence its purest statement, I revisit the earlier Romantic doubling of antinomian anti-hero and demonic nemesis at the site of its inauguration in British fiction, in Matthew Lewis's paradigmatically transgressive Gothic novel *The Monk* (1796). In contrast to the dissociated state of Hogg's Robert Wringhim, Lewis's Ambrosio acts out, with excessive zeal, the perverse will-to-eroticism analysed by Praz (in whose gallery of satanic-sadistic types, indeed, Ambrosio figures: Praz 60,

112). Agonizingly bound to his desires and sensations, in a frenzy of libidinal overdrive, Ambrosio rushes headlong into ever-deeper gulfs of depravity following his sexual congress with a young woman (Matilda), who has at first disguised herself as a male novice (Rosario), and is eventually revealed to be a demon. The antinomian theme is not theorized or stated as a principle, as it is in Hogg's or Poe's fiction, but is established instead as an institutional condition for the action, in which the repression of vital urges in Catholic monastic discipline produces sexuality as the reaction to a prohibition. In other words, the denial of a natural drive recreates it as perverse, such that sexuality must always realize itself transgressively, as a symptomatic rapacity and violence. What is fascinating in *The Monk* is how tightly, despite (or perhaps because of) its technical rawness, Lewis's novel constellates a set of logical and symbolic declensions in which the aesthetic is locked into the body and, specifically, to sexuality as a pathological condition.

The raging wildfire of Ambrosio's passion subsides into shame, ennui and disgust as soon as it is consummated:

> The burst of transport was past: Ambrosio's lust was satisfied; Pleasure fled, and Shame usurped her seat in his bosom. ... He looked forward with horror; his heart was despondent, and became the abode of satiety and disgust. He avoided the eyes of his Partner in frailty; a melancholy silence prevailed. (*Monk* 223)

The same erotic and affective rhythm – rampant desire switching to melancholic aversion – governs his later rape of Antonia:

> The very excess of his former eagerness to possess Antonia now contributed to inspire him with disgust; and a secret impulse made him feel how base and unmanly was the crime which he had just committed. He started hastily from her arms. She, who so lately had been the object of his adoration, now raised no other sentiment in his heart than aversion and rage. (*Monk* 385)

Lewis plots this structure of erotic feeling through the familiar aesthetic categories of Gothic fiction, theorized by Edmund Burke in his *Philosophical Enquiry into the Origin of Our Ideas of the Sublime and Beautiful* (1757) and later systematized by Ann Radcliffe in her posthumous essay "On the Supernatural in Poetry" (1826). Terror is analogous with a sublime erotic transport, sustained by obscurity, distance and deferral, which collapses into horror as soon as it is realized as physical experience, fixed in the sensate body. From horror it slides irresistibly into disgust, the affective state that most fully engages Lewis's poetic attention. Thus Lorenzo, wandering in the catacombs beneath the convent, finds his senses stimulated and his imagination aroused in the enveloping darkness:

> Carried away by his eagerness to clear up this mystery, and to penetrate into which he was impelled by a movement secret and unaccountable, Lorenzo heeded not this circumstance till he found himself in total solitude. (*Monk* 359)
>
> [...]
>
> A deep abyss now presented itself before [him], whose thick obscurity the eye strove in vain to pierce ... Nothing was discernible, save a flight of rough unshapen steps which sank into the yawning Gulph and were soon lost in darkness. (*Monk* 367)

So, of course he goes down those steps: darkness activates the imagination, which activates in turn the will to understanding – to interpretation. But then a glimmer of candle-
light reveals the wretched Agnes, shackled and starving amid decomposing corpses:

> Lorenzo stopped: he was petrified with horror. He gazed upon the miserable Object with
> disgust and pity. He trembled at the spectacle; he grew sick at heart: his strength failed
> him, and his limbs were unable to support his weight. (*Monk* 369)

Terror expands the faculties: horror contracts and freezes.

There is another striking thing to note here. The state of imaginative and erotic excite-
ment, associated with sublimity and terror, is predicated on a latency or indetermination
of the sexual object. Ambrosio delights in the company of Rosario/Matilda before she
reveals herself as female. That revelation triggers the sexual act, and Ambrosio's reciprocal fall into masculinity, the precipitate of a catastrophic dimorphism which fixes the
two sexes in opposed physiological economies and temporalities:

> Possession, which cloys Man, only increases the affection of Woman. … [As Matilda's]
> passion grew ardent, Ambrosio's grew cold; the very marks of her fondness excited his
> disgust, and its excess served to extinguish the flame which already burned but feebly in
> his bosom. (*Monk* 235)

To be sexed is to be imprisoned in the body (hence the persistent tropism of the Gothic
body to incarceration), which becomes fully physical (is totalized *as* body) in its desub-
limation to a corpse – in the most unforgettable scenes of the novel, a disfigured or
rotting corpse. The alluring phantasm of beautiful form is reduced to excremental matter: a reduction that is bound, in its most extreme scenario, to biological reproduction.
(Here *The Monk* stakes out an antithetical position to the regenerative, emancipatory
scenarios of perverse eroticism imagined, in Sha's analysis, by Blake and Shelley.) Thus
Agnes, chained in the catacomb, lays her hand on "something soft" which turns out to be
a "corrupted human head" (*Monk* 403); nurses the "mass of putridity" that was her still-
born child (*Monk* 412); and, in the novel's most reliably stomach-turning line, awakens
to "[find] my fingers ringed with the long worms which bred in the corrupted flesh of
my Infant" (*Monk* 415). Lewis's Gothic hierarchy of the senses sets hearing at the top,
with its imaginative affordances of obscurity, indirection and indetermination, followed
by sight, with its potentially deceptive attachment to a particular object. Lowest of all –
but most vividly evoked in Lewis's writing – comes touch, the medium of the disgusting.

The Monk plays out, I am suggesting, a scandalous declension of the empiricist protocols
of the British aesthetic tradition, as represented by Burke. Here it is vision – paradigmatically the medium of sensuous cognition, or of the aesthetic as a mode of knowledge
– that occupies the unstable middle zone between sublime audition and disgusting tactil-
ity. A beautiful image, the archetypal aesthetic object, occupies the etiology of Ambrosio's perverse career. Early in the novel, he fixes his sexually aroused gaze on an icon of
the Madonna in his cell: "Oh! if such a Creature existed, and existed but for me! Were I
permitted to twine round my fingers those golden ringlets, and press with my lips the
treasures of that snowy bosom!" (*Monk* 41). The image becomes flesh in the person of

Matilda, who reveals that she sat as the painter's model with the design of seducing Ambrosio. Lastly, Matilda turns out to be no mortal but a demon sent to tempt him. The sequence of substitutions – image to sexual body to devil – plots a standard Protestant satire of Catholic idolatry, but also, more interestingly, a parody of the empiricist model of aesthetic experience, through the serial collapse of a symbolic order into its referential objects. The downward arc is plotted in the movement from Ambrosio's fantasy of "golden ringlets" he can "twine round my fingers", eliding the central, normative symbolic object, the wedding ring, to Agnes's "fingers ringed with the long worms which bred in the corrupted flesh of my Infant". Ambrosio rationalizes his fascinated gaze:

> "What charms me, when ideal and considered as a superior Being, would disgust me, become Woman and tainted with all the failings of Mortality. It is not the Woman's beauty that fills me with such enthusiasm; It is the Painter's skill that I admire, it is the Divinity that I adore!" (*Monk* 41)

He is deluded, of course. In the Gothic regime of Lewis's novel, devotional and aesthetic contemplation are alike *interested*, determined, in Burke's phrase, by "some quality in bodies, acting mechanically upon the human mind by the intervention of the senses" (Burke 102). It is an aesthetic stance that *The Monk*, with its unrelenting sensationalism, reproduces in its readers, binding us to its rhythm of excitation and disgust. The programmatic contrast is with the Gothic romances of Ann Radcliffe, which suspend their narrative drive for elaborate descriptions of sublime landscape. These model the imperilled heroine's intuition of a transcendental design beyond the scene she contemplates:

> Here, gazing upon the stupendous imagery around her, looking, as it were, beyond the awful veil which obscures the features of the Deity, and conceals Him from the eyes of his creatures, dwelling as with a present God in the midst of his sublime works; with a mind thus elevated, how insignificant would appear to her the transactions, and the sufferings of this world. (*Italian* 87)

Ellena's appeal to a supreme order, in defiance of a present state of tyrannous lawlessness, charges her vows of refusal with a redemptive force.

Aesthetic and Symbolic

Ambrosio is a weak figure in the gallery of antinomian rebels, after all, a hapless product of the prohibition he violates. He never voices his defiance of moral and religious law as a rational principle of self-determination, and remains, instead, the dupe of an infernally bioengineered libidinal drive. No less than was the case with Hogg's Wringhim, his desire turns out never to have been his own. Aesthetic response is ensnared in a deluded erotic purpose that stays blind to its determination – always already captured by a symbolic order, sentenced to collapse into its sensual ground.

I return, for the last part of this essay, to Poe, who gives us a pure statement of the antinomian imperative in one of his best tales, "The Black Cat". More decisively than in "The Imp of the Perverse", Poe defines the perverse in formal terms, as the defiance of a prohibition:

> Who has not, a hundred times, found himself committing a vile or a stupid action, for no other reason than because he knows he should *not*? Have we not a perpetual inclination, in the teeth of our best judgment, to violate that which is *Law*, merely because we understand it to be such? ("Black Cat" 599)

Law, in other words, becomes knowable as a prohibition through our violation of it – a negation of a negation. This logic weighs on the narrator's challenge to his readers at the opening of the story: to interpret its escalating sequence of unmotivated acts of violence as "an ordinary succession of very natural causes and effects" ("Black Cat" 597). He offers his alcoholism as an alibi for lazy readers: it is an explanation that explains nothing, if the story is simply a record of intoxicated hallucinations. In a fit of drunken irritation, the narrator mutilates his pet cat, and later, "in cold blood", he hangs it, "*because* I knew that it had loved me, and *because* I felt it had given me no reason of offence … *because* I knew that in so doing I was committing a sin" ("Black Cat" 599). The category of "sin" is produced by the ex-post-facto rationalization of a senseless act.

A feline *doppelgänger* (the story's variant of the Romantic familiar demon) then takes the original cat's place. The narrator's spasm of violence towards this second cat is discharged onto his wife, who unluckily gets in the way of the fatal blow. As in *The Monk*, the protagonist's transgressive career is entangled with a semiotically intensified iteration – here, a reiteration – of the image. The succession of banal domestic cruelties is made uncanny by an accompanying series of symbolic apparitions or portents. Their cryptic iconic force disrupts the possibility of our reading "an ordinary succession of very natural causes and effects" ("Black Cat" 597), not least because they raise to the surface of the tale the question of reading as an interaction between the aesthetic (the sensuous apprehension of a form) and the symbolic (the interpretation of its meaning or purpose).

After the narrator has hanged the original cat in the garden, his house catches fire and burns down. When the flames are extinguished, an image becomes visible on the bedroom wall:

> I approached and saw, as if graven in *bas relief* upon the white surface, the figure of a gigantic *cat*. The impression was given with an accuracy truly marvellous. There was a rope about the animal's neck. … The falling of other walls had compressed the victim of my cruelty into the substance of the freshly-spread plaster; the lime of which, with the flames, and the *ammonia* from the carcass, had then accomplished the portraiture as I saw it. ("Black Cat" 600)

A rational explanation for the uncanny image, barely plausible here, breaks down in the cases that follow. All of them scramble the categories of the natural, the artificial, and the supernatural in the constitution of the aesthetic object and its symbolic status. The first two, in which the image *develops* into its significant form, evoke the brand-new technology of photography – or, in Poe's phrase, "photogeny" ("Daguerreotype" 37). The first instance is analogous to the daguerreotype process, introduced into the United

States in 1839, four years before the publication of Poe's story. Alert to the new invention (he would sit for his own portrait at least six times before his death in 1849), Poe published an essay on the daguerreotype in the Philadelphia newspaper *Alexander's Weekly Messenger* in January 1840:

> The results of the invention cannot, even remotely, be seen – but all experience, in matters of philosophical discovery, teaches us that, in such discovery, it is the unforeseen upon which we must calculate most largely. It is a theorem almost demonstrated, that the consequences of any new scientific invention will, at the present day exceed, by very much, the wildest expectations of the most imaginative. ("Daguerreotype" 38)

Poe's commentary captures the uncanny, quasi-magical aura of the new technology at the historical moment of its inauguration. Photography's seemingly unmediated truth to nature yields a perfect instance of aesthetic purposiveness-without-purpose: "The source of vision itself has been, in this instance, the designer" ("Daguerreotype" 38).

The second image, the anomalous white patch on the second cat's breast, rather resembles calotype (far less current in the United States in the period), with its production of the image in negative:

> The reader will remember that this mark, although large, had been originally very indefinite; but, by slow degrees – degrees nearly imperceptible, and which for a long time my Reason struggled to reject as fanciful – it had, at length, assumed a rigorous distinctness of outline. It was now the representation of an object that I shudder to name … it was now, I say, the image of a hideous – of a ghastly thing – of the GALLOWS! ("Black Cat" 602-03)

The form that develops is now an image *from the future*. It externalizes the motif of purpose or design that seems so signally lacking as a subjective, regulative principle in the narrator's sequence of feckless actions. After – pointlessly – murdering his wife, the narrator entombs her body in the cellar wall. For the first time, it seems, he has a plan. The last of the tale's dire portents makes its appearance when the police tear the wall down, in response to a ghastly cry from within:

> The corpse, already greatly decayed and clotted with gore, stood erect before the eyes of the spectators. Upon its head, with red extended mouth and solitary eye of fire, sat the hideous beast whose craft had seduced me into murder, and whose informing voice had consigned me to the hangman. I had walled the monster up within the tomb! ("Black Cat" 606)

The excavation uncovers an appalling Gothic mutation of the figure of a Classical Greek Herm, a semi-anthropomorphous, phallic boundary-marker erected to ward off evil from the household. This obscene phallic vision is a final revelation of the symbolic order in its absolute case, that of external necessity or law. Law in its essence, law as such, discloses itself as at once abstract allegorical form and gruesome physiological matter, excessively meaningful and yet mysterious – for (again) whose design or purpose is expressed here? At last the deed we have done returns to make its claim upon us as our own: as an aesthetic and symbolic appearance that – now – judges us.

Works Cited

Burke, Edmund. *A Philosophical Enquiry into the Origin of Our Ideas of the Sublime and Beautiful.* Ed. Adam Phillips. Oxford: Oxford UP, 1998.

Byron, Lord [George Gordon]. *The Major Works.* Ed. Jerome J. McGann. Oxford: Oxford UP, 2000.

Dostoevsky, Fyodor Mikhailovich. *Crime and Punishment.* Trans. Constance Garnett. New York: Collier, 1917.

Duncan, Ian. "Don Giovanni Automaton". *The Politics of Romanticism: Selected Papers from the Bamberg Conference of the German Society for English Romanticism.* Ed. Pascal Fischer and Christoph Houswitschka. Trier: WVT, 2019. 81-89.

Gigante, Denise. *Life: Organic Form and Romanticism.* New Haven: Yale UP, 2009.

Goethe, Johann Wolfgang von. *Goethe's Faust.* Trans. and ed. Walter Kaufmann. Garden City, NJ: Doubleday, 1963.

Hogg, James. *The Private Memoirs and Confessions of a Justified Sinner.* Ed. Ian Duncan. Oxford: Oxford UP, 2010.

Lewis, Matthew. *The Monk.* Ed. Howard Anderson. Oxford: Oxford UP, 1983.

Makdisi, Saree. *William Blake and the Impossible History of the 1790s.* Chicago: University of Chicago Press, 2002.

Mee, Jon. *Dangerous Enthusiasm: William Blake and the Culture of Radicalism in the 1790s.* Oxford: Clarendon Press, 1992.

---. "Is there an Antinomian in the House? William Blake and the After-Life of a Heresy". *Historicizing Blake.* Ed. Steve Clark and David Worrall. London: Palgrave Macmillan, 1994. 43-58.

Milton, John. *Poetical Works.* Ed. Douglas Bush. Oxford: Oxford UP, 1969.

Nietzsche, Friedrich. *On the Genealogy of Morality.* Trans. Carol Diethe, ed. Keith Ansell-Pearson. Cambridge: Cambridge UP, 2007.

Poe, Edgar Allan. "The Daguerreotype". *Classic Essays on Photography.* Ed. Alan Trachtenberg. New Haven: Leetes Island Books, 1980.

---. "The Black Cat". *Poetry and Tales.* Ed. Patrick Quinn. New York: Library of America, 1984. 597-606.

---. "The Imp of the Perverse". *Poetry and Tales.* Ed. Patrick Quinn. New York: Library of America, 1984. 826-32.

Praz, Mario. *The Romantic Agony.* Trans. Angus Davidson. Oxford: Oxford UP, 1951.

Radcliffe, Ann. "On the Supernatural in Poetry". *New Monthly Magazine* 16.1 (1826): 145-52.

---. *The Italian.* Ed. Frederick Garber and Nick Groom. Oxford: Oxford UP, 2017.

Sedgwick, Eve Kosofsky. *Between Men: English Literature and Male Homosocial Desire.* New York: Columbia UP, 1985.

Sha, Richard C. *Perverse Romanticism: Aesthetics and Sexuality in Britain, 1750-1832.* Baltimore: Johns Hopkins UP, 2008.

Thompson, E. P. *Witness Against the Beast: William Blake and the Moral Law.* New York: The New Press, 1993.

Alexander Schlutz

"A poor, imprisoned animal." Persons, Property, and the Unnatural Nature of the Law in E.T.A. Hoffmann's *The Entail*[1]

> Mine, yours.
> "This is my dog," said those poor children. "That is my place in the sun."
> Here is the beginning and the image of the usurpation of the whole earth.
> Blaise Pascal, *Pensées*

I

In a survey article on "Where the Evidence Leads: Gothic Narratives and Legal Technologies" in a 2007 special issue of *European Romantic Review* on Romanticism and the Law, Diane Long Hoeveler and James D. Jenkins chart the course of representations of legal issues in British Gothic novels from the 1780s to the 1820s. They uncover an underlying concern with the modernization of the legal system in Britain characterized by the clash of traditional, divine-rights-based, authoritarian views of the law and emerging rationalistic and utilitarian approaches. Hoeveler and Jenkins identify three stages in the entanglement of Gothic fiction and legal technologies over the course of the article; a first one, encompassing the decades of the 1760s and 1770s, concerned with the shift from an oral-based to a print-based culture, in which the demonization of legal practices of the *ancien régime* allow the readers of Gothic novels to measure the modernizing progress of their culture; a second phase in the 1790s, which sees a shift in focus towards legal issues in the private realm, mainly towards the legal rights of women; and finally, a third stage in the early 1800s, in which concern with the law in Gothic novels serves not only a didactic purpose but becomes a crucial part of the narrative itself (in form of trial-scenes and similar set pieces), as the British reading public becomes more and more interested in true-crime narratives. Hoeveler and Jenkins ultimately conclude that no clear progression towards legal modernization can be traced in the Gothic archive, mainly because of a nostalgia for a pre-modern, providential universe in texts that are too mired in Gothic literary conventions to truly push a progressive legal agenda (Hoeveler and Jenkins 330).

The German Gothic text with which I am concerned in this chapter, E.T.A. Hoffmann's short novel, *Das Majorat / The Entail*, published in 1817,[2] not only does not fall into

---

1   A longer version of this chapter first appeared in Clason, Christopher, ed. *E.T.A. Hoffmann. Transgressive Romanticism*, copyright Liverpool UP, 2018. The original text is reproduced with permission of Liverpool UP through PLSclear.

2   *The Entail* is one of the *Night Pieces* (*Nachtstücke*), Hoffmann's second collection of stories, published at a time when he was working again in a legal capacity as a councillor

Hoeveler and Jenkins's taxonomic categories, but deeply unsettles the underlying assumption of progressive legal modernization that informs them. Hoffmann, whose storytelling is driven by the self-reflexive principles of Romantic narrative irony, is never in danger of being bound by any of the Gothic's conventions, which are always staged as artificial in his texts and made visible as such to his readers. Hoffmann, in other words, *plays* with the Gothic, and in a story that has as its title an instrument of Prussian land and inheritance law, this kind of serious jest serves to make visible the socially constructed nature of not just pre-modern but of *all* legal conventions, which reveal their fictional character in Hoffmann's literary treatment. With this radical mode of questioning, Hoffmann's text participates in the differently-focused, post-Kantian philosophical discussion about the law in turn-of-the-nineteenth-century Germany. In this debate, as Ulrike Zeuch puts it in her introductory essay for a special issue of the *Internationales Archiv für Sozialgeschichte der deutschen Literatur* on Law and Literature around 1800, the *limits* of positive law, as well as "the then controversially discussed question, whether justice, as a standard to judge an action could even exist beyond codified law" are the central topics (Zeuch 82; my translation). Specifically, Hoffmann's text calls into question the fundamental legal distinctions between persons and property and between human beings and animals in a way that is of uncanny relevance today.

Even on the narrative surface level, nostalgia for a chivalric world is absent from Hoffmann's text, in which the institution of the entail by the Baron Roderich von R. inexorably leads to the complete eradication of the family line he meant to preserve. In two generations, all members of the von R. family have died mostly violent deaths, all of which are either directly or indirectly connected to the entail and the authoritarian 'law of the father' embedded in the very walls of castle *R..sitten.* In Hoffmann's hands, however, the Prussian entail laws are not simply narrative material to be used in a Gothic plot, they are *themselves* revealed as essentially Gothic in nature: they operate in a realm beyond ordinary human experience where the dead hold sway and the living must follow their command. In this sense, they are a special case in land law of "the vanity and presumption of governing beyond the grave" that Thomas Paine calls in *The Rights of Man*, in the context of parliamentary and governmental reform in Britain, "the most ridiculous and insolent of all tyrannies" (Paine 55). For Roderich, the law of which he avails himself to make his will legally binding is no more than an extension of a providential order that controls our actions, a fate that he, with the help of astrological apparatus and his faithful steward Daniel, can read in the stars. As such a reader of celestial omens and, to use the technical legal term, a 'free testator' able to control the future of his property, Roderich, whose name is derived from Old High German *hrod* (fame) and *ric* (power), seeks to assume divine authority. Like an author aware of the literary conventions that

---

for the Berlin *Kammergerichtshof*, the city's court of appeals, to which he had been appointed in 1816.

prescribe the options of his characters, Roderich makes a providential order that is illegible for mere mortals visible to them in the form of a legal document.[3] By highlighting the literariness of legal conventions, Hoffmann avoids the temptation to suggest, in the way Hoeveler and Jenkins hoped to find in the British Gothic, that a modernized legal system might be able to avoid such tyrannical groundings of the law. In an essay on Hoffmann's *Entail*, Peter König elaborates on this central point by drawing on Giambattista Vico's constructivist conception of the law as a form of poetic creation that, just like literature and art in general, produces realities rather than reflects them. Roman law, König points out, was for Vico a "strict poem", operating by means of a network of legal fictions, the legal concept of a "person" foremost among them (König 206). The Latin *persona*, originally the mask used by an actor on the stage, allows for the creation of a role, and persons for Vico, as König reminds us, are consequently "masks that have been given rights" (König 206; my translation). This "constructivist character of the law", however, is usually hidden from individual actors in the political world, König points out, and only becomes visible in times of deep social disruption such as the end of the *ancien régime* in Europe. The immense bloodshed and violence of the French Revolution and the subsequent Napoleonic wars undermine any Enlightenment or Romantic optimism, König suggests, and raise the inevitable question of what actually constitutes the driving forces behind historical developments (König 207).

In Hoffmann's story, these ghosts of history can be encountered in the knight's hall of R..sitten, where, after the ceiling of the castle's original court room has collapsed, the local court of law is now located. Here judicial decisions are made and recorded, and justice dispensed by the current baron, Roderich's grandson, maybe unsurprisingly also named Roderich. To help his readers understand why such ghosts cannot be laid to rest Hoffmann undertakes – among other things – a literary investigation of one of the most fundamental distinctions of any legal system, that between persons and property.

---

3   For a helpful introduction to this instrument of German land law and an overview of its history, see Riedl, esp. 19-23. The translation of "Majorat" with "Entail", a convention I follow in this chapter, is ultimately misleading, as these two legal instruments are, despite their similarities (the exclusion of women from property inheritance foremost among them), not in fact identical in structure and purpose. Most importantly, the *Majorat*, a special form of a *Familienfideikommiß* (family trust commission), specifies that succession must take place through the first-born male and hence cements the Roman laws of primogeniture. As such, it was mainly employed by donors of the petty aristocracy who sought to protect the family's land holdings. The English entail laws, by contrast, were originally developed specifically to *counteract* the laws of primogeniture, as Sandra Macpherson demonstrates, and were, as part of English common law, meant to give the donor a freedom of alienation precluded by the automatic line of succession through the first-born male. For that reason, Macpherson writes, "by the seventeenth century entails were primarily favored", not by aristocratic families, but "by the newly gentried, successful lawyers, merchants, or tradesmen, who'd amassed fortune enough to purchase an estate", and the eighteenth-century critique of entail laws in England pitted, not Whigs against Tories, but Whig commercialists against Whig landowners (Macpherson 7).

II

We discover the Gothic space of the knight's hall through the eyes and ears of Theodore, a young jurist and the first-person narrator of the first half of Hoffmann's text, whose name is a wink to Horace Walpole's *Castle of Otranto* (1764), where the name of the true heir of the family property is also Theodore. Theodore accompanies his great-uncle, the old family advocate V. on one of his yearly trips to R..sitten, and for Theodore, just as for the reader, the family history that lies hidden here is a mystery only to be revealed in the novel's second half. Here, in the knight's hall, we learn much later and by a spiralling and self-reflexive narrative route, did the founding violence of Hoffmann's story take place. Roderich's dead body lay in state here, and here did Roderich's older son Wolfgang theatrically confront the corpse of his tyrannical father, asking "which will, which power reaches beyond the grave" (*Entail* 248),[4] words that are again reminiscent of Paine's indictment of monarchical and aristocratic power in *The Rights of Man*. Here, Wolfgang would soon succumb to insatiable greed, seeking a fortune he presumes his father has kept hidden from him. And here, Wolfgang would be pushed to his death only a few weeks later by the old steward Daniel, falling into empty space through a door, now walled shut, to be crushed among the rubble of his father's collapsed astronomical tower, where, at Daniel's insinuation, he believed the treasure to be buried. Daniel in turn had been working to bring about Wolfgang's demise together with Wolfgang's younger brother Hubert, who, denied an inheritance and in love with the same woman as his older sibling, had become consumed by jealousy and hatred. At castle R..sitten, the scene of capital crime, to which Daniel's ghost is forced to return on each full moon, and the seat of judgement occupy the same space, and the rule of law takes shape from a space of violent transgression, where literary precedent from Shakespeare to Schiller seems to determine the course of action.

Through Theodore, who finds himself alone here on the first night of his stay, Hoffmann depicts the knight's hall as a highly aestheticized, self-consciously Gothic space: the full moon shines through the medieval stained-glass windows, walls and ceiling are covered by curiously carved wood panelling, wind and sea provide the requisite, seemingly supernatural soundscape, and the overall atmosphere, combined with his own youthful receptivity, increased by several glasses of hot punch, gives Theodore the impression of being on the brink of the spirit world, an "alien realm" ("ein fremdes Reich") that "might now visibly and audibly open" (*Entail* 207). That alien realm then indeed does open up, after Theodore, who instantly recognizes the potential of the setting for the reading of a Gothic novel and its likely conduciveness to the greatest amount of aesthetic pleasure such an act of reading can provide, immerses himself in Schiller's *The Ghost-Seer*, itself an iconic example of the German tradition of the genre.

---

4   The page numbers for citations from Hoffmann's text refer to the standard German *Deutscher Klassiker Verlag* edition. All translations of Hoffmann in this chapter are mine.

Despite the fact that Hoffmann explicitly creates the R..sitten knight's hall as a repetition of pre-existing Gothic imagery, this place of uncanny repetitions has its own distinctive atmosphere, setting Hoffmann's atmospheric description apart from the models with which he plays.[5] That distinctive difference is created by the peculiar paintings that adorn the walls of the knight's hall. Theodore describes them as follows:

> From the great paintings, which for the most part represented the wild turmoil of bloody bear and wolf hunts, jutted heads of animals and human beings carved in wood that had been placed on the painted bodies, so that, particularly with the flickering and shimmering lighting provided by the fire and the moon, the whole lived in dreadful truth. (*Entail* 206)

The ambiguous formulation "dreadful truth" ("grauliche Wahrheit") refers to both the true-to-life, *trompe-l'œil* effect of the multi-media artworks that burst through the safe, two-dimensional representational pictorial space, suggesting the realism of the bloody violence they depict, *and* it implies that what is represented here brings an otherwise hidden, dreadful truth to life. That dreadful truth is not only the "bloody turmoil" of the violence depicted, but particularly the fact that in that violence human beings and animals, the killed and their killers, become indistinguishable – the German "Gewühl" suggests a mass of twisting bodies in which individual ones are no longer discernible. Who is killing whom and why in this bloody confrontation, resembling mortal combat more than a hunt, is unclear, and the paintings make visible what would remain hidden in any real-world medieval knight's hall. They present a Hobbesian state of nature marked by universal violence, a founding fiction that in turn underwrites the authoritarian structures of political and legal institutions meant to prevent its return. Pointedly, the underlying question is one of ownership and property, since the hunt in the medieval aristocratic context is no longer a matter of subsistence, but a social privilege, reserved to the rightful owners of the woods or fenced-in park where such hunting can legally take place. As Christine M. Korsgaard points out, in an article that seeks to discover in Kantian philosophy a conceptual foundation for animal rights, the "legal bifurcation" that divides the world into persons and property

> is not based on some principled argument that proves that everything that is not a person is properly regarded as property. Instead, the traditional theory of rights simply starts from the unargued assumption that everything in the world except people, including non-human animals, is a possible piece of property. (Korsgaard 646)

As aesthetic fictions, the paintings in the knight's hall at R..sitten reveal the hidden violence behind that "unargued assumption" and depict the "bloody turmoil" through which human beings emerge as persons distinct from other sentient beings who may be used and instrumentalized as property.

---

5   For a discussion of the centrality of repetition for the (German) Gothic and Hoffmann's repetition of such repetitions as a poetological reflection of the genre as a whole, see Schmitz-Emans. In the case of *The Entail* and the scene in the knight's hall in particular, Hoffmann's intertextual play would itself be famously repeated by Edgar Allan Poe in "The Fall of the House of Usher".

The names of Roderich's sons, Wolfgang and Hubert, make it clear that this kind of foundational violence can easily be reactivated in the legal distinctions between human persons themselves: Hubert, a direct reference to St Hubertus, the patron saint of the hunt, and Wolfgang, whose name means "the wolf's path" (from the Old High German *wulf* – wolf, and *gang* – path, or journey), repeat the "bloody turmoil" of the knight's hall paintings, and link through their legally induced sibling rivalry the violence of the human/animal distinction with the potentially destructive effects of legal instruments on human relationships.

Roderich's faithful servant Daniel, the ghost haunting the knight's hall, is the spectral and uncanny embodiment of the simultaneity of both concerns. As a revenant, he is detectable for Theodore only by means of sound. Daniel's identity is of course unknown to Theodore when he first hears his voice in the knight's hall, and he announces himself with a sighing and moaning in which, Theodore tells us, "lies the expression of the deepest human suffering, of inconsolable sorrow" (*Entail* 208). Yet, despite the unmistakable humanity of these sounds, Theodore's first reaction is to explain the pain they communicate as that of an animal: "Ha! that is some locked up, sick animal on the lower floor" (*Entail* 208). By deciding that the sounds he hears must be exclusively those of an animal, Theodore seeks to "clarify" his perceptions and to hold his existential dread at bay. If we read the meaning of Theodore's name, "gift of God", from the Greek *theos*, God and *doron*, gift, as a reference to the God-given, rational soul and free, autonomous will that separates human beings from the animal world in the Western tradition, then Theodore must here fear for the gift of that distinction, and with it for his very name, identity, and sanity.[6]

As Theodore hopes for clarification of his very being, he hears again, this time "louder, deeper sighs, uttered as if in the terrible fear of mortal danger" (*Entail* 208), sounds that communicate to him the presence of a fellow creature in the direst need. And once more, Theodore can only think to protect himself by attempting to force a distinction where none can be heard:

> "Yes, it is a poor, imprisoned animal – I will now call loudly, I will stamp vigorously with my foot on the ground, everything will instantly be silent, or the animal below will make itself more clearly audible in its natural sounds." (*Entail* 208)

As he attempts to assert his autonomy through call and gesture, commanding either silence or submission to an imposed set of categories, it never occurs to Hoffmann's

---

6   Fittingly, this fear emerges in the confrontation with Daniel, whose name means in turn "God be my judge" or "judge of God" in Hebrew. Daniel reminds us that we assume the imaginary, metaphysical position from which such distinctions could be determined, and judgements proclaimed, at our great peril. "Daniel, Daniel, what are you doing here at this hour!" are Wolfgang's last words before he will plummet to his death, words with which Wolfgang's son Roderich will inadvertently kill Daniel himself years later, and which echo in uncanny repetition throughout Hoffmann's text (*Entail* 278).

deeply unsettled first-person narrator that he might need to heed the call for assistance made upon him by a voice whose "nature" he cannot identify.

Theodore could have read about such calls in Johann Gottfried Herder's "Treatise on the Origin of Language" from 1772, the opening sentences of which run as follows:

> *Already as an animal, the human being has language.* All violent sensations of his body, and the most violent of the violent, the painful ones, and all strong passions of his soul immediately express themselves in cries, in sounds, in wild, inarticulate noises. A suffering animal, as much as the hero Philoctetes, when overcome with pain, will whine!, will groan!, even if it were abandoned, on a desolate island, without the sight, the trace, or the hope of a helpful fellow creature. (Herder 65-66; italics in original)

This natural "language of sensation", Herder claims is shared by all "sensitive beings", and its purpose is to elicit sympathy and support in a hostile physical universe (Herder 66).

Through Herder's effort to adduce the "language of sensation" as proof of the fundamental interconnectedness of all sentient beings by means of sympathy, another, more Rousseauian view of the "state of nature" to be negotiated in the knight's hall, and the "natural law" to be derived from it comes into view. In the *Discourse on the Origin and Foundations of Inequality Among Men* of 1755, Rousseau proposes two pre-rational principles as "the first and simplest operations of the human Soul", self-preservation on the one hand, and the "repugnance to see any sensitive Being perish or suffer, principally those like ourselves" on the other (Rousseau 14-15). From this perspective one might say that Theodore is now caught between both these impulses and can come down on the side of self-preservation, driven as he is predominantly by fear in this instance, only by making an "unnatural" distinction between human and animal suffering. Unable to do so, as the groans he hears defy classification, Theodore remains paralyzed, and his individual freedom and autonomy become inaccessible: tongue-tied and immobilized, he can neither call nor stomp his feet and cannot help but bear witness to the suffering in which he is now implicated.

III

Only much later in Hoffmann's text do we witness the confrontation between Daniel and Wolfgang in the knight's hall that leads to the murder Daniel subsequently re-enacts compulsively. By now, the central role of both the person/property and the human/animal distinction in this 'primal scene' will no longer come as a surprise. It occurs the day after Wolfgang confronts the dead body of his father. Daniel, who was Roderich's right hand and, as the castellan of R..sitten, his highest-ranking servant, finds his standing imperilled and voices his fear that, given Wolfgang's conflict with his master, he will probably be let go, despite his old age and long-standing service. Wolfgang responds with overt disdain that while he will not turn his father's old servant out of doors, he has indeed no intention to rely on his services, and that Daniel may "enjoy his keeping well enough without work" (*Entail* 249-50).

Hoffmann's word for such voluntary "keeping" of a former servant in old age, "Gnaden-brot", literally "bread of mercy", sets the tone for what follows, for the same word is also used for the keeping of an old domestic animal like a dog or horse who can no longer be profitably put to work but has rendered its services ably for so long that it deserves gratitude and cannot be simply disposed of like a mere thing. In *The Metaphysics of Morals* of 1797, Immanuel Kant asserts, immediately after strongly condemning unwarranted cruelty against animals for purposes of scientific experimentation, that "gratitude for the long service of an old horse or dog (just as if they were members of the household) belongs *indirectly* to a human being's duty *with regard to* these animals" (Kant, *Metaphysics* 193; italics in original). As a "*direct* duty, however", Kant claims, "it is always only a duty of the human being *to* himself" (Kant, *Metaphysics* 193; italics in original). This is so because, according to Kant, "a human being has duties only to human beings (himself and others), since his duty to any subject is moral constraint by that subject's will" (Kant, *Metaphysics* 192). Only human beings can be moral persons, in other words, and a sense of obligation towards animals is from a Kantian perspective a misplaced projection of an obligation towards oneself onto the animal.[7] Daniel, deeply wounded by Wolfgang's remark, senses instantly that Wolfgang, who strips him of his value as a person and a servant in high standing, implicitly likens him to a domestic animal. If Kant suggests we treat domestic animals in long-standing service "as if they were members of the household," the hierarchical inequality of that "as if" cuts both ways and means that human persons with whom we stand in an unequal social relationship can for all practical purposes be denied their personhood and be relegated to the status of "mere" animals as well (Kant, *Metaphysics* 193).

For Kant, only the moral personhood of human beings gives them a dignity and hence a value above all price, while everything else is ultimately fungible and can be replaced in a process of economic exchanges. In the *Groundwork of the Metaphysics of Morals* of 1785 he had written that "[i]n the kingdom of ends" – i.e. the moral state in which all persons are citizens as well as sovereigns, able to legislate through their rational choices by submitting to the moral law – "everything has either a *price* or a *dignity*. What has a price can be replaced by something else as its *equivalent*; what on the other hand is raised above all price and therefore admits of no equivalent has a dignity" (Kant, *Groundwork* 42, italics in original). In the *Metaphysics of Morals*, in the section "On Servility" Kant makes explicit that

> [i]n the system of nature, a human being (*homo phenomenon, animal rationale*) is a being of slight importance and shares with the rest of the animals, as offspring of the earth, an ordinary value *(pretium vulgare)*. (Kant, *Metaphysics* 186; italics in original)

---

7   Cruel treatment of animals degrades one's own humanity on the Kantian view, and re-fraining from such conduct, while a direct duty to oneself, is only an indirect one with respect to the animal, who, in Kant's view, does not have the requisite free will and per-sonal autonomy to exert moral constraint in others directly. Kant, in other words, seeks to secure a binding moral foundation for our conduct with regard to animals without giv-ing up on the traditional hierarchies of the human/animal relationship.

Just like the earth itself, everything produced by and from it, including rational animals such as human beings in a strictly phenomenal sense can become personal property to be bought, sold and controlled by means of land and inheritance law. Their distinctive difference from animals, their understanding and their ability to set themselves ends, Kant continues, may mean that some human beings are valued more highly than others, but since what is in question here is only their extrinsic value, i.e. their *usefulness*, that merely means that they can fetch a higher price in a system of exchange ("Verkehr") in which the supreme value is the medium of exchange itself:

> it gives one man a higher value than another, that is, a *price* as of a commodity in ex-
> change with these animals as things, though he still has a lower value than the universal
> medium of exchange, money, the value of which can therefore be called preeminent.
> (Kant, *Metaphysics* 186; italics in original)

Only as a *person* can a human being escape the power of money:

> But a human being regarded as a *person*, that is, as the subject of a morally practical
> reason, is exalted above any price ... he possesses a *dignity* (an absolute inner worth) by
> which he enacts *respect* for himself from all other rational beings in the world. He can
> measure himself with every other being of his kind and value himself on a footing of
> equality with them. (Kant, *Metaphysics* 186; italics in original)

Not sure anymore what the "other being[s] of his kind" might be, Daniel must now fear the loss of all dignity and respect. Being a "rational animal", Daniel understands, is not enough to secure equality among human beings, and in his role as a servant, he is ulti-mately not distinguishable from a domestic animal.

Daniel's shocked protest at that realization has an incendiary effect on Wolfgang, who, about to leave the hall, is now overcome by an irrepressible rage at Daniel's words and screams a threat that confirms Daniel's animal status: "I should cast you out like a rabid dog" (*Entail* 250). Terrified by Wolfgang's outburst, Daniel has fallen to his knees very close to him, so that Wolfgang, possibly inadvertently, completes the humiliation by kicking Daniel in the chest so that the old man falls to the ground "with a hollow cry" (*Entail* 250). As Daniel gathers himself up with difficulty, he "utter[s] a strange sound, similar to the howling whimper of a deadly wounded animal" and "pierce[s] Wolfgang with a look glowing with fury and despair" (*Entail* 250). In this strange sound, the same Theodore will hear again in the knight's hall several decades later, Wolfgang might hear the agonized expression of his inalienable kinship with Daniel, whom he deeply wounds here as an *animal*, precisely by inflicting the verbal and physical abuse on him against which a mere animal – a rabid dog, say – has no ability to speak up. As a *person*, Daniel cannot feel pain, for persons and their rights are only masks, while the pain he *does* feel as that mask is ripped from his face can no longer sound through it ("per-sonare") to be perceived as human. Were he not blinded by his own rage, Wolfgang might recognize this pain as his own, as Herder would have him do, particularly because the violent passion he displaces here onto his dead father's servant originates from the patriarch's denial of Wolfgang's own personal autonomy and dignity. Instead, Wolfgang tosses Daniel a bag of money as he leaves the room, signalling once again that the old servant does not have the inestimable value of a person in the Kantian kingdom of ends, but only a market price. His affective state reduced to a deadly combination of pain, fury, and despair, the only form of communication still available to Daniel is violence.

By insinuating to his master that a great treasure lies buried beneath the rubble of the collapsed tower, Daniel plants the seed in Wolfgang's mind that leads the latter obsessively to the door of the knight's hall overlooking the abyss through which Daniel will push him to his death with a powerful kick, screaming wildly, "Down with you, you rabid dog!" (*Entail* 282) The sound of animal agony that paralyzes Theodore in the knight's hall is hence both Daniel's *and* Wolfgang's and levels all distinctions between victim and perpetrator, master and servant, human and animal, hunter and hunted.

IV

Theodore, it will be remembered, remains suspended in the R..sitten knight's hall, unable to either respond to Daniel's animal voice, or to assert his own agency and personhood. In this state of paralysis, instead of the "natural sounds" he hopes for, he distinctly hears a supernatural voice that apparently issues from one of the portraits on the walls, warning him, "No further – no further, or you are lost to the dreadful horror of the spirit world" (*Entail* 208). The following day, the effect of this voice still haunts Theodore, who tells us that he

> felt as if touched by an unknown power, or it seemed to me rather as if I had already brushed the circle and that only one more step were needed to transgress it and to perish irredeemably, as if only the summoning of all my power could protect me against *that* horror, which usually only gives way to incurable madness. (*Entail* 209-10; italics in original)

It is particularly pertinent in the present context that for Rousseau the distinction between the state of nature and civil society lies in the invention of private property and the drawing of an imaginary circle around a plot of common ground. Here are the opening lines of part two of the *Second Discourse*:

> The first person, who, having fenced off a plot of ground, had the idea to say *this is mine* and found people simple enough to believe him, was the true founder of civil society. What crimes, wars, murders, what miseries and horrors would the human Race have been spared by someone who, uprooting the stakes or filling in the ditch, had shouted to his fellows: Beware of listening to this impostor; you are lost if you forget that the fruits belong to all and the Earth to no one! (Rousseau 43; italics in original)

If we take Theodore's suspension as an unresolvable contradiction inherent in the Rousseauian state of nature between the pre-rational principles of sympathy and self-preservation, heightened by the fear induced by the Hobbesian state of nature surrounding him in the knight's hall, then the step Theodore is warned not to take, the step that will break his paralysis but will take him into the magic circle from beyond which there is no return, may very well be the claiming of private property as an entry into the security of a civil society where insanity and violence are the hidden law that rules our everyday interactions. The fact that this warning is uttered by a speaking portrait again directly connects the R..sitten knight's hall to Horace Walpole's *The Castle of Otranto*, where that Gothic convention is established, and hence links it to the very origins of the Gothic. In Walpole's text, Theodore's namesake is ultimately revealed as the rightful heir of Otranto, and it is quite likely that Hoffmann's narrator and protagonist is warned here by the collective spirit of the genre not to accept the concept of personal property however legitimized, and to reject the temptation of an identity based on ownership altogether.

In the brief coda to Hoffmann's long story, Theodore returns to R..sitten many years later, on his journey home from St Petersburg, where he had fled to escape "the storm of war that roared devastatingly over all of Germany" (*Entail* 283). Theodore discovers that castle R..sitten now lies entirely in ruins, while the property of the extinct von R family has reverted back to the state. In an ironic fulfilment of part of Roderich's original will, stones of the castle have been used to build a lighthouse that now shines its horizontal light to guide ships across the storm-tossed sea. That transformation, however, does not suffice to put Daniel's ghost to rest: From an old peasant with whom he enters into conversation Theodore learns that "gruesome wailings" ("grauenvolle Klagelaute") (*Entail* 284) can still be heard among the castle's ruins. Today, we can hear in them not only the global conflagrations that would follow, but the pain of a whole biosphere in danger of collapse. Like Hoffmann's "[p]oor, old, short-sighted Roderich", we are realizing too late that we "conjured up" an "evil power ... that poisoned to death at its first sprouting the stock [we] thought to plant for eternity with strong and solid root" (*Entail* 282).

Works Cited

Herder, Johann Gottfried von. "Treatise on the Origin of Language". *Philosophical Writings*. Ed. and trans. Michael N. Forster. Cambridge: Cambridge UP, 2006, 65-164.

Hoeveler, Diane Long and James D. Jenkins. "Where the Evidence Leads: Gothic Narratives and Legal Technologies". *European Romantic Review* 18.3 (2007): 307-37.

Hoffmann, E.T.A. *Nachtstücke*. Ed. Hartmut Steinecke and Gerhard Allroggen. Frankfurt a.M.: Deutscher Klassiker Verlag, 2009.

Kant, Immanuel. *Groundwork of the Metaphysics of Morals*. Ed. and trans. Mary Gregor. Cambridge: Cambridge UP, 2008.

---. *The Metaphysics of Morals*. Ed. and trans. Mary Gregor. Cambridge: Cambridge UP, 1996.

König, Peter. "Der Poetische Charakter des Rechts: Das Majorat von E.T.A. Hoffmann". *Internationales Archiv für Sozialgeschichte der deutschen Literatur* 31.2 (2006): 203-17.

Korsgaard, Christine M. "Kantian Ethics, Animals, and the Law". *Oxford Journal of Legal Studies* 33.4 (2013): 629-48.

Macpherson, Sandra. "Rent to Own: Or, What's Entailed in *Pride and Prejudice*". *Representations* 82.1 (2003): 1-23.

Paine, Thomas. *Political Writings*. Ed. Bruce Kuklick. Cambridge: Cambridge UP, 1989.

Riedl, Peter Philipp. "Die Zeichen der Krise: Erbe und Eigentum in Achim Arnims *Die Majoratsherren* und E.T.A. Hoffmanns *Das Majorat*". *Jahrbuch der Eichendorff-Gesellschaft* 52 (1982): 17-50.

Rousseau, Jean-Jacques. *Discourse on the Origins of Inequality (Second Discourse). Polemics, and Political Economy*. Ed. Roger D. Masters and Christopher Kelly. Trans. Judith R. Bush et al., vol. 3. Hanover, NH: University Press of New England, 1992.

Schmitz-Emans, Monika. "Wiederholung der Wiederholung. E.T.A. Hoffmanns *Die Räuber* (1820/21) als metaliterarische Erzählung im Kontext der Schauerliteratur". *Populäre Erscheinungen: Der Deutsche Schauerroman um 1800*. Ed. Barry Murnane and Andrew Cusack. München: Fink, 2011, 309-25.

Zeuch, Ulrike. "Recht und Literatur um 1800 im Kontext des *law and literature movement*". *Internationales Archiv für Sozialgeschichte der deutschen Literatur* 31.1 (2006): 77-84.

Sebastian Domsch

Transgressing (Story)Worlds: Polidori, Byron, and *The Vampyre*

While the notion of boundaries and their transgression in Romanticism is frequently explored in terms of social norms and rules (from political radicalism to sexual taboo and beyond), one area that has yet to come into focus through this conceptual framework is the cultural practice of creating narrative storyworlds. There are two main aspects here. The first is that of the boundaries between authors and their narrative worlds, the second is whether authors become the sole proprietors of their storyworlds, so that consequently any attempt by a different author to use elements from that storyworld or to even continue it is an act of transgression. In other words, this paper wants to look at the territorial power politics of writing, and particularly narrative in the Romantic age, focusing on a fascinating example of narrative transgressions by looking at John Polidori's 1819 short novel *The Vampyre*.

This investigation is part of a larger project that attempts to create a systematic account, as well as a history of, our engagement with storyworlds. When it comes to the aspect of boundaries, in the most simple sense, in the case of fictional worlds recipients need to address the question whether two acts of narrating,[1] both creating 'a' storyworld, can share territory, whether two stories can be 'set in the same world' and more importantly, how that sharing is regulated.

There are two main ways to conceptualize the 'regional politics' of storyworlds, ways that either regard storyworlds as *self-contained* or as *additive*. The extreme version of the idea of self-contained fictional worlds would claim that each narrative act creates its own distinct and complete storyworld that is absolutely different from all other storyworlds. Different narrative texts might use the same proper names for existents[2] in their storyworld, but they are not identical, according to this view, as they exist in different and self-contained worlds. Thus, Bram Stoker's Dracula is not the same as the character embodied by Bela Lugosi or Christopher Lee, though they share the same name and many properties.[3]

---

1 This could mean the act of creating and publishing a novel, or telling a tale to an audience. Of course, already the definition of what constitutes such an 'act' is under debate, as in the case of publishing several novels that form a narrative series, or publishing a single novel in a serialized format etc.

2 In narratology, this term refers to everything that has an existence in the storyworld; this can be characters, places, objects, but also properties, such as 'time runs backwards' etc.

3 This idea is for example apparent in the acceptance that two stories about the 'same' character will contain an event that can, logically speaking, only happen once, such as the character's death.

The idea of additive storyworlds, on the other hand, is that multiple narrative acts can add to the creation of a single storyworld. This conception should be further subdivided into an *authorial/canonical* and an *appropriative* form. The canonical form, on the one hand, privileges original authorship and clearly distinguishes between authors and readers, with only authors, or rather: the right author, being allowed to legitimately add to the storyworld. In its most restricted form, there is only one author, who is usually the original creator of the storyworld (e.g. Arthur Conan Doyle as author of the 'canonical' Holmes stories). In the era of story-franchises, the right of authorship can also be conferred on (multiple) authors by a copyright holder such as a publishing company. The appropriative form, on the other hand, takes the position that a fictional world is principally open to additions from every reader, who has the right to become an author at any time, a position that is taken, for example, by writers of fan fiction.

According to the guiding hypothesis of my general research project, throughout the history of narrative, the diverging concepts about as well as the attitudes towards storyworlds and their boundaries have been in competing use, and their dominance or negligence has been closely tied to the dominant media, as well as to general currents in the history of ideas.

Thus, for example, oral storytelling traditions necessarily rely on an additive-appropriative concept of fictional worlds. Oral narratives are constantly being re-told, with inevitable variations that still leave the story's identity and integrity untouched in the minds of the listeners – because there is no concept of an integrity with clear-cut borders. With writing, in contrast, texts become fixed: once a text is written down, it can be performed time and again without variations. This has consequences for the recipients' attitudes towards storyworlds: The idea of the integrity of fictional worlds gains strength.

Print further strengthened the process of creating hierarchies of authority. Printed text was fixed even further than written text, which remained a more fluid object of revisions and rewritings. Thus, print created for example a clear-cut differentiation between authoritative text (the printed text) and non-authoritative text (hand-written marginalia). We can see this played out in the publication history of *The Vampyre*. In the context of the ghost-story contest, Byron had written his original idea in manuscript and did not publish it. While theoretically this act should secure the artistic originality for himself, in actual practice this is trumped by the power of the printed word. It is because Polidori writes and publishes his version of the story (and because it is published with the claim that it is by Byron himself) that Byron feels compelled to add his own fragment to a published collection of his poems. Only in that form can he maintain his ownership of his own text, not in a legal sense, but in the eyes of a public that has come to regard print as more authoritative than writing.

Print also accelerates the development of writing into a business, a profession within a market economy, and therefore it creates the necessity for regulations of this market and its commodities, the texts. It is in the eighteenth century that a real book market develops that can sustain professional authors. And backed by the emerging copyright law, these authors regard themselves as the owners of their creations, who have an absolute control over them. This is an important, though less often considered, element in the development of the concept of Romantic authorship.

But print also brought with it a new factor, one working simultaneously against the compartmentalization of the fictional worlds that it reinforced, and that is also contained in the commercialization of the literary market. A successful oral storyteller would be able to tell his story again and again, with each performance varying from the other, with constant revisions and additions. But though a printed text can of course be re-read, its fixed nature leaves a desideratum for novelty within familiarity: Readers wanted more, but of the same, creating a demand. This is where the idea of fictional expansion, of the sequel comes to prominence. Sequels of course have existed much longer than print, but the eighteenth century experiences an unprecedented surge of continuations of popular books that were characteristically not written by their original authors.

To repeat, it is the eighteenth-century literary market with its copyright laws and printing technology and widening readership that calcifies the boundaries between storyworlds, establishes the author as legal as well as commercial proprietor of her creations, and creates the demand for varied repetition and expansion in fiction. As David Brewer has argued, another major shift can be observed in the change from an eighteenth-century focus on narrative characters that are understood to belong to a common cultural repertoire to an emphasis on (commercially successful and legally protected) authors that hold monarchical power:

> Yet in order to be perceived as possessing the necessary charisma to bind together a virtual community, authors needed first to be granted a proprietary, monarchic authority over their own creations. Toward this end, nineteenth-century readers actively collaborated in the enclosure of the textual commons, even when it meant abandoning their own claims upon a given character. (Brewer 194)

This corresponds to what David Riede has described as the desideratum of Romantic authorship more generally, which is "an authority apparently beyond argument" (Riede 29). This authority rested not only on the recently established copyright laws, but also on the Romantic emphasis on originality. No longer a product of careful study and imitation of exemplary models, the ideal work of art now becomes a creation that is wholly new and absolute in its individuality. Both of these attributes, newness and uniqueness, are the preconditions for the author's property rights to her creation. Edward Young writes in his *Conjectures on Original Composition*:

> Thyself so reverence, as to prefer the native growth of thy own mind to the richest import from abroad; such borrowed riches make us poor. The man who thus reverences himself, will soon find the world's reverence to follow his own. His works will stand distinguished; his the sole property of them; which property alone can confer the noble title of an author. (*Conjectures* 24)

The conflation of the celebration of authorial genius and the quasi-legal status of the product of that genius will become most consequential in the future, since the notion of the original Romantic author as sole and inimitable creator becomes "deeply embedded in Anglo-American copyright law" (Aoki 1322-23).

While these tendencies enshrined the author as the absolute proprietor of a literary work of art, they also cemented the differentiation between the concrete form of expression and the underlying 'ideas' or content that is used as 'raw material', with a clear emphasis on 'expression'. And this idea/expression dichotomy is to this day an important aspect of laws about copyright and intellectual property.[4] The belief that developed during Romanticism is that for such an original author

> everything in the world must be made available and accessible as an 'idea' that can be transformed into his 'expression' which thus becomes his 'work'. Through his labour, he makes these 'ideas' his own; his possession of the 'work' is justified by his expressive activity. As long as the author does not copy another's expression, he is free to find his themes, plots, ideas, and characters anywhere he pleases, and to make these his own (this is also the model of authorship that dominates Anglo-American laws of copyright). Any attempts to restrict his ability to do so are viewed as censorship and as an unjustifiable restriction on freedom of expression. (Coombe 211)

An anonymous author in the *Cambridge Review* notes in an 1889 article on plagiarism how this development has led to the point where critics see themselves as some kind of police force that guards the particular poetic expression of authors:

> The whole body of critics [is] placed, as it were, like trusty watch-dogs around the works of every author, past or present, suffering no man to approach without a growl of warning. And so many are they in number, as well as keen in scent, that the wariest intruder can scarcely approach their charges without being marked and apprehended. (Anon. 1889)

As we can see, the ideas about authorship that develop in the context of Romanticism also bring an intense negotiation about the legal and economic relation between an author and their creation. One of the consequences of this is that it establishes at least some authors' personas as trademarks, an effect that is explainable as a combination of the Romantic notion of original authorship with the development of a media landscape that accelerates the potential speed of a writer's success and the extent and dissemination of 'press coverage'. And certainly, no author is more important for this development in the early nineteenth century than Byron. As Antoine Lilti writes, "the momentous irruption of Lord Byron onto the public stage was, undeniably, an important step in celebrity culture" (Lilti 229). Interest in Byron's texts was inextricably tied to the interest in Byron's person, which was of course facilitated by Byron's use of the autobiographical in his fictional writing. This already meant a systematic eroding or transgression of the author/character-divide, both from the perspective of the writer and from that of his readers. In Byron's celebrity, one that was fuelled not least by his own willingness to blur the

---

4   "The natural law roots of the idea/expression dichotomy are ... striking ... [The idea/expression dichotomy] speaks directly to the natural law doctrines of inherent possessability. Expressions such as the text of a work are the proper subject of copyright because they are sufficiently concrete for the law to transform them into property. By contrast, ideas are so incorporeal that the law cannot make them into property" (Yen qtd. in Aoki 1325).

boundaries between himself and his literary heroes, we can see something like the invention of autobiographic reading, or what Tom Mole calls an "hermeneutics of intimacy" (Mole).

Before this development, texts are read rather as constituting the author's personality. This is what happened when readers declared Jonathan Swift to be mad, or at least an unremitting misanthrope, because of reading *Gulliver's Travels*. But in the case of Byron, the emphasis shifts, in that for an intrigued audience, his personality was a (somewhat mysterious) fact that existed outside of his texts, but that found expression in these texts and could therefore be glimpsed by a careful perusal that knew how to relate textual clues to already known biographical information. As early as 1821, the *London Magazine* claimed that interest in Byron was more 'personal' than 'poetic':

> Numerous readers read Byron's poems in the hope of better understanding his secrets and his mysteries, his flaws and his prominence, as a way to satisfy their curiosity about such a celebrated and fascinating figure. Byron's celebrity was not a biographical episode apart from his poetic work and his place in literary history; it was an essential element. As a legacy, Byron left not only the image of a romantic hero, melancholy and in revolt, or a body of poems that would be admired by a generation of readers, but also a form of almost voyeuristic poetic exchange between the curious reader and a shameless author who risked being accused of exhibitionism. The poetic fiction turned out to be a good way to feed the system of celebrity because of Byron's clever ability to carefully handle one aspect of the ambiguity. (Lilti 231)

Reviewing *Childe Harold's Pilgrimage* 3 on 23 November 1816, the *Portfolio* knew what kind of text it was dealing with, and dissected the new 'species of distinction':

> Indeed it is the real romance of [Byron's] life, immeasurably more than the fabled one of his pen, which the public expects to find in his pages, and which not so much engages its sympathy, as piques its curiosity, and feeds thought and conversation. The Noble Poet, in the mean time, is content with – it should be said is ambitious of this species of distinction; the booksellers, printers, and stationers, all profit by the traffic to which the exhibition gives rise; and thus every party is a gainer in this remarkable phenomenon of the time. (Anon. 1816, 73)

So people read Byron *out of* his fictionalized works, but that meant that they were only too eager to read him *into* the fictionalized works of others as well. One of the most prominent examples is of course Lady Caroline Lamb's first novel, *Glenarvon*, published in 1816, and featuring the rakish character of Lord Ruthven, who goes on to ruin the innocent Calantha (a self-portrait of the author) and himself. But in the same year, John Polidori takes over the name "Lord Ruthven" for his vampiric title character in a curious act of multiple-storyworld transgression that I want to look at somewhat closer in the following.

John Polidori's *The Vampyre* was inspired by a fragmentary story of Byron's, "Fragment of a Novel" (1816), and in turn inspired a 'vampire craze' across Europe via a number of adaptations through novels, plays and opera, and is an excellent example to highlight the complex relations between authorship, storyworlds, Romantic notions of originality versus imitation and the transgressive nature of fictional creation in general.

When Byron started into his self-imposed exile on the Continent in 1816, he took with him the twenty-one-year-old John William Polidori as his personal physician. Polidori had studied medicine, writing a dissertation on somnambulism, but because he was still too young to get his license for practising in London, and because he had literary ambitions, taking a prolonged trip with the celebrated and notorious Byron must have seemed like a once-in-a-lifetime chance. On a biographical level, it turned out to be a complete disaster: Byron and Polidori did not get along well, and Byron fired him just a few months into the trip. Polidori then tried and failed to get work in Italy, returned home to England with the hope of succeeding either as a physician or as a writer. A few years later, he committed suicide, possibly over a gambling debt.

Yet in between these dates lay the stuff of literary legends. There is the fabled meeting of Byron and Polidori with Percy Bysshe Shelley, Mary Godwin, and Claire Clairmont at the Villa Diodati near Geneva. There is the persistent bad weather in the 'year without summer' (see Klingaman and Klingaman), forcing the party indoors, and inspiring the ghost-story writing contest, proposed by Byron. There is Mary's nightmare vision of an unholy creation, and her sitting down to write "It was on a dreary night of November that I beheld the accomplishment of my toils", words that were the seed of her first novel, *Frankenstein*, to be published in 1818. But of course, Mary was not the only one who participated. Polidori started a tale as well that would eventually be published as *Ernestus Berchtold; or, The Modern Oedipus* in 1819, a text that has hardly resonated through literary history. And Byron started his own story, though he quickly became bored with it and abandoned the project. He must have shown his unfinished drafts to his companions, though, because at some point after their falling out, Polidori used elements of this story and fused them with an unflattering caricature of Byron himself. The result is his short novel *The Vampyre*, the manuscript of which found its way back to England while Polidori was still in Italy, where it is published without Polidori's knowledge and under Byron's name. The book, which is generally panned by the critics, nevertheless becomes commercially very successful, prompting Polidori to republish it later with careful revisions. Several stage adaptations follow, and a new tradition of vampire writing is born, though one that would for the longest time forget about its origins. As Skarda puts it: "The first vampire story in English fiction told less about ghoulish rituals of blood-sucking and heart-staking than about the failure to actualize one man's dreams of literary fame" (Skarda 249).

The story of *The Vampyre* is concerned mainly with the relationship between Aubrey, a promising but somewhat naïve young Englishman, and the mysterious Lord Ruthven, who appears in many ways like a parody of the Byronic hero, as created by Byron himself. As the narrator describes him, he is

> a nobleman, more remarkable for his singularities, than for his rank. He apparently gazed upon the mirth around him, as if he could not participate therein. It seemed as if, the light laughter of the fair only attracted his attention, that he might by a look quell it, and throw fear into those breasts where thoughtlessness reigned. (*Vampyre* 39)

Both men agree to travel on the Continent, but Aubrey soon leaves Ruthven in disgust at his immoral behaviour in Rome. He travels on, and they meet again in Greece, where Aubrey has been told about local legends of vampires by the beautiful Ianthe. Shortly after, Ianthe is killed, possibly by such a vampire, and Aubrey and Ruthven continue their journey. They are attacked by bandits, and Ruthven is mortally wounded in the fight. He gives very precise instructions for his own burial and makes Aubrey promise not to tell anybody about him and his death for a year. Aubrey returns to London, only to find Ruthven is there as well and very much alive, although he had seen him dead. Bound by his promise, he cannot but watch Ruthven be celebrated by society and court his own sister. Indeed, the worst comes to pass, and Ruthven and Aubrey's sister are engaged to marry on the day the oath ends. Aubrey has a breakdown, and just before he dies, he writes a letter to his sister revealing Ruthven's history, but it does not arrive in time. Ruthven marries her, and on the wedding night, she is discovered dead, drained of her blood – and Ruthven has vanished, now truly revealed as the vampire.

While this summary makes it sound like one of the cheaper pulps that can be found at a train station's newsstand, I want to suggest that from the perspective of literary history, Polidori's text is a singularly transgressive act, particularly in relation to the notion of storyworlds. First of all, it 'borrows' its original idea from Byron's unpublished text in an act that wavers between plagiarism and idea theft (see Skarda 264).

Then, it assumes (albeit unwittingly) a different authorship through the original publication, claiming to be by Byron. But it also wilfully transgresses the boundary between fictional and factual by clearly relating the fictional villain to the real Byron, a relation that is paradoxically made apparent by borrowing the fictional name from Lamb's scandalous *roman à clef*. Interestingly enough, Polidori writes about his young hero: "He thought, in fine, that the dreams of poets were the realities of life" (*Vampyre* 40). This is of course a standard trope in literature that goes back at least to *Don Quijote*, but it acquires an additional poignancy in this context, because Polidori's text borrows characteristics of the Byronic hero, through which already Byron had ambiguated the boundary between factual and fictional. And he does all of this to create a character that will become one of the prime archetypes of transgression, both in terms of content, and in terms of storyworld creation: the modern (Romantic? Byronic?) vampire.

As in the case of Victor Frankenstein and his creature, a Romantic writer here creates a new kind of archetypal character that is particularly connected to the Gothic mode. This mode and its roots in myth and legend are used to create (recognizable) archetypes, but in contrast to folkloristic storytelling these archetypes are now 'humanized', because they are treated narratively like realist characters with emotional complexity and moral ambiguity. Their archetypal character, with a more or less clearly defined set of pre-existing traits or components, makes them easily recognizable even through infinite variations. And indeed, the traumatic 're-appearance' of Lord Ruthven after his supposed death in Polidori's story is echoed not only by similar reappearances within later stories, but across the spectrum of popular narrative in general, where the vampire has become one of the major 'hauntings' of popular culture. But in contrast to the de-individualized stock figures of myth, the humanized character of the Romantic archetypes elevates them, because it makes them interesting in an empathetic way. We process them like (realistic) narrative characters, which in turn means that the recognition involved in their frequent re-appearances becomes much more specific, because the recognition contains not just their mythological characteristics, but a whole literary heritage. Even if we have never read the original source texts, we are still dimly aware that these characters have already come (or should we say: have already transgressed) from other texts, and they bring some of that baggage along.

Vampires had always existed in European folklore, with varying and recurring features – but the Polidori-tradition is recognizably distinct; this is a new breed of vampires, one that is radically different from its folkloristic ancestors and yet forms a recognizable literary family. To take an example that comes much later in the literary history of vampires: in Anne Rice's *Interview with the Vampire* (1976), the clearly Byronic vampire Louis travels to Transylvania in search of his roots, in an obvious nod to Bram Stoker, but also to the fact that the vampire has its origin in folkloristic archetypes. But what Louis finds there are only mindless animated corpses, which he kills in disgust, in a symbolic act that differentiates him from this tradition, or rather, that characterizes him as a specific sub-set of that tradition. Because as a literary figure, Anne Rice's Louis is a descendant of a family line that was epitomized by Bram Stoker, but that really started with Polidori, and that had its roots in a caricature of the Byronic hero.

Where the traditional vampire is a ghoulish and subhuman monster that mindlessly preys on those close to him, the Byronic vampire is human if mysterious in appearance, aristocratic, elegant and arrogant. The stereotypical Byronic disdain for common humanity is hereby turned into the hunter-prey relationship of the supernatural monster and normal humans. The typical black spot in the past that haunts the Byronic hero and keeps him from achieving happiness is elevated into a literal and supernatural curse. By the way, it is interesting to note that Byron himself, when he invoked the figure of the vampire in *The Giaour*, rather relied on the folkloristic tropes:

> But first, on earth as vampire sent,
> Thy corse shall from its tomb be rent:
> Then ghastly haunt thy native place,
> And suck the blood of all thy race;
> There from thy daughter, sister, wife,
> At midnight drain the stream of life;
> Yet loathe the banquet which perforce
> Must feed thy livid living corse:
> Thy victims ere they yet expire
> Shall know the demon for their sire,
> As cursing thee, thou cursing them,
> Thy flowers are withered on the stem. (*Giaour* ll. 755-65)

To come back to Polidori's textual practice, it is striking that the original debate often turned around the notion of 'expression' and Romantic ideas of authenticity, in the sense of 'are these really the words of the poet?' Thus the *Edinburgh Monthly Review* fumed that the act of appropriating the name of the esteemed poet was worse because the text itself fell so far below the 'expression' that would have been associated with the name:

> Did the wretched bungler, who has foisted his own mass of putrid sentiments on the public, not perceive, that by bringing it into immediate comparison with the living and glowing images of genius, he furnished the most effectual exposure of the imposition, which the admirers of Lord Byron's works could desire? (Anon. 1819)

So contemporaries attacked Polidori because he would presume to sell his own expression for that of Byron. But what eventually emerges through literary history is a shift from (poetic) expression towards an underlying or unifying idea that – because of its transgressive nature – cannot be contained: because this idea encompasses notions of literary style and generic conventions, the merging of a celebrity persona and a recognizable character type with recurring traits, and the further merging with a (non-realistic) narrative archetype that in itself is all about transgression (transgressing the boundary between life and death, and transgressing/invading the boundary between aggressor and victim). The resulting mix has proved immensely fertile, in that it laid the groundwork for the modern archetype of the vampire, a form that was most visibly codified by Bram Stoker, and that has by now transgressed any literary or narrative boundary imaginable. "*The Vampyre* is not *Dracula* (1897), but it made Bram Stoker's masterpiece possible" (MacDonald and Scherf 11).

So whose achievement is this? Who gets to claim intellectual ownership of the tradition of the Byronic vampire? Is it Byron, who served as a double inspiration, both through his literary work and through his public persona? Is it Polidori, who amalgamates the different influences into an incredibly fruitful germ (while never really understanding what he did, and creating a text (or, in the legal understanding, an 'expression') of only modest literary value? Is it Stoker, who takes up the tradition and uses it as the basis of a genuine literary masterpiece, by finding a congenial expression for the originality of the underlying idea? Personally, I rather like the irony that the best truth is possibly 'all of them', that the enduring literary myth of the modern vampire, born out of the epitome of individualism and the deification of the lonely but supreme self is in the end a collaborative creation. It is only fitting that the modern literary vampire should be born out of multiple transgressions.

Works Cited

Anon. "Childe Harold's Pilgrimage, Canto III". *Portfolio*, 23 November 1816.

---. "On Plagiarism". *Cambridge Review*, 21 February 1889.

---. "The Vampyre, a Tale". *Edinburgh Monthly Review*, 1 May 1819.

Aoki, Keith. "(Intellectual) Property and Sovereignty: Notes toward a Cultural Geography of Authorship". *Stanford Law Review* 48.5 (1996): 1293-355.

Brewer, David A. *The Afterlife of Character, 1726-1825*. Philadelphia: University of Pennsylvania Press, 2005.

Byron, Lord [George Gordon]. *Selected Poems of Lord Byron*. Ed. Paul Wright. London: Wordsworth Editions, 2006.

Coombe, Rosemary J. *The Cultural Life of Intellectual Properties: Authorship, Appropriation, and the Law*. Durham, NC and London: Duke UP, 1998.

Klingaman, William K. and Nicholas P. Klingaman. *The Year Without Summer: 1816 and the Volcano That Darkened the World and Changed History*. New York: St. Martin's Griffin, 2013.

Lilti, Antoine. *The Invention of Celebrity*. Transl. Lynn Jeffress. Cambridge: Polity Press, 2017.

Macdonald, D. L. and Scherf, Kathleen. "Introduction". John Polidori. *The Vampyre: A Tale, and Ernestus Berchtold; or, The Modern Oedipus*. Ed. D. L. Macdonald and Kathleen Scherf. Peterborough: Broadview, 2008. 1-29.

Macfarlane, Robert. *Original Copy: Plagiarism and Originality in Nineteenth-Century Literature*. Oxford: Oxford UP, 2007.

Mole, Tom. *Byron's Romantic Celebrity: Industrial Culture and the Hermeneutics of Intimacy*. Basingstoke: Palgrave Macmillan, 2007.

Polidori, John. *The Vampyre: A Tale, and Ernestus Berchtold; or, The Modern Oedipus*. Ed. D. L. Macdonald and Kathleen Scherf. Peterborough: Broadview, 2008.

Rice, Anne. *Interview with the Vampire*. New York: Knopf, 1976.

Riede, David G. *Oracles and Hierophants: Constructions of Romantic Authority*. Ithaca: Cornell UP, 1991.

Skarda, Patricia L. "Vampirism and Plagiarism: Byron's Influence and Polidori's Practice". *Studies in Romanticism* 28.2 (1989): 249-69.

Wiley, Michael. "Romantic Amplification: The Way of Plagiarism". *ELH* 75.1 (2008): 219-40.

Young, Edward. *Conjectures on Original Composition*. Ed. Edith J. Morley. Manchester: Manchester UP, 1918.

Jonathan Gross

"No *hopes* for *them* as *laughs*": William Beckford in the Margins of Robert Southey's and Lord Byron's Visions of Judgement

In a letter to Augusta Leigh on December 19, 1816, Byron wrote with insight about laughter, religion, and the nature of moral judgement:

> I remember a methodist preacher who on perceiving a profane grin on the faces of part of his congregation – exclaimed "no *hopes* for *them* as *laughs*" and thus it is – with us – we laugh too much for hopes – and so even let them go – I am sick of sorrow – & must even content myself as well as I can – so here goes – I won't be woeful again if I can help it. (*Byron's Letters and Journals* [*BLJ*] 5:144)

It was not the first time he used the anecdote. The phrase appears in a note to *Hints from Horace* (l. 382) and in a letter on September 2, 1811. "In the mean time I *hope & laugh* in Spite of *Johnny Stickles*" (*BLJ* 9:160), Byron wrote to Davies, mentioning the name of the "methodist preacher" he would allude to in his letter to Augusta. Eight years later he suggested the phrase as epigraph for his mock-dedication to *Don Juan*. "Take for the Motto 'No Hopes for them as laughs' – Stickles's Sermons. – You will recollect the passage. ---" (*BLJ* 11:172).

Laughter, for Byron, was a form of transgression, something "profane" people did when they had the temerity to "grin" during a service. Triple rhymes in *Don Juan* (Wellington/Villainton) could be funny and even transgressive, but the deeper question was the ontological status of laughter itself. What was laughter good for, and who had the right to laugh? Most importantly, who was the "we" he alluded to in these letters? Byron, Augusta, or Lady Byron? Were Byron and Augusta laughing at Lady Byron? Was shared laughter a form of satire? There is evidence that Lady Byron smiled when she read *Don Juan*, and even gave others permission to laugh. "Writing to Theresa Villiers on July 15, 1819 about her appearance as Donna Inez, the hero's prim mother-in-law", Miranda Seymour notes, "Annabella remarked that Byron's satire was 'so good as to make me smile at myself – therefore others are heartily welcome to laugh'" (Seymour 134). Perhaps a smile differs from a laugh, since the latter is more irreverent. Lady Byron can smile, but she good-naturedly (or helplessly) allows others to laugh at her evangelical ways.

Begun before he wrote *Cain* and finished at the same time as "Heaven and Earth" and other minor works, this masterful satire, "The Vision of Judgement" reflects a view of Heaven that has been called "sharply conceived, [and] firmly constructed" by Emrys Jones (Jones 1-2), and "angry" by Peter Cochran (Cochran, online version of Lord Byron's *Vision of Judgement* 3). I would argue that the poem is "laughing", a strategy he employed by using a source no other critical commentators on the poem mention:

William Beckford's notes, recently made available since 1987 through the Pierpont Library's acquisition of William Ray's bequest. Taking his cue from the ever-irreverent Beckford, as Byron had once done in *Childe Harold's Pilgrimage*, Canto 1, he refuses to be woeful about the last judgement: his or George III's.

Robert Southey and William Beckford

Robert Southey was Poet Laureate from 1804-21 and wrote "A Vision of Judgement" in April 1821 to herald George III's entry into heaven when he died on January 29, 1820. Percy Bysshe Shelley upbraided George III in "England in 1819"; Southey blessed him in 1821, while Thomas Moore, James Henry Leigh Hunt and William Hazlitt had viewed him for the better part of a decade as highly injurious to England's reputation, especially during the American and French revolutions. I argue that Byron read Beckford's marginalia to assist him in responding to Robert Southey's high praise for the recently deceased monarch. In his note to the *Two Foscari*, and in his letters to John Murray (1817), Byron revealed that he was irritated by Southey's gossip. Southey had claimed that Byron and Percy Bysshe Shelley were in a league of incest with Mary Godwin and Claire Clairmont the previous summer in Geneva (Jump 122-36). Byron's poem was as much a running commentary on his dispute with Robert Southey, then, as it was a depiction of George III. He does not attempt to imitate the Laureate's style, as Andrew Rutherford has shown, "but makes his plot appear ridiculous by presenting it in a completely different style, transforming the whole tone, feeling, and significance of the original work" (Rutherford 226).

In 1821, Southey's poem set off a series of reactions from Shelley, Moore, and the group Southey referred to as a Satanic school of poetry (de Montluzin 19-22). "Southey's famous digression on the 'Satanic School', while obviously aimed at Byron, was in large measure adapted from a review of Thomas Moore's *Epistles, Odes, and Other Poems* that he had published some fifteen years earlier in the Annual Review for 1806", Nicholas Joukovsky observes (Joukovsky 498). Beckford seems to have known this, for he inserts Moore's name even though it does not appear in Southey's Preface to "A Vision of Judgement". Byron explained his political strategy to Thomas Moore on October 1, 1821, leaking the argument of his own satire. "In this it is my intent to put the said George's Apotheosis in a Whig point of view, not forgetting the Poet Laureate for his preface and his other demerits". Once Byron's poem appeared, even Wordsworth entered the fray, noting "one article which I was induced to publish in a London newspaper, when Southey and Byron were at war" (Joukovsky 496). Wordsworth's essay was intended for the *Morning Post*, a conservative daily that indicates that Southey's transgressions against good taste transcended politics. "Wordsworth, writing to Henry Crabb Robinson on 23 January 1821, clearly predicted that Southey's work would produce a storm of protest, though he seems to have been more concerned about Tory opinion than about the predictable attacks of the Whig and Radical opposition" (Joukovsky 498).

The Morgan Library Copy of the Poem

Gordon Ray's 1987 bequest of the Southey volume to the Pierpont Morgan library occurred too late to be incorporated into Andrew Nicholson's edition of Byron's complete miscellaneous prose. For this reason, Beckford's marginalia has never been included in any close reading of Byron's satire. I argue that Byron used Beckford's marginalized reading of Southey as the basis for his own. My focus on Beckford's marginalia to Southey's poem promises to provide new insight into an unpublished aspect of this widely publicized contest between Byron and Southey. Having written his own "Vision" of the afterlife, in 1777, Beckford read Southey's with a trained eye. As he had done with *Vathek*, Byron benefited from Beckford's witticisms that exposed the blindness of Southey's vision.

The Morgan copy once belonged to Byron, Heather Jackson writes. "It contains a transcription, in ink, not necessarily made in Byron's lifetime, of Beckford's satirical but defensive annotations" (Jackson 43). We should be sceptical about whether Byron saw this transcription in his "lifetime", Jackson argues. Perhaps. But why would a poet order a transcription he never intended to read? Why is the manuscript bound with Byron's crest mark on the spine? What if Byron waited to receive Beckford's copy to finish his own verse satire on Southey (cf. Jackson 41)? In fact, that appears to be exactly what happened. Byron wrote the first 38 stanzas very quickly in May, and then continued the poem, almost without interruption, in September. Why the gap in time? Byron may well have been waiting for Beckford's notes to arrive. "Southey's Vision with this preface did not appear until April 11, 1821. When Byron read it, he made a skillful counter-attack in a long note added to the appendix of his drama of *The Two Foscari*, on which he was working in June and July (2:933)" (Joukovsky 502). Four months went by. "According to his own memorandum on the manuscript, the poem was begun on May 7, 1821, but left off the same day – resumed about the 20th of September of the same year, and concluded as dated – that is, on 4 October" (Joukovsky 502).

The key point here is that Byron put the poem aside. "On 26 August Byron wrote to Shelley from Ravenna telling him that he and the servants were already 'in all the agonies of packing'", Fiona MacCarthy notes. During those weeks he wrote "The Irish Avatar", "Heaven and Earth" and "The Vision of Judgement" (MacCarthy 402). With his books packed, it seems unlikely that his sources were Quevedo Redivivus's "Third Vision" (Spain 1665; London 1815), Fielding's *Journey from this World to the Next*, Pulci's *Morgante Maggiore*, Swift's *Tale of a Tub* and Chaucer's *Wife of Bath's Tale*, as he suggested in his own preface, though he used these precedents to justify a dialogue in heaven where "saints, etc., may be permitted to converse in works not intended to be serious" (Jones 1-2). Jones cites the *Apocolocyntosis, or the Ludus de Morte Claudii Caesaris* ("The Apotheosis of Claudius") as a source. Just as he had concealed sources in the past by drawing attention to other ones, Byron borrowed Beckford's marginalia for his verse satire.

Little is known about the provenance of the copy of Beckford Byron owned, for it is not included in any editions of Byron's "The Vision of Judgement" by Coleridge, McGann, Nicholson, or Cochran. Beckford biographers have not discussed Beckford's marginalia to Southey's poem, nor do his remarks appear in any checklist of Beckford's works. Despite much evidence for someone having transcribed Beckford's commentary for Byron, Heather Jackson leaves it an open question whether Byron read the marginalia by 1822. And yet, the proof of Byron's ownership remains: Byron's signature on the first pages, his crest on the binding, and Morgan's purchase of the volume at a high price. All of these factors suggest an illustrious provenance that gave this book value as a collector's item, as determined by the shrewd acquisitions staff at the Pierpont Morgan library.

Having read Isaac D'Israeli's *Literary Character of Men of Genius* in detail in 1818, Byron read Beckford's commentary for the purpose of penning his own poem. Such a speculation fits Byron's previous writing strategies. Though no plagiarist, as Isaac D'Israeli explained, he composed poems that were a palimpsest of other texts. He did this in *English Bards* (Gross, Watson 131-39), *Childe Harold's Pilgrimage*, and *Don Juan*. He blended epigraphs, wrote footnotes alluding to Beckford's *Vathek* in *The Giaour*, and penned letters suggesting sources not mentioned in *Don Juan*, such as Thomas Hope's *Anastasius*. "Byron's written reaction to *Anastasius* was muted", Peter Cochran writes, "a sure sign, in one so secretive, that he was studying it assiduously" (Cochran 1995, 38). The same strategy applies to Beckford's marginalia to Robert Southey's poem. I consider four factors that show Byron's borrowing from Beckford's marginalia: (1) Beckford's patronizing attitude towards Southey, (2) his light-hearted dismissal of Southey's charge of Satanic poets (in contrast to Byron's enraged reaction in his letters), (3) his satire of George III's diction (4) and his decision to make Junius and Wilkes important figures in his satire.

Beckford's First Marginal Note to Southey's Preface to "A Vision of Judgement": Games of Crambo

In order to consider the influence of Southey on Byron's imagination, it is helpful to discuss Byron's long-running admiration of Beckford as guide and influence. As Heather Jackson wrote of Beckford, "He particularly relished being able to turn a writer's own words against him or her, to expose prudery or affectation" (Jackson 87). In the text, I am considering, Beckford's marginalia is particularly powerful for not being included on the flyleaf, a point I will return to later. For now, it is helpful to note that Beckford's gathering of choice passages highlighted absurdity, making ludicrous applications of serious statements (Jackson 87). For example, Southey writes in his preface to *A Vision of Judgement*, "[n]otwithstanding this explicit declaration the duncery of that day attacked me as if I had considered the measure of *Thalaba* to be in itself essentially and absolutely better than blank verse. The duncery of this day may probably pursue the same course on the present occasion. With that body I wage no war, and enter into no explanations" (Beckford's edition of Southey's *Vision of Judgement* xiv). Beckford pounced on Southey's pompous use of the word "duncery" and his decision to take no prisoners, turning it against him. "Quite the reverse", Beckford notes, "but the Duncery of this day, will approve the Poet Laureates' crambo" (Beckford's note to Southey's *Vision of Judgement* xiv). What does Beckford mean by "crambo"?

One is tempted to assert that "crambo" is a polite version of the Scottish tradition of "flyting", or, as James Montgomery said of *English Bards and Scotch Reviewers*, an English version of a "game-cock spectacle" (Montgomery 2:703-04). According to the *OED*, however, crambo is an English word that dates back to 1711, when Addison wrote of "A Cluster of Men and Women ... diverting themselves at a Game of Crambo" (*OED*). In 1728, Jonathan Swift noted "His Similies in Order set, And ev'ry Crambo he cou'd get", while in 1786, Burns wrote "Amaist as soon as I could spell, I to the crambo-jingle fell" (*OED*). For Burns, poetry is itself a self-enclosed game of crambo, in which one poet tilts swords with other poets. Again in 1786, Burns used the term to describe the "crimbo crambo rime" (*OED*). Theoretically, a strategy of bout-rimes, also invented by Addison, might be described as a non-patriarchal but brotherly version of Harold Bloom's anxiety of influence (Bloom 3). In his own preface to "The Vision of Judgement", Byron sees himself playing a game of crambo with Southey:

> It hath been wisely said, that "One fool makes many;" and it hath been poetically observed, "That fools rush in where angels fear to tread." – *Pope*

> If Mr. Southey had not rushed in where he had no business, and where he never was before, and never will be again, the following poem would not have been written. (Cochran, online version of Lord Byron's *Vision of Judgement* 3)

Byron fully understood how reading and marginalia precipitate a game of crambo, transforming a polite English parlour game into a Scottish battle of wits. He adopts a "flyting" tone, consistent with Renaissance Scottish verse, as T.S. Eliot observed (Eliot 601-19; Speer). Other examples of writing contests abound in the Romantic period, though they were more polite and mutually supportive. James Henry Leigh Hunt initiated sonnet writing contests that produced "To the Nile" and "On the Grasshopper and the Cricket". Another example was Shelley's game of crambo with Horace Smith that produced "Ozymandias" (Holmes 361). Keats was anxious to stay away from such games of crambo, however, recognizing that he needed to preserve his poetic voice: "I refused to visit Shelley, that I might have my own unfettered Scope" (Holmes 361). Further, Byron glosses Beckford's "crambo" by making use of his own deflating rhetoric. Southey has been mocked, Byron explains, so he calls Byron "Satanic" in retribution. "I wish to touch upon the *motive*, which is neither more nor less, than that M^r.S. has been laughed at a little in some recent publications", Byron writes in his preface to the poem, "as he was of yore in the 'Anti-jacobin' by his present patrons. Hence all this 'skimble scamble stuff' about 'Satanic,' and so forth. However, it is worthy of him." (Preface, "Vision of Judgement", Cochran, online version of Lord Byron's *Vision of Judgement* 4). Byron's phrase, "skimble scamble" wonderfully captures the casual, *ad hominem* tone of "The Vision of Judgement", with its mixture of low and high subjects, vernacular, newspaper allusions to Junius and heaven, George III, and the future of England's monarch. – "*Qualis ab incepto*". There is "no hopes for them as laughs". In the same way that the Methodist minister alluded to in Byron's letter to Augusta Leigh does not wish to have smirking ten-year old boys laughing at his sermons, so too Southey does not like being laughed at. Verbal jousting, crambo, is thus a form of half-serious, playful revenge.

Crambo dates back to 1711. The game is a jingle that carries its own song. It requires two players. By the time, Byron wrote *Don Juan*, he was engaging in what Bakhtin would call "heteroglossia" in his study, *The Dialogic Imagination*, or what we might consider as a game of crambo with Southey and Wordsworth (Bakhtin 34; Robinson). For Bakhtin, who rejected the monoglossia of Saussure's closed linguistic system, "the combination of existing statements or speech-genres to construct a text. Each novel [and the same might be said of Byron's poem] is constructed from a diversity of styles and voices, assembled into a structured artistic system which arranges difference in a particular way" (Robinson). As Byron puts it in the last stanza of Canto 1 of *Don Juan*, "The four first rhymes are *Southey's every line*: For God's sake, reader! *take them not* for mine". If crambo is unique to poetry, Beckford implies that Southey has chosen unpoetic words that, however accurate, disrupt the poem, which has aesthetic rules of its own. In fact, these writers alter the definition of poetry itself, as Byron put it in the first Canto of *Don Juan* (*DJ*):

> "Go, little book, from this my solitude!
> I cast thee on the waters – go thy ways!
> And if, as I believe, thy vein be good,
> The world will find thee after many days."
> When Southey's read, and Wordsworth understood,
> I can't help putting in my claim to praise – (*DJ* 5:222)

For Byron, Beckford, and Southey, language is a social world, not a closed system, as Saussure had believed. "In a situation of heteroglossia, the dominant perspective, or one's own perspective, is itself defamiliarized", Andrew Robinson explains. "This happens because it is made visible from the perspectives of others, as well as one's own. It ruptures the mythological relationship to language, showing the gap between words and their meanings" (Robinson). Byron's poem is not a solitary work of poetry, any more than an epic poem is: it is a social text, with social meanings. "Vision of Judgement" then exhibits the appropriate tension between the universal and particular. As Stuart Peterfreund has shown, Byron sought to write himself into history when composing "The Vision of Judgement" (Peterfreund 275). Byron's appropriation of Beckford's marginalia gave him the tools to do so.

Beckford's Marginalia to Southey's Preface

While Southey presents himself as in complete rhetorical control of his poem, Beckford questions that authority. Southey has turned poetry into a poetic discursive field in which readers must guess the next rhyme. Beckford shrewdly objects to Southey's metrical choices. "To write in hexameters (which Southey defends in a long preface) was tantamount to courting abuse", David Radcliffe notes (Radcliffe online). The Poet Laureate's crambo thus refers to the poetic system he has created, the hexameters he uses to express it, and the position of Poet Laureate which predetermines his crambo praise. To read the preface is to confront Southey's parade of erudition, his showy logorrhea. "The English line greatly exceeds the ancient one in literal length, so that it is actually too long for any page, if printed in types of the originary proportion to the size of the book, whatever that may be. The same inconvenience was formerly felt in that fine measure of the Elizabethan age, the seven-footed couplet; which, to the diminution of its powers, was, for that reason, divided into quatrains, (the pause generally falling upon the eight syllable,) and then converted into the common ballad stanza" (Beckford's "Marginalia" to Southey's *Vision of Judgement* 3). So far so good. But what follows mixes formalist analysis with xenophobia, poetics with ethnocentricity. "The hexameter cannot be thus divided, and therefore must generally look neither like prose nor poetry. This is noticed as merely a dissight, and of no moment, our poetry not being like that of the Chinese, addressed to the eye instead of the ear" (Beckford's "Marginalia" to Southey's *Vision of Judgement* xv). The *OED* defines "dissight" as "Something unpleasant to look upon, an unsightly object, an eyesore", in short, the opposite of the picturesque. China and India are proscribed nations whose very language excludes them from poetic games, an attitude discernible in *Curse of Kehema* and *Thalaba the Destroyer*. For Southey, the objection is linguistic: "Our poetry, not being like that of the Chinese". In the poem, as opposed to the preface, Southey compares John Wilkes's forehead to India's (Gárdos 298-307). Unable to confront the plunder of Warren Hastings, and the impeachment trial conducted so successfully by Richard Sheridan and Edmund Burke, both Whigs, Southey blames the radical London mayor John Wilkes for the graft, and India for the crime perpetrated upon it. The England of Southey's *Vision of Judgement* prides itself on not being French, Catholic, or Asian, however much Lords and Ladies might don Turkish hats and Albanian (Colley 25). In constructing an Anglo-Saxon heaven, Southey self-righteously excludes other religions, including Catholicism, Judaism and Islam. Critics such as Balint Gardos have taken a different view. "Room is left for the possibility, in other words, that Southey is more open to non-Western ways of thinking than he is usually given credit for," maybe in this poem "truth is dependent on social circumstances". India appears as a "disturbing and fascinating alterity" (Gárdos 298-307) in *The Curse of Kehama* (1810), but it remains a question, however, whether delight in the wildly exotic really amounts to openness towards "alterity".

At the very least, Beckford's next series of marginalia in the PREFACE to Southey's poem exposes Southey's lack of humour. In his marginalia, Beckford was responding to a specific passage from the prose introduction. He lamented

> Men of diseased hearts and depraved imaginations, who, forming a system of opinions to suit their own unhappy course of conduct, have rebelled against the holiest ordinances of human society, and hating that revealed religion which, with all their efforts and bravadoes, they are unable entirely to disbelieve, labour to make others as miserable as themselves, by infecting them with a moral virus that eats into the soul! The school which they

have set up may properly be called the Satanic school; for though their productions breathe the spirit of Belial in their lascivious parts, and the spirit of Moloch in those loathsome images of atrocities and horrors which they delight to represent, they are more especially characterized by a Satanic spirit of pride and audacious impiety, which still betrays the wretched feeling of hopelessness wherewith it is allied. (Beckford's "Marginalia" to Southey's *Vision of Judgement* xx-xxi)

Southey had objected when Jeffrey lumped himself, Wordsworth, and Coleridge into a "school", though he does the same to Byron, Moore, and Shelley. Southey wrote that there could be no "stronger proof of want of discernment or want of candour than in grouping together three men so different in style as Wordsworth, Coleridge and myself under one head. It is ridiculous enough to be thus coupled with Wordsworth, a man who probably despises my talents as much as the Reviewers despise his" (Speck 94). Beckford pounced on Southey's hypocrisy in redeploying Jeffrey's "Lake poets" designation into an attack on a "Satanic school":

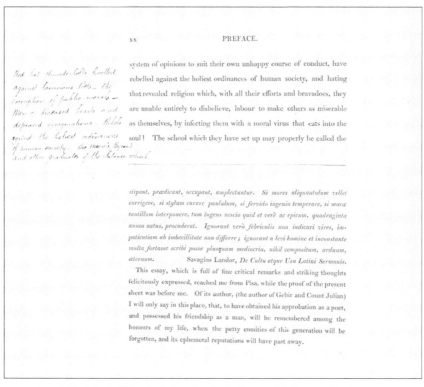

Fig. 1. Beckford's "Marginalia" to Southey's *Vision of Judgement*, Preface, xx.

Xx Red hot thunderbolts levelled
against lascivious Poets – the
corruption of public morals –
Men of diseased hearts and
depraved imaginations – Rebels
against the holiest ordinances
of human society – the Moore's, Byron's
and other graduates of the Satanic school. (Beckford's "Marginalia" to Southey's *Vision of Judgement* xx)

On the very next page he writes

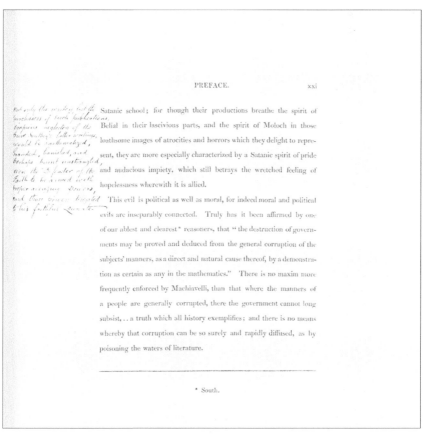

PREFACE.   xxi

Satanic school; for though their productions breathe the spirit of
Belial in their lascivious parts, and the spirit of Moloch in those
loathsome images of atrocities and horrors which they delight to represent, they are more especially characterized by a Satanic spirit of pride
and audacious impiety, which still betrays the wretched feeling of
hopelessness wherewith it is allied.

This evil is political as well as moral, for indeed moral and political
evils are inseparably connected. Truly has it been affirmed by one
of our ablest and clearest* reasoners, that "the destruction of governments may be proved and deduced from the general corruption of the
subjects' manners, as a direct and natural cause thereof, by a demonstration as certain as any in the mathematics." There is no maxim more
frequently enforced by Machiavelli, than that where the manners of
a people are generally corrupted, there the government cannot long
subsist, ... a truth which all history exemplifies; and there is no means
whereby that corruption can be so surely and rapidly diffused, as by
poisoning the waters of literature.

_____

* South.

Fig. 2. Beckford's "Marginalia" to Southey's *Vision of Judgement*, Preface, xxi.

> Not only the writers, but the
> purchasers of such publications,
> impious neglectors of the
> pure Southey's latter writings,
> would be anathematized,
> branded, banished, and
> perhaps burnt unstrangled,
> were the Defender of the
> Faith to be armed with
> proper avenging powers,
> and those powers delegated
> to his faithful Laureate. (Beckford's "Marginalia" to Southey's *Vision of Judgement* xxi)

Southey's target is too broad, Beckford implies, including "not only the writers, but the /
purchasers of such publications". Having purchased Southey's poem, Beckford could
see the irony of Southey attacking his own audience. Southey calls them "impious ne-
glectors of the pure Southey's latter writings", referring to Southey as the "Defender of
the / Faith" who is "armed with / proper avenging powers". Southey appears in Beckford's view as an avenging angel, and Byron focuses on this aspect of his lack of self-
knowledge, his unchristian anathematizing, branding, banishing, and strangling in a version of crambo gone bad. Adopting the same strategy, Byron shows how Southey's hu-
mourlessness exposes him to the whip of satire and becomes its own form of "duncery".

Beckford's Marginalia to Southey's Poem

So far I have limited my commentary to Beckford's marginalia in Southey's PREFACE.
In the poem itself, Beckford pounces on Southey's misguided use of place names. Many
of Southey's place names are from the north of England, and might arguably be said to
give the poem a Gothic quality, as if mixing English locality with a vision of heavenly
transcendence. Here's Southey, mixing realism and romanticism in exceedingly effective ways:

> Under the woods reposed; the hills that, calm and majestic,
> Lifted their heads in the silent sky, from far Glaramara
> Bleacrag, and Maidenmawr, to Grizedal and westermost Withop.
> Dark and distinct they rose. The clouds had gather'd above them
> High in the middle air, huge, purple, pillowy masses,
> While in the west beyond was the last pale tint of the twilight; (Beckford's edition of
> Southey's *Vision of Judgement* 1:8-13)

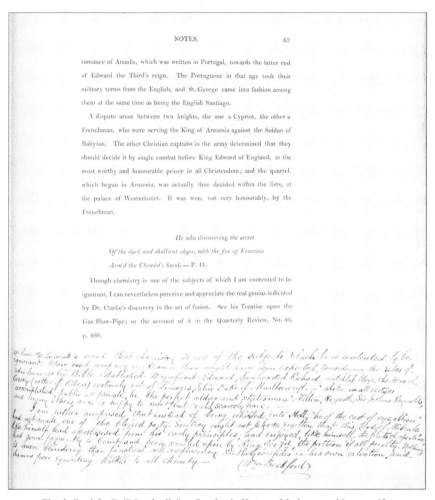

NOTES. 63

romance of Amadis, which was written in Portugal, towards the latter end
of Edward the Third's reign. The Portugueze in that age took their
military terms from the English, and St. George came into fashion among
them at the same time as being the English Santiago.

A dispute arose between two knights, the one a Cypriot, the other a
Frenchman, who were serving the King of Armenia against the Soldan of
Babylon. The other Christian captains in the army determined that they
should decide it by single combat before King Edward of England, as the
most worthy and honourable prince in all Christendom; and the quarrel,
which began in Armenia, was actually thus decided within the lists, at
the palace of Westminster. It was won, not very honourably, by the
Frenchman.

He who discovering the secret

Of the dark and ebullient abyss, with the fire of Vesuvius

Arm'd the Chemist's hand. — P. 41.

Though chemistry is one of the subjects of which I am contented to be
ignorant, I can nevertheless perceive and appreciate the real genius indicated
by Dr. Clarke's discovery in the art of fusion. See his Treatise upon the
Gas Blow-Pipe; or the account of it in the Quarterly Review, No. 46.
p. 466.

Fig. 3. Beckford's "Marginalia" to Southey's *Vision of Judgement*, Notes p. 63.

Beckford's marginal note focuses on the ludicrous nature of the specific, consonant-bedevilled words as universal place-holders for Southey's heavenly vision. In his own vision of 1777, Beckford was careful to speak in general terms of mountains rather than "Glarmar" and "westernmost Withop": "I happened accidentally to open my Casement the Moon shone bright in the clear Sky illuminating the Mountains", Beckford wrote,

I stole away silently from the gay circle of Company and passing swiftly the Garden of Flowers the Orange trees and the Grove betwixt the House and the Rocks set my feet to some steps cut in their solid sides. Luckily I had mounted the hundred steps which lead to the first flat Crag of the Mountain before a dark grey Cloud fleeting from the North veiled the Moon and obscured the light which conducted me. (Beckford's edition of Southey's *Vision of Judgement* l)

Beckford contrasts his own practice with Southey's:

– from the Glaramara,
Bleacrag and Maidenmawr, to Guizedal
and Westermost Withop. (Beckford's "Marginalia" to Southey's *Vision of Judgement* ll. 8-9)

Read on its own terms, Southey might be praised for transforming unpromising, unpoetic place names from northern England into an Ossianic epic vision, replete with majesty and specificity. Ariosto, Milton, and other visionary poets also used the specific cities and towns such as Ferrara, Florence, and Rome to evoke the universal.

That is not how William Beckford views Southey's practice, however. Beckford repeats Southey's language only to mock it. Heather Jackson has argued that someone has written Beckford's marginalia into Byron's copy of Southey's poem (to return our attention to the Morgan copy of Southey's poem). Her objection is that flyleaf entries were turned into marginalia, thereby changing their character. "The second unusual feature of this copy", she writes, "is that the transcription is not in fact an exact facsimile, for the notes have been copied onto the relevant pages of the text rather than being kept to the flyleaves. In a few cases, when Beckford's note is a direct critical remark, this procedure may work; but when – as is more often the case – his note is simply an echo of the text, it doesn't. 'Firm in his Father's steps hath the Regent trod, was the answer' does not provide much illumination for 'Right in his Father's steps hath the Regent trod, was the answer: / Firm hath he prov'd and wise' in the text. These are properly 'index' notes. They don't belong in the margins" (Jackson 41).

I would argue otherwise. It is precisely because Beckford's marginalia appears in the margins that we can appreciate his wit. To begin with Beckford's note is never "simply an echo of the text". Beckford corrects Southey's diction, substituting "right" for "firm". Jackson misquotes Beckford's marginalia, missing the subtlety of Beckford's critique. He has changed Southey's language suggesting that one should, properly speaking, be "Firm in his father's steps" not "right" in them. Beckford plays schoolmaster. I have consulted the original copy at the Pierpont Morgan library to make this determination, supported by photographs of the manuscript.

> Thou, said the Monarch, here? Thou, Perceval, summon'd before me? …
> Then as his waken'd mind to the weal of his country reverted,
> What of his son, he ask'd, what course by the Prince had been follow'd
> Right in his Father's steps has the Regent trod, was the answer:
> Firm hath he proved and wise, at a time when weakness or error
> Would have sunk us in shame, … (Beckford's "Marginalia" to Southey's *Vision of Judgement* ll. 114-20)

Beckford replaces "Firm" for "Right". Southey's diction is so imprecise that the words can be exchanged with little loss of meaning, Beckford implies. Coleridge reviewed Southey's "Joan of Arc" in similar terms, lamenting Southey's poor choice of words.

Byron learned from Beckford's notes to pay attention to detail, for verbal lapses reveal Southey's poor writing skills.

Another occasion occurs later in the poem, where Beckford also questions Southey's choice of words.

> Suc'bus & Incubus ugly such names suit
> Better than mountains in my poor Opinion.
> (W.B.) (Beckford's "Marginalia" to Southey's *Vision of Judgement* 2, commentary on l. 10 of Southey's poem)

Taking the tone of a schoolmaster, Beckford condescends to Southey by emphasizing not his politics but his poetic diction. After this he faults George III's repetitive speech:

> The Ghost of Geo. 3rd asking the
> Ghost of Perceval – What –
> What of his son –
> (Beckford's "Marginalia" to Southey's *Vision of Judgement* 9)

Byron picks up on Southey's exposure of George III's stammer: "No", quoth the Cherub, "George the third is dead", Byron wrote (stanza 18, ll. 137-38):

> "And who is George the third?" replied the Apostle. *"What George? What third?"* (Byron, *Vision of Judgement* ll. 139-40 in *Complete Poetical Works [CPW]*)

emphasizing the British king's lack of importance, while mocking George III's verbal tics.

Mistaking Southey for the previous Laureate, the much-ridiculed H. J. Pye, he exclaims, with the repetitiousness that was habitual with him in life,

> What! What!
> Pye come again? No more – no more of that". (Byron, *Vision of Judgement* in *CPW* l. 736)

Both Southey and George III suffer from provinciality, suggesting that Heaven is pre-occupied with England when they could care less: "What George? What third?" Though he craves sycophancy, George III is bored by such sycophants and cannot distinguish Pye from Southey: "Pye come again? No more – no more of that".

My penultimate example of Beckford's marginalia in Southey's *A Vision of Judgement* concerns the adamantine gates. Beckford finds Southey's use of the word "Ho!" so amusing that he repeats it ("Ho!" and "A grand angelic Ho", l. 22 and 32 of Southey's poem), reminding us, as Freud noted of Heinrich Heine and others, that jokes flourish when the same words appear in a new context (Freud 40).

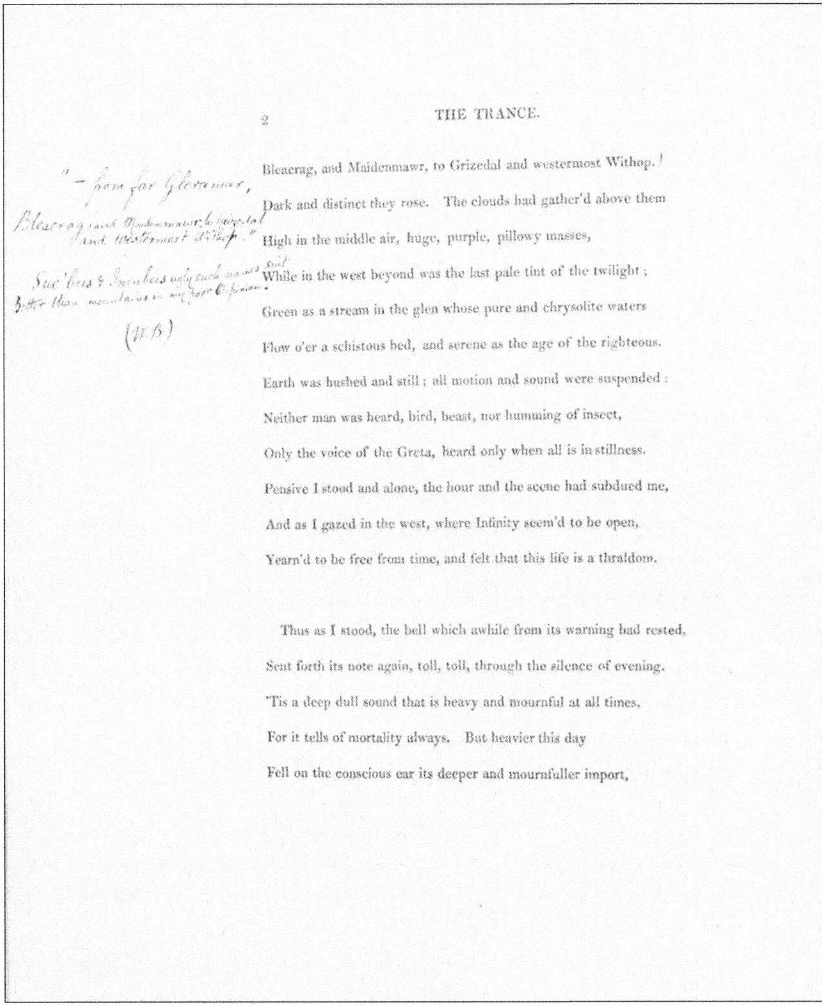

2 THE TRANCE.

"— from far Glenmar, Bleacrag, and Maidenmawr, to Grizedal and Westermost Withop."

Suc'bus & Incubus only such names suit better than mountains in my poor Opinion.

(W.B)

Bleacrag, and Maidenmawr, to Grizedal and westermost Withop.)
Dark and distinct they rose. The clouds had gather'd above them
High in the middle air, huge, purple, pillowy masses,
While in the west beyond was the last pale tint of the twilight;
Green as a stream in the glen whose pure and chrysolite waters
Flow o'er a schistous bed, and serene as the age of the righteous.
Earth was hushed and still; all motion and sound were suspended:
Neither man was heard, bird, beast, nor humming of insect,
Only the voice of the Greta, heard only when all is in stillness.
Pensive I stood and alone, the hour and the scene had subdued me,
And as I gazed in the west, where Infinity seem'd to be open,
Yearn'd to be free from time, and felt that this life is a thraldom.

Thus as I stood, the bell which awhile from its warning had rested,
Sent forth its note again, toll, toll, through the silence of evening.
'Tis a deep dull sound that is heavy and mournful at all times,
For it tells of mortality always. But heavier this day
Fell on the conscious ear its deeper and mournfuller import,

Fig. 4. Beckford's "Marginalia" to Southey's *Vision of Judgement*, Poem, p. 2, ln. 9.

By repeating Southey's words in the margin, Beckford damns with faint praise, turning Southey's "Ho!" into a Beckfordian laugh at Southey's diction, rather than a solemn greeting between angels, as it purports to be in Southey's poem. The two quotations below, from different parts of the same section, emphasize the repetition of the word "Ho!":

> O'er the adamantine gates an Angel stood on the summit.
> Ho! He exclaim'd, King George of England cometh to judgement!
> Hear heaven! ... (Southey, *Vision of Judgement* 4:21; 217-19)

Later in the poem George III stands in judgement:

> Ho! He exclaim'd, King George of England standeth in judgement!
> Hell hath been dumb in his presence. Ye who on earth arraign'd him,
> Come ye before him now, and here accuse or absolve him!
> For injustice hath here no place. (Southey, *Vision of Judgement* 6:359-62)

Why did Beckford laugh at Southey's "grand angelic Ho!"? The *OED* defines "ho" as: "A call to stop or to cease what one is doing. *to say* or *cry ho*: to stay, cease, check oneself. *Obsolete.*" "Ho" is not quite "ha-ha", in other words. Rather, "Ho" marks someone as present. Though Southey opts for the elevated term, Beckford detects another possibility: "A cry of sailors in heaving the anchor up, etc.; also used as the burden of a song. †*with heave and how (ho), figurative* with force, with might and main (*obsolete*)" (*OED*). Far from a greeting, "ho" becomes a form of dispatch. After all, a "heave-ho" action is what gets George III, though not Southey, into heaven. Beckford redeploys "Ho", having a laugh at Southey's expense.

An "angelic Ho!" mixes insubstantial with substantial things in an absurd, self-satisfied manner. In doing so, Beckford shows not only Southey's illiberality but his provincialism. Beckford tacitly suggests that the word "Ho!" might not be quite appropriate for the Heavenly vocabulary he wishes to emulate. By turns undignified and provincial, Southey's language implies that English is the default language of Heaven. The angels, as we will soon see, do not even know who George III is. "What George, what third?" they cry in Byron's poem, imitating his stammer. By not commenting, by merely repeating Southey's absurd use of the word "Ho!", Beckford damns with a marginal silence. He calls attention to Southey's absurdity, even as Southey wishes to focus the reader's attention on a sublime moment. More formal in his own satire of George III, Byron used the word "ho" nineteen times in his poetry, but never in *The Vision of Judgement*. Perhaps he was following Beckford's proscription against the word.

In moving from the "Gate of Heaven" to the Accusers, we learn a different lesson about humour. Beckford mocks Southey's serious tone, showing that to expose someone as without humour is itself humorous. Southey's punishment of squinting Wilkes and vizored Junius is so over the top that the poem effectively hoists Southey on his own petard. Southey cruelly mocks Junius' deformity, and Junius' (Sir Philip Francis') necessary self-concealments. Why is Junius iron-vizored, for example, the poem encourages us to ask? Beckford comments as follows in his marginalia:

> A guilty Pair – squinting Wilkes
> And iron vizored Junius, swing
> Into blackest-Hell for slandering their
> Holy immaculate Sovereign. Sons of
> Faction be warned, and ye, ye slanderers,
> Learn ye justice. (Beckford's "Marginalia" to Southey's *Vision of Judgement* ll. 334-40)

William Beckford writes this in response to a particularly virulent description of John Wilkes who shares with Southey a change of principle and attitude towards George III (Cash 234-35). Like Robert Southey, Benjamin Franklin disliked John Wilkes (Cash 143, 221) and worried about the London crowd over whom he presided as mayor (Goodwin 188, 234; Van Doren 381, 438, 464). Wilkes knew how to play politics for a laugh, an especially effective strategy among humourless leftists.

> Caitiffs, are ye dumb? Cried the multifaced Demon in anger;
> Think ye then by shame to shorten the term of your penance?
> Back to your penal dens! ... And with horrible grasp gigantic
> Seizing the guilty pair, he swung them aloft, and in vengeance
> Hurl'd them all abroad, far into the sulphurous darkness.
> Sons of Faction, be warn'd! And ye, ye Slanderers! Learn ye
> Justice, and bear in mind that after death there is judgement.
> Whirling, away they flew. (Southey, *Vision of Judgement* 5:334-41)

Byron and Beckford found something highly objectionable in Southey's pompous use of heavenly language to level accusations against sinners, a kind of intolerant judgement and vision that was at the very heart of the misprision of English morality. Southey had suddenly become the arbiter of England's heaven, dispensing judgement like Job's accusers, unsympathetic by virtue of his mean-spirited style. Though Dante had levelled the same power in the *Divine Comedy*, Southey's stature as Poet Laureate was more compromised, precisely because, as Wordsworth suggested on June 24, 1817, he had become a "tool of power" in such documents as his "Letter to William Smith, Esq. MP" (Wordsworth; qtd. in Joukovsky 499). Beckford showed, and perhaps suggested to Byron, that Southey's brand of Christian morality was parochial, condescending towards the very countries, cultures and religions (India, Spain) that he treated with bluff self-confidence (Joukovsky 499). *Thalaba the Destroyer* (1801), *Madoc* (1805), and *Curse of Kehama* (1810) were rife with ethnocentric judgements that inspired Byron's wrath.

Beckford brought Byron's attention to Southey's treatment of Wilkes, which is even stranger than Byron suggested. Why did Southey depict Wilkes's face as Indian for example? When Beckford portrayed a green-faced Giaour in *Vathek*, he did so, in part, to satirize England's claims to India. Southey, by contrast, underscored British superiority, a humourless posture that particularly irked Byron and Beckford, who had been treated as social pariahs for their transgressive sexuality at home. One of the few "slanderers" to escape judgement is George Washington, who exhibits an appropriately humble attitude that earns George III's admiration (Southey, *Vision of Judgement* 6:70). Where Junius is compared to Hindu gods, Washington is compared to "Fabius, Aristides, and Solon, and Epaminondas", the latter of whom was a Theban general and statesmen who led Greece out of Spartan subjugation (Southey, *Vision of Judgement* 6:23). The other figures Southey allows into heaven are Thomas Chatterton, and the American painter Washington Allston, a strange compilation of individuals who bear the Christian mark of "meekness" so flagrantly violated by prideful poets like the sceptic Byron and the self-proclaimed atheist, Shelley. Progressive on such issues as the rights of North

America's indigenous people, the slave trade, and the French Revolution, Southey became increasingly intolerant as the paid defender of Tory values and Poet Laureate. Byron repeatedly questioned Southey's sincerity, portraying him as a pen for hire in both *The Vision of Judgement* and *Don Juan*.

Southey's idiosyncratic preference for Thomas Chatterton, as a fellow poet from Bristol, exposes his whimsical view of heaven, over which he is the arbitrary judge. So too Washington Allston, whose famous portrait of Coleridge and biblical scenes such as "Elijah in the Desert", endeared him to Southey. Allston befriended and was admired by Henry Wadsworth Longfellow, Samuel Coleridge, Sophia Peabody (Hawthorne's wife), and many others. Southey's inclusion of Allston and Washington in heaven suggests that his view of the United States and of revolution itself was more nuanced than Byron allowed. Both Byron and Southey admired Washington's restraint and heroism, and Southey even has George III reach across the political aisle, or Atlantic in this case, and greet him in heaven, a radical move that Byron's more polarized Whig/Tory poem did not allow. Southey's "A Vision of Judgement" was more compassionate and enlightened in this sense, a truly heavenly vision, whereas Byron's was more decidedly terrestrial. Was Byron's a failure of imagination, a failure of nerve or, finally, a failure of belief?

I conclude with a discussion of Beckford's final manuscript note to Southey's *A Vision of Judgement*. No longer content to employ *sprezzatura*, Beckford assaults Southey's ignorance in a final note that anticipates Byron's Preface to his own *The Vision of Judgement*.

> We have the Laureate's word that chemistry is one of the subjects of which he is contented to be ignorant. More good company in Heaven than might have been expected, considering the rules of admission as by Bible established. Magnificent Edward, Lionhearted Richard, matchless Eliza, the Hero of Cressy (rather of Poitiers), certainly not of Limoges. John Duke of Marlborough – "alike in all virtues accomplished, public or private, he the perfect soldier and statesman." Milton, Hogarth, Sir Joshua Reynolds, and many others one is happy to meet, but could scarcely have. –
> I am rather surprised that instead of being whirled into Hell, "he of the cast-of-eye oblique" had not made one of the blessed party. Southey ought not to have forgotten that this Lord of Misrule, like himself, had apostasized from his early principles; had enjoyed, like himself, the fruits of repentance, had gone frequently to Court, and been smiled upon by King Geo 3rd, the pattern of all purity. Nothing is more blinding than fanatical self-complacency. Southey confides in his own salvation, and damns poor squinting Wilkes to all eternity. – (Wm Beckford) (Beckford's "Marginalia" to Southey's *Vision of Judgement* 63)

Beckford dutifully notes all the figures that Southey left out of Heaven: Milton, Hogarth, Reynolds. William Wordsworth added William Pitt and Samuel Johnson (Joukovsky 496). "In enumerating the glorified spirits of the reign of George 3d admitted along with their earthly sovereign into the New Jerusalem", Wordsworth wrote to Henry Crabb Robinson on 23 January 1821, "neither Dr Johnson nor Mr Pitt are to be found. Woe to the Laureate for this treasonable judgement!" (qtd. in Joukovsky 500).

Wordsworth disliked Southey enough to accuse him of a "treasonable judgement" because Southey omitted Johnson and Pitt from his poem. Beckford went one step further, suggesting that there was something irreligious about Southey's charge of treason. As Beckford put it, "Southey ought not to have forgotten that this Lord of Misrule, like himself, had apostasized from his early principles" (Beckford's "Marginalia" to Southey's *Vision of Judgement* 20). Like Byron, Wordsworth defines Southey's vision solely in terrestrial terms: treason is an act committed against Tories, which suggests a failure of imagination on both Byron and Wordsworth's part. Southey was writing a very different poem and could not be taxed for not writing the one Byron and Wordsworth would have written themselves.

If satire is parasitic, feeding off a host text, one wonders whether Byron's poem can truly be said to stand as a satire in its own right, a literary masterpiece. One also wonders whether Byron's poem was not parasitic in a different sense, using Beckford's marginalia for his own attack on Southey, harvesting Beckford's best lines on "apostasy". Perhaps. If Whig journalists charged Tory political opponents with apostasy, Byron deserves credit for weaving the conceit into an effective charge dating back to "Lines to a Lady Weeping", when he faulted the Prince Regent for such conduct in 1812. And before Byron there was Junius who memorably used the word "apostasy" in his 13th letter, "Philo Junius to the Printer of the Public Advertiser" (49-56), referring to his opponent as "an apostate by design" (Junius 51). "He became minister by accident; but deserting the principles and professions which gave him a moment's popularity, we see him, from every honourable engagement to the public, an apostate by design." Beckford used apostasy as a verb. Nevertheless, neither Beckford nor Byron's name appear in the *OED* entry under "apostate" or "apostasized" (*OED*), though Disraeli's *Vivian Grey* (1827) does. Disraeli knew Byron's work through his father Isaac D'Israeli's friendship with John Murray, Byron's publisher. To the Disraelis, Byron was a family friend, even a marginal commentator on Byron's "English Bards and Scotch Reviewers" (Watson 131-39). In *Vivian Grey*, Disraeli wrote that "[n]o one is petted so much as a political apostate, except, perhaps a religious one" (*Vivian Grey* 237), a Byronic sentiment worthy of Byron's *Cain* or his satiric references to religion in *Childe Harold's Pilgrimage* Canto 1. Byron's attack on Southey blends the two meanings of apostasy, religious and political, by setting his poem in heaven, or just outside it.

Beckford puns on blindness – moral and physical, suggesting that "squinting Wilkes" has more vision than the Southey who suffers from a "fanatical self-complacency: that blinds him". Byron blends history and myth, inserting himself into an argument about heaven with historical characters. Charging Wilkes with being a "lord of misrule", Beckford notes, Southey does not see the mote beaming in his own eye (Beckford's "Marginalia" to Southey's *Vision of Judgement* 62-63). In his own "Vision" of 1777, Beckford was careful to avoid the pride such complacency encourages, indicating his own terror of falling into damnation: "Surely my time is not yet come surely I am reserved to fall from the precipices of the Andes or the more probable precipices of Ambition exclaimed my Vanity when I attained a Summit from whence I looked down on the dreadful rock

I had surmounted." Beckford's "Vision", in short, contrasts with Byron's and Southey's in being the most modest of the three (Beckford's edition of Southey's *Vision of Judgement* 3). Beckford's sympathy, needless to say, is with the damned,

> haggard wretches abandoned by the mercy of Heaven a miserable few shrinking from Mankind and burying themselves in this gloom to work mischief and pour destruction on those who ages past may have offended them. – Revenge the baneful passion, is their Soul and for which they blot their names from the Book of Life and sacrifice an Eternity of Happiness. Hark! Was not that their yell amongst the mountain Peaks on high. (Beckford's edition of Southey's *Vision of Judgement* 3)

Having written his own vision in 1777, Beckford was particularly interested in Southey's lapse of taste in using place names and such colloquial words as "Ho!" instead of "Hark!" when writing about the afterlife. Beckford attacks Southey for his pride, especially for assuming he can damn others to eternity. Byron takes an identical position in a letter to John Murray, carefully distinguishing between Southey's views, which he is entitled to change, and Southey's unfortunate proclivity for damning others for changing theirs (*BLJ* 9:43). Though they disagreed publicly on other matters, Wordsworth shared Byron's concern that Southey could be charged with being a paid sycophant of George III. In his private correspondence and in an article he never published on the dispute between Byron and Southey, Wordsworth worried about "the force of a charge which his enemies will bring against the author of being too obsequious to the throne the aristocracy [sic], and to persons in office, or in plain terms, a tool of power" (Wordsworth; qtd. in Joukovsky 499). Wordsworth's egotism made it difficult for him to love anyone, including Hazlitt, Coleridge, and Southey himself, writing a tepid epitaph on the occasion of Robert Southey's death that enraged Caroline Bowles (Speck 143). Probing deeper than Wordsworth, Hazlitt thought Southey a disappointed idealist whose self-love was his defining sin, not an unusual trait for writers and Romantic poets generally, and one from which Byron was not immune, despite Byron critics who crow that their poet won the exchange: "not truth but self-opinion is the ruling principle of Mr. Southey's mind", Hazlitt wisely noted. "The charm of novelty, the applause of the multitude, the sanction of power, the venerableness of antiquity: pique, resentment, the spirit of contradiction, have a good deal to do with his preferences" (Hazlitt 241-51). Hazlitt's neologism, "self-opinion", wonderfully captures Southey's character, as does Hazlitt's charge of "pique, resentment, the spirit of contradiction". Of course, James Henry Leigh Hunt charged Lord Byron with "the spirit of contradiction" in his biography of the poet (Hunt 155), and was caricatured by Dickens as a sponging ingrate, Mr. Skimpole, for doing so (*Bleak House* 185). Yet even John Stuart Mill observed that Southey "seems to me to be a man of gentle feelings and bitter opinions" (*Letters* 1:212). Southey's tendency to damn others reflects a mirror on his own character, and supports what his contemporaries wrote about him.

Byron often threw his readers off the true inspiration for his works. For example, he sought a copy of Coleridge's unpublished "Kubla Khan", Beckford's additional *Vathek* tales, and Thomas Hope's *Anastasia* for *Don Juan* (Jones 1-19). Previous critics have noted how neither Geoffrey Chaucer, Quevedo Redivivus, nor Jonathan Swift are precise guides to Byron's satire; not even Seneca's *Ludus* and Chaucer's *Julius Exclusus* are perfect fits. While these models are important guides to Byron's strategy, as is the Italian art form developed by Ariosto, they bury the sly, concealed Beckfordian notes to Southey. My essay has argued that Beckford's notes also influenced the satirical strategy and tone of Byron's poem, and did so, not as endnotes or on a flyleaf, as Heather Jackson contends, but in the margins through a direct encounter with Southey's poetic voice. During an eight-month period, from his home in Venice at the Palazzo Mocenigo, Byron met Thomas Moore, read Moore's *Fudge Family* and Beckford's marginalia on Southey's poem, and made those poetic strategies his own, creating a highly original strand of satire, that was, like all great poetry, highly derivative – rendered mythological, because transmogrified by Byron's pen (Peterfreund 275).

Works Cited

Bakhtin, Mikhail. *The Dialogic Imagination: Four Essays*. Austin: University of Texas Press, 1982.

Beckford, William. *Vathek and Other Stories: A William Beckford Reader*. Ed. with an introduction by Malcolm Jack. New York: Penguin, 1993.

---. "Marginalia" to *Robert Southey's A Vision of Judgement*. Pierpont Morgan Library. London: Longman, Hurst, Rees, Orme, and Brown, 1821.

Bjelajac, David. *Washington Allston: Secret Societies and the Alchemy of Anglo-American Painting.* Cambridge: Cambridge UP, 1997.

Bloom, Harold. *The Anxiety of Influence: A Theory of Poetry*. New York and Oxford: Oxford UP, 1973

Byron, Lord [George Gordon]. *The Complete Poetical Works.* Ed. Jerome J. McGann and Barry Weller. 7 vols. Oxford: Clarendon Press, 1980-92.

---. *The Works of Lord Byron*. Ed. Rowland E. Prothero. London: John Murray, 1904.

Byron's Letters and Journals. Ed. Leslie A. Marchand. 12 vols. Cambridge, MA: Harvard UP, 1973-82.

Cash, Arthur H. *John Wilkes: the Scandalous Father of Civil Liberty*. New Haven, London: Yale UP, 2006.

Cochran, Peter. "Byron, Don Juan, and Russia". *A People Passing Rude: British Responses to Russian Culture.* Ed. Anthony Cross. London: Open Book Publishers, 2012. 37-52.

---. "The Vision of Blasphemous Judgment". *The Keats-Shelley Review* 9 (1995): 37-50.

---, ed. Online version of Lord Byron's *Vision of Judgement.* n.d. https://petercochran.files.wordpress.com/2009/03/the_vision_of_judgement3.pdf (accessed 12 June 2021).

de Montluzin, E. L. "Southey's 'Satanic School' Remarks: An Old Change for a New Offender". *Keats-Shelley Journal* 21.2 (1972-73): 29-33.

Dickens, Charles. *Bleak House*. Ed. George Ford and Sylvère Monod. London: W. W. Norton, 1977.

Eliot, T. S. "Byron". *From Anne to Victoria: Essays by Various Hands*. Ed. Bonamy Dobrée. London: Cassell & Company Ltd., 1937. 601-19.

Freud, Sigmund. *The Joke and Its Relation to the Unconscious*. London: Penguin, 2003.

Gárdos, Balint. "Marginalia and Marginal Figures in the Romantic Age". *The Ana-ChronisT* 17 (2012): 298-307. *Gale Literature Resource Center*. link.gale.com/apps/doc/A514177301/LitRC?u=depaul&sid=bookmark-LitRC&xid=d715c858 (accessed 12 June 2021).

Gerdts, William H. *A Man of Genius: The Art of Washington Allston, 1779-1843*. Boston: Museum of Fine Arts, 1979.

Goodwin, George. *Benjamin Franklin in London: The British Life of America's Founding Father*. London: Weidenfeld & Nicolson, 2016.

Gross, Jonathan. "Byron's Marginalia in Isaac Disraeli's *Literary Character of Men of Genius*". *Byron and Marginality*. Ed. Norbert Lennartz. Edinburgh: Edinburgh UP, 2019. 116-40.

Hazlitt, William. "Robert Southey". *The Spirit of the Age*. Ed. Ernest Rhys. London: J. M. Dent & Sons; New York: E. P. Dutton & Co., 1934. 241-51.

Holmes, Richard. *Shelley: The Pursuit*. New York: New York Review of Books Classics, 2013.

Hunt, James Henry Leigh. *Lord Byron and Some of His Contemporaries*. London: Henry Colburn, 1828.

Jackson, Heather. *Marginalia: Readers Writing in Books*. New Haven: Yale UP, 2002.

Jones, Emrys. "Byron's Visions of Judgement". *The Modern Language Review* 76.1 (1981): 1-19.

Joukovsky, Nicholas. "Wordsworth's Lost Article on Byron and Southey". *The Review of English Studies* 45 (1994): 496-516.

Jump, J.D. "Byron's Vision of Judgment". *Bulletin of the John Rylands Library* 51 (1968): 122-36.

Junius. *Stat Nominis Umbra: A New Edition*. London: Vernor, Hood and Sharpe, 1810.

MacCarthy, Fiona. *Byron: Life and Legend*. New York: Farrar, Straus and Giroux, 2002.

Mill, John Stuart. *The Earlier Letters of John Stuart Mill, 1812-1848*. 2 vols. London: Routledge & Kegan Paul, 1963.

Montgomery, James. "Review of English Bards and Scotch Reviewers". *Eclectic Review* (May 1809). *The Romantics Reviewed: Contemporary Reviews of British Romantic Writers, Part B: Byron and Regency Society Poets*. Ed. Donald H. Reiman. 5 vols. New York: Garland, 1972. 2:703-04.

Nicholson, Andrew, ed. *Lord Byron: The Complete Miscellaneous Prose*. Oxford: Clarendon Press, 1991.

Peterfreund, Stuart. "The Politics of 'Neutral Space in Byron's Vision of Judgement". *Modern Language Quarterly* 40.3 (1979): 275-91.

Radcliffe, David. "The Vision of Judgment. By Quevedo Redivivus. Suggested by the Composition so entitled by the Author of 'Wat Tyler.'" n.d. http://spenserians.cath. vt.edu/TextRecord.php?&action=GET&textsid=36351 (accessed 12 June 2021).

Robinson, Andrew. "In Theory Bakhtin: Dialogism, Polyphony and Heteroglossia." *CeaseFire* (July 29, 2011): n.p. https://ceasefiremagazine.co.uk/in-theory-bakhtin-1/.

Rutherford, Andrew, ed. *Byron: The Critical Heritage*. London: Routledge, 2000.

Seymour, Miranda. *In Byron's Wake: The Turbulent Lives of Lord Byron's Wife and Daughter, Annabella Milbanke and Ada Lovelace*. London: Pegasus Books, 2018.

Speck, W.A. *Robert Southey: Entire Man of Letters*. New Haven: Yale UP, 2006.

Speer, Roderick S. "Byron and the Scottish Literary Tradition". *Studies in Scottish Literature* 14.1 (1979). https://scholarcommons.sc.edu/ssl/vol14/iss1/16.

Storey, Mark. *Robert Southey: A Life*. Oxford: Oxford UP, 1997.

Van Doren, Carl. *Benjamin Franklin*. New York: Viking, 1938.

Watson, Alex. *Romantic Marginality: Nation and Empire on the Borders of the Page*. London: Pickering & Chatto, 2012.

Denise Gigante

Transgressing the Sacred Frontier of Culture

> The science of taste and of cultural consumption begins with a transgression
> that is in no way aesthetic: it has to abolish the sacred frontier
> which makes legitimate culture a separate universe.
> Pierre Bourdieu, *Distinction: A Social Critique of the Judgement of Taste*

This chapter will consider how the concept of taste, both as an aesthetic philosophy and a cultural practice, transgressed (and still transgresses) the very distinctions it makes possible.[1] In *Distinction: A Social Critique of the Judgement of Taste* (Bourdieu 7, quoted in epigraph), Pierre Bourdieu suggests that to approach taste through the lens of social science, the researcher becomes a transgressor: in order to see how consumerism works either to confer social distinction or else to negate it by revealing unconscious socioeconomic biases, he must first demystify the idea of culture, reducing it from an abstract ideology into a set of socially embedded choices and practices. Yet, as this chapter aims to show, the sociologist waving the flag of ideological transgression arrives late at a frontier that has already been crossed. The modern practice of taste was always a bourgeois phenomenon linking the ideology of aesthetic disinterestedness, or the appreciation and judgement of beauty with an objective, detached attitude, to the competitive and self-interested motivations of consumerism.

While today we tend to think of museums as the sacred spaces of "legitimate culture", it is worth remembering that private, individual collectors preceded institutional curators as custodians and shapers of culture. Many of those same collectors preceded the sociologist in self-consciously transgressing the sacred frontier of culture, not in the name of analytical science however, but on the vanguard of a more expansive aesthetic praxis. This chapter will explore those private spaces, curatorial in nature, in which individualized – and intentionally transgressive – tastes were defined and celebrated. Given that the phenomenon of the private library was at the centre of the collecting impulse that began to define cultural connoisseurship in eighteenth century, the three sections of this chapter shall focus on diverse genres of collecting as showcased in private libraries – ornamental, gastronomical, and bibliomaniacal – described in literary essays. For from Joseph Addison to the French founder of modern gastronomy (Alexandre Balthazar Laurent Grimod de la Reynière) to the bibliophile Charles Lamb, literary essayists were taste-makers. What we shall find in this essayistic prehistory of Bourdieuvian taste is that all genuinely taste-making activity was and is by nature transgressive.

---

1   I here revisit and revise material previously considered in "Transgressions in Taste". This
    version is printed with permission of The Licensor through PLSclear.

An Ornamental Library

In the English literary tradition, Joseph Addison was among the first of those who attempted to instruct a general reading audience in the principles of middle-class taste. His *Spectator* essays appeared at a time when the category of fine art was expanding from the five traditional genres of painting, sculpture, music, architecture, and poetry to include new aesthetic domains compatible with consumerism. One of these was the phenomenon of literary prose (fine writing, or *belles lettres*), which Addison's *Spectator* essays modelled. Another was the social phenomenon of the tea table, a domestic equivalent of the coffeehouse for mixed company involving ornamental and conversational arts. In the tenth number of *The Spectator*, Addison advised his readers, for their own improvement, "to order this Paper to be punctually served up, and to be looked upon as a Part of the Tea Equipage" (*Spectator* 10, 1:45). Porcelain and silver *objets d'art* formed part of that equipage, as did the imported luxury of tea, which like coffee (and to a lesser degree, hot chocolate) was associated with the European coffeehouse culture of Enlightened discourse – itself an expansion of the rarefied domain of culture per se.

Writing on Thursday, April 12, 1711, Addison recounts a visit Mr. Spectator has paid to the library of a lady, whom he names Leonora. Leonora's finely bound books are mixed up on her shelves with decorative objects such as Oriental tea dishes, porcelain vases, and a silver snuff box in the shape of a book. The books are in a "beautiful Order", but that order is ornamental insofar as it is external to the ideational content of the books (*Spectator* 37, 1:153). Rather than digesting her books into divisions of abstract knowledge, for example, or arranging them alphabetically by author, she has grouped them according to physical size: folios, quartos, octavos, duodecimos, and (in a decorative framework to contain them) pamphlets and unbound papers. One might posit that the lady's marginalized status as a female reader provides the opportunity for her transgressive approach to literary tradition, and to culture more generally. For by treating her books as decorative objects, Leonora has scrambled the traditional categories of the fine arts constituting high culture:

> At the End of the *Folio's* (which were finely bound and gilt) were great Jars of *China* placed one above another in a very noble piece of Architecture. The *Quarto's* were separated from the *Octavo's* by a pile of smaller Vessels, which rose in a delightful Pyramid. The *Octavo's* were bounded by Tea Dishes of all Shapes, Colours and Sizes, which were so disposed on a wooden Frame, that they looked like one continued Pillar indented with the finest Strokes of Sculpture, and stained with the greatest Variety of Dyes. (*Spectator* 37, 1:153)

Poetry here sits next to the plastic arts, which in turn form architectural pyramids and pillars. Leonora has arranged her books according to their material characteristics as ornamental objects.

Just as she jumbles the categories of art on her shelves, moreover, she confounds literary genres. The Spectator is amused to find French romances, for example, brushing shoulders with prayer books. What he discovers in Leonora's library is not only a collection of objects formed without regard to the traditional hierarchy of the arts, but evidence of the more everyday arts (including tea-drinking, letter-writing, and face-patching) associated with a culture of taste in which connoisseurship is complicit with commodity culture. Rather than critical annotations or manuscript commentary, for example, the Spectator discovers in the Lady's copy of John Locke's *Essay Concerning Human Understanding* an array of black silk patches. Patches were used cosmetically, either to hide blemishes or else to stand out on their own as beauty spots. Leonora has adapted them as bookmarks, or perhaps pointers to literary "beauties": linguistic felicities or ornamental features of belletristic texts that the connoisseur could identify – and the more subtle the beauty, the finer the taste of the reader sensitized to it. The culture of taste gave rise to the phenomenon of polite reading, an aesthetic practice suited to mixed company, and as the patches in her copy of Locke's philosophical treatise suggest, Leonora's library bears marks of gendered reading.

At first glance, it might seem that the Spectator is mocking the frivolity of the female reader as incapable of serious cogitation. Yet, unlike the solitary meditations of the philosopher, the practice of taste, Addison insisted, took place in polite society where the genders mingled. "I shall be ambitious to have it said of me", Addison's Spectator announced in *Spectator* 10, "that I have brought Philosophy out of Closets and Libraries, Schools and Colleges, to dwell in Clubs and Assemblies, at Tea-tables, and in Coffee houses" (*Spectator* 10, 1:44). The silk patches that pepper Leonora's copy of Locke's philosophical treatise can be seen, from this perspective, as mocking the narrowness of philosophical pedantry, a form of rational discourse that set itself apart from polite conversability. For Addison, the purpose of polite literature was to *gently* stimulate the intellectual faculties. In *Spectator* 411, he explains that the pleasures of the imagination derived from polite literature "do not require such a Bent of Thought as is necessary to our more serious employments, nor, at the same time, suffer the Mind to sink into that Negligence and Remissness, which are apt to accompany our more sensual Delights, but, like a gentle Exercise to the Faculties, awaken them from Sloth and Idleness, without putting them upon any Labour or Difficulty" (*Spectator* 411, 3:539). Pedantry, by contrast, was any species of technical or specialized talk involving the sweaty fatigues of mental labour and ill-suited to a lay audience that included women.

Flipping through Leonora's copy of *Artamène, ou le Grand Cyrus*, a ten-volume French romance published in the mid-seventeenth century, the Spectator discovers a hairpin stuck in one of the pages. Like the patches in her copy of Locke's *Essay Concerning Human Understanding*, this pin is a mark of gendered reading as well as a placeholder. It suggests that in addition to arranging her books on her shelves for visual gratification, the lady has been reading them and paying careful attention to their contents, seemingly with the purpose of revisiting them. If tasteful reading, according to Addison, was less intellectually demanding than learned inquiry, it was likewise intellectually superior to reading for sensational gratification. The pleasures of the imagination derived from polite literature encompassed *both* the intellectual pleasures of understanding and the corporal pleasures of visceral aesthetic delight. Locke's *Essay* represents one extreme of the category of polite literature (on the side of heavier mental satisfaction), while the French novel *Artamène* represents the other (on the lighter side of entertainment). Leonora's library positions her as a reader somewhere in the middle, navigating between the two extremes in a sea of belletristic reading. Rather than a caricature of bad taste, she represents a challenge to heteronormative standards of taste.

The Spectator goes on to observe that Leonora's books are bound in expensive leather with gilt-edged leaves, and that her collection includes other *objets d'art* fashioned from expensive materials such as lacquered wood and porcelain. Like the gilt edges of her books, the highly polished superficies of these objects in her library emphasize the role of surface beauty as ornamentation. The ornamental aesthetic departs from classical ideals of beauty as inherent in form. Kant describes this ideal in his 1790 *Critique of Judgement* when he states that anything superadded to, or intended merely as an embellishment of, beauty disrupts the perception of teleological, self-fulfilling form necessary to a judgement of the beautiful. "[I]f the ornament itself does not itself consist in beautiful form", he writes, "but is merely attached, as a gold frame is to a painting ... then it impairs genuine beauty" (Kant 72). Like his other examples of ornament in the fine arts, a frame that seems a natural extension of the picture it contains *can* contribute to aesthetic pleasure, but only to the degree that the ornament submits itself to formal purposiveness, thereby diminishing its own status as an ornament:

> what we call *ornaments* (*parerga*), i.e. what does not belong to the whole presentation of the object as an intrinsic constituent, but [is] only an extrinsic addition, does indeed increase our taste's liking, and yet it too does so only by its form, as in the case of picture frames, or drapery on statues, or colonnades around magnificent buildings. (Kant 72)

Such ornaments can be seen as excessive effervescences of the pure line of beauty theorized as immanent form.

Indeed, in the Romantic period the ornamental stood in relation to the beautiful as a form of excess. "It is not to be supposed that any one, who holds that sublime notion of Poetry which I have attempted to convey", Wordsworth wrote in his "Preface to *Lyrical Ballads*", "will break in upon the sanctity and truth of his pictures by transitory and accidental ornaments" (Wordsworth 141-42). Such ornamentation, having little to do with the formal immanence of beauty, characterized the eighteenth-century culture of *belles lettres*. The belletristic mode of literary criticism consisted of identifying beauties and blemishes, in an effort to perceive ever finer distinctions that might be missed by a less sharpened sensibility, which served to multiply the pleasures of the imagination. Belletristic literary reviews took the form of a string of extracted beauties punctuated with commentary. Selections of belletristic texts were frequently published under the title of Beauties. The man of taste collected beauties, copying passages from his reading into his commonplace books and placing bound Beauties on his shelves. The concept of the beautiful as an assemblage of empirical beauties was, in short, the basis of the belletristic aesthetic.

Beauties were likewise part of the ornamentality characterizing the literary periodical essay in English, although ornamentality *to excess* detracted from beauty, slipping into the category of the Gothic or grotesque. Odd conceits, such as Addison found in Metaphysical Poetry, and shaped poems (in the form of an egg or wings, for instance), were considered species of false wit (see *Spectator* 58-63, 1:244-74). True wit lay in the kind of rhetorical beauties that Addison identified in his series of *Spectator* papers on *Paradise Lost*.[2] Yet the materialized form of ornamentality the Spectator finds in Leonora's library, like "concrete" poems shaped like objects, veered out of good taste into the grotesque. "That Part of the Library which was designed for the Reception of Plays and Pamphlets, and other loose Papers", the Spectator claims, "was enclosed in a kind of Square, consisting of one of the prettiest Grotesque Works that ever I saw, and made up of Scaramouches, Lions, Monkies, Mandarines, Trees, Shells, and a thousand other odd Figures in *China* Ware" (*Spectator* 37, 1:153). The Mandarins decorating the container for Leonora's unbound papers are clearly Chinese, but whether the monkeys are Indian, African, Asian, or East Asian matters little: national differences collapse into the more general category of the Oriental associated with the aesthetics of ornamentality. Revising Edward Said's category of "Orientalism" by shifting the frame of reference from race to rank, David Cannadine proffers the term "Ornamentalism" as a descriptor for British imperialism.[3]

The Lady's Library in *Spectator* 37 appears to the Spectator as excessively ornamental, conveying Oriental notions of beauty into the neoclassical culture of taste. The Mandarins look out over a decorative "Japan table", which supports more ornamental items that threaten to swallow up (or snuff out, in the case of the silver book-shaped snuff box) the ideal of the literary in a grotesquerie of consumer culture (*Spectator* 37, 1:153). The very co-presence of Oriental monkeys and Mandarins on an ornamental paper tray is itself an uncomfortable juxtaposition, suggesting an outside to tasteful society that has infiltrated its centre through the global flow of commodities. Literature, rather than serving as an idealized, privileged sphere of culture, appears to be mixed up with consumerism as everyday taste practice. Addison's Spectator looks askance at the lady's ornamental, Orientalized taste at the same time as he is strangely drawn to it, his tone of bemused condescension stopping short of outright critique.

What distinguishes the grotesque is above all its *mixed* nature (comic and tragic, animal and human, Oriental and Occidental), and the Spectator concludes his visit to Leonora's library with this observation: "I was wonderfully pleased with such a mixt kind of Furniture, as seemed very suitable both to the Lady and the Scholar, and did not know at first whether I should fancy my self in a *Grotto*, or in a Library" (*Spectator* 37, 1:153-54). Etymologically, the term grotesque is derived from "grotto", and this obser-

---

2   Addison's twelve weekly *Spectator* papers devoted to the specific beauties of *Paradise Lost* are numbered 303, 309, 315, 321, 327, 333, 339, 345, 351, 357, 363, and 369.

3   See Said, Cannadine, and more recently, Cheng, who has revisited Cannadine's topic along the lines of gender.

vation by the Spectator leads, by way of association, to another visit he pays to the lady, this time in a grotto at her country home. Grottoes were standard features of landscape aesthetics, and although Addison does not explicitly mention Leonardo Da Vinci's *Lady of the Rocks*, when his Spectator visits Leonora in her country home, he describes her as if she were such a lady: "The Rocks about her are shaped into Artificial Grottoes covered with Wood-Bines and Jessamines" (*Spectator* 37, 1:158). He does name the lady Leonora, and Leonardo's painting of the Madonna enclosed in a grotto made an impression when he visited the Palace at Versailles on his European Grand Tour (where the painting then hung), the picture gallery being the part of the Palace that he enjoyed most (cf. Addison, *Guardian* 101, 14:237).

We might say that the Spectator's lady in her grotto, first in the form of an ornamental library and then amidst landscaped ornamentation, represents both legitimate culture *and* the dangers of aesthetic extravagance. By virtue of being a lady, she was after all excluded from the hegemonic subjectivity of the Enlightenment Man of Taste, and his axiomatic standards of beauty: an exclusion that granted her a certain transgressive freedom to expose the artificiality of those standards. By reining in his own imaginative pleasures to criticize the lady's transgressions, Addison seems to find himself confined within the prison of Spectatorial taste. For while from the Spectator's viewpoint the lady's ornamental aesthetics exceed the bounds of good taste, the authorial perspective seems to recognize (and thus force us to consider) the relativity of any universal standard that would determine those bounds. When Addison claims that the Spectator was "wonderfully pleased" with the ornamental wonders of the Lady's Library, we might believe him (*Spectator* 37, 1:153). Then again, we might recognize his irony as a defence against the recognition that her transgressions in taste are invitations to his own. As Leonora's library lays bare, the British culture of taste was predicated upon global, commercial exchange with cultures whose aesthetic standards differed from, transgressed, and challenged its own.

A Gastronomical Library

By the end of the eighteenth century, and particularly with the invention of the restaurant as an institution of public discretionary dining following the French Revolution, the category of culture had expanded to encompass such formerly paradoxical taste practices as food and wine connoisseurship.[4] Gastronomy emerged as a genre of critical discourse suited to culinary artistry, allowing formerly unthinkable transgressions between taste and its poor cousin, appetite.[5] The engraved frontispiece to the opening volume of the *Almanach des gourmands* by the French gastronome Alexandre Balthazar Laurent Grimod de la Reynière depicts *The Library of a Nineteenth-Century Gourmand*.

---

4   On the invention of the restaurant, see Spang.
5   For a fuller explication, see my introduction to *Gusto*.

Fig. 5. *The Library of a Nineteenth-Century Gourmand* (*Bibliothèque d'un Gourmand du XIXᵉ Siècle*), frontispiece to vol. 1 of Alexandre Balthazar Laurent Grimod de la Reynière, *Almanach des gourmands*.

The shelves of this library contain not the disembodied voice of literature speaking from the sacred sphere of culture, but objects to be consumed literally: not books to be read, that is, but food to be eaten.

After a century of disinterested aesthetic taste discourse, Romantic gastronomes flaunted, rather than denied, bodily appetite. From their perspective, disinterestedness was a veneer of detachment out of sync with the "gusto" of the more robust man of taste. In his 1816 *Round-Table* essay on gusto, William Hazlitt had recourse to the continental term for taste (*gusto, goût*) to describe a more full-bodied form of taste experience, one that was compatible with passion (Hazlitt 332-33). The library of a nineteenth-century gourmand in the opening number of Grimod's *Almanach des gourmands* (1803), much like the lady's library in *Spectator* 37, challenges the disinterested attitude of aesthetic taste experience – and in so doing, the gap between culture and consumerism.

Etymologically, the eater and the thinker came together in the figure of the gastronome, who was defined by his stomach (from Greek, *gaster*) as much as his mind (from Greek, *nomos*). In his description of the frontispiece depicting the gastronome's library, Grimod catalogues the various taste-objects visible on the shelves: "a suckling pig, various sorts of pâtés, enormous saveloys, and other such delicacies, along with a good number of bottles of wine and liquor, jars of fruit, either crystallized or preserved in brandy, and so forth".[6] Unlike the porcelain jars in Leonora's library in *Spectator* 37, these jars are ter-racotta, which is to say functional rather than ornamental. The chief sensory mechanism of gastronomy is chemical rather than optical, working through gustatory and olfactory rather than visual sensation. Thus, the less distracting the objects containing the food and drink on display, the better. For a similar reason, Grimod explains, a dumbwaiter rather than a flesh-and-blood waiter stands next to the table in the gourmand's library, ensuring that "no servants shall disturb this solitary diner" (Grimod qtd. in Gigante, *Gusto* 283).

In pioneering new codes of etiquette, Grimod departed from the standard practice of service *à la française* (in which a number of dishes were arranged at one time on the table over a series of several relieves) in favour of dinner *à la russe* (in which the meal was served one dish at a time, as has become standard practice in restaurants and fine dining today). In his explanation of the frontispiece, Grimod explains that the sideboard in the background of the main dining table in the gourmand's library holds the next in-stallment of the meal in reserve. The art of fine dining sought to give each culinary taste-object the kind of mental space that art objects today are given in museums, where cu-rators are careful not to crowd the walls with too many paintings and to encourage ex-periencing them singularly in succession.

Fig. 6. *Les méditations d'un Gourmand*, frontispiece to vol. 4 of
Alexandre Balthazar Laurent Grimod de la Reynière, *Almanach des gourmands*.

---

6   As translated from Grimod de la Reynière by Michael Garval in Gigante, *Gusto* 283.

The frontispiece to the fourth volume of the *Almanach des gourmands* featured the gourmand in his study. Here, the bookshelf behind him has transformed into a multi-levelled sideboard. Grimod captures him at a moment when he has paused in his writing to contemplate the stuffed calf's head on the pedestal table before him: "The calf's head seems to preoccupy his own", Grimod writes cheekily in his description of the image. He again catalogues the various dishes that have been sent to the gourmand from the leading restaurateurs in Paris: a truffled red partridge, a wild boar's head, a sponge cake, a truffled turkey, a mortadella, a Bayonne ham, a capon seasoned with coarse salt, an Italian cheese and sausages, a foie gras pâté, some Abbeville biscuits from Mademoiselle Rose des Gardens, etc. These culinary artists counted on the gastronome to pronounce judgement, which would be printed in the *Almanach*, where the first form of the restaurant review appeared.

The few books scattered around the gourmand's study are classics of culinary literature: *The Learned Cook, Healthful Pastry-Making, The Modern Confectioner*, and *Comus's Gifts*. The last mentioned (*Les dons de Comus*), named after the Greek god of feasting, was the bible of the *nouvelle cuisine*, a culinary revolution that began in the 1740s as an effort to produce more delicate fare than the heavy, meat-laden meals to which medieval and early-modern diners had been accustomed. The pesudonymous Launcelot Sturgeon, who was Grimod's greatest English imitator in the literary genre of gastronomy, had "The Meditations of a Gourmand" copied by William Hughes, an English engraver, as the frontispiece for his *Essays, Moral, Philosophical and Stomachical, on the Important Science of Good-Living*. Sturgeon took the logic suggested in Grimod's depiction of the gastronome's study to its logical conclusion:

> We cannot help thinking, that it would be productive of the most important results to society, if children, instead of reading Ovid's *Metamorphoses*, were instructed in those of Mrs. Glasse, and then proceeded through a regular course of culinary classics, including the whole range of English literature from *Murrel's Kickshawes* and *May's Accomplishede Cooke*, down to *Simpson's Bills of Fare*, until they reached the French *Cours Gastronomique*, and were able to enjoy the *Almanach des Gourmands*, as a book of amusement as well as study. (Sturgeon 177-78)

In the end, such a library defined by one consuming passion might not be so far from the Romantic literary sensibility after all.

The gastronome, as a transgressive Man of Taste, was a type of Romantic explorer. The reader of *Frankenstein* will recall that the polar explorer Robert Walton read nothing but travel adventures during his formative years, leading him into unexplored terrain, just as his alter ego Victor Frankenstein read wildly in alchemical literature, setting him on a scientific quest to discover the secret of life. Examples abound in Romantic literature of characters who, reading unsystematically and to excess, guided by a reigning passion, transgress the frontier from known fields of knowledge into the unknown. So too, the English gastronome William Kitchiner – culinary chemist, master chef, and gastronomical writer – explicitly compared the figure of the gastronome to that of the explorer in his *Apicius Redevivus; or the Cook's Oracle* (1817), a best-selling cookbook.

"I have not presumed to insert a single composition without previously obtaining the *'imprimatur'* of an enlightened and indefatigable *COMMITTEE OF TASTE*", he wrote, borrowing Grimod de la Reynière's device of the Tasting Jury (a variant of the literary periodical club), which granted *légitimations* to the dishes it approved, and added that the gourmands of his committee

> were so truly philosophically and disinterestedly regardless of the wear and tear of teeth and stomach, that their Labour – appeared a Pleasure to them. – Their laudable perseverance ... has hardly been exceeded by those determined spirits who lately in the Polar expedition braved the other extreme of temperature, &c. in spite of Whales, Bears, Icebergs, and Starvation. (Kitchiner 4)

Kitchiner, like other gastronomers, revised the concept of aesthetic disinterestedness to suit the gastronomical mission: the art of culinary judgement here involves not only disembodied (mental) taste, but the grinding, swallowing, and assimilation of food – all features of the digestive labour that exceeded the bounds of traditional taste experience and that Kitchiner would address in another gastronomical work, *Peptic Precepts: Pointing out Agreeable and Effectual Methods to Prevent and Relieve Indigestion, and to Regulate and Invigorate the Action of the Stomach and Bowels* (1821).

Gastronomy was a new and blatantly transgressive stage in the history of taste, and the literature of gastronomy offered a new canon or measure of connoisseurship in a culture of consumption. Gastronomical writers of the nineteenth century used the language and conventions of taste philosophy to stage a resistance to the opposition between the intellectual and the material that traditionally characterized aesthetic experience, just as bibliomaniacs, who fetishized the book as a physical taste-object, would do. The dandyism of men and women of such self-consciously transgressive tastes characterized European Romanticism, which was not only the Age of Gastronomy but also, let us now consider, the Age of Bibliomania.

A Bibliomaniacal Library

The bibliomaniac was a close cousin to the gastronome as a man of transgressively material tastes. The equivalent to Grimod de la Reynière in the field of bibliomania was the Reverend Thomas Frognall Dibdin, author of *The Bibliomania; or, Book-Madness* (1809). Dibdin, who was affiliated with the leading book collectors of his day, popularized the mania for old and rare books through his bibliographical writings. His best-known work, *The Bibliomania*, took the form of an epistle to the English bibliomaniac Richard Heber, a wealthy book connoisseur who was known for filling not merely one, but *eight* houses with books ([Livermore] 195). "Heber the Magnificent", as Sir Walter Scott dubbed him, filled his shelves with more volumes than many major university libraries in Europe, including those in Bologna, Prague, Vienna, Leipzig, Copenhagen, Turin, Dublin, and Edinburgh (Scott qtd. in Lockhart 2:280; [Livermore] 195). Regardless of the wear and tear of stagecoach travel, he was known to traverse four or five hundred miles in pursuit of a single volume; likewise, in one fell swoop on a book-buying expedition to Paris, he purchased a library of thirty thousand books, a larger collection than any major American university library, except for Harvard, had amassed by mid-century (Edwards 1859, 2:137). "Probably no private person ever organized so extensive an intercourse with booksellers and auctioneers, both at home and abroad", book historian Edward Edwards observed, "and his interest in the pursuit was as keen as ever during the latest days of his life" (Edwards 1859, 2:137).

Richard Heber's bibliomania was a form of excessive literary consumerism tied to anti-quarianism, and the obsessive nature of the antiquarian's collecting habits. His was bibliomania of the grand style, just as Grimod de la Reynière's extravagant, five-hour dinners were a gastronomical legacy of the *ancien régime*. Heber modelled a passion for books, much as Grimod modelled a gourmet attitude, from the top down, opening the sacred sphere of art to consumerism as a mode of cultural self-fashioning. It is against this background that I would like to consider the library of the Romantic essayist Charles Lamb as a still more radically transgressive venture in taste. Singed with smoke, soaked with gin, sprinkled with crumbs, stripped of engravings, detached from their covers, bescribbled, Lamb's books constituted a famously motley collection. They self-consciously defied all expectations of the Gentleman's Library, defined as a collection of finely bound works of "standard literature" (the nineteenth-century phrase for canonical European literature) arranged in a tasteful private space.

Like the antiquarian books that fed the bibliomania, circulating through auctions and old book dealers, Lamb's idea of a book resisted the generic nature of the commodity. Likewise it resisted the consumerist notion that taste could be purchased. The catalogue of what Lamb called *biblia a-biblia* ("books which are no books") included not only fancy notebooks, encyclopedias, and almanacs, but works of "standard" literature – moral philosophy, economic and population essays, dry-as-dust histories, or as Lamb put it in the voice of Elia, "all those volumes which 'no gentleman's library should be without'" (Lamb, "Detached Thoughts on Books and Reading", in Lamb 1903, 2:172). To some, it might seem that the principle guiding the formation of his library was downright perversity. His friend Henry Crabb Robinson remarked that the books from his library were such that "a delicate man would really hesitate touching" (Crabb Robinson 77, 10 January 1824). An American admirer, Evert Augustus Duyckinck, after having seen sixty volumes from Lamb's library for sale in a book store in New York, observed: "The appearance of them was shocking – positively so bad that a *genius* for getting together the worst possible bound bad copies was involved in the collection" (Duyckinck, unpublished letter). Yet, those same dilapidated volumes from Lamb's bookshelves were covered with marginalia and other markings by Lamb and his literary friends (chiefly among them, Samuel Taylor Coleridge) that made them unique, restoring the printed, reproducible book to its status as originary art. The manuscript markings connected the material substance of the book to its immaterial literary content, which in Lamb's case largely resisted the standards of popular, middle-class taste.

Rather than a collection made mainly for display, the books of Lamb's library were read and reread – to the exhaustion of the book and its binding often more than its reader. By the light of day, Lamb himself was embarrassed by them. "We have got our books into our new house", he wrote to his friend Thomas Hood after moving from Islington to Enfield in 1827: "I am a dray horse if I was not ashamed of the indigested dirty lumber, as I toppled 'em out of the cart" (Lamb 1935, 3:131, 18 September 1827). Yet Lamb loved these books with a passion that veered into the romantic; his essayistic persona Elia refers to his folios as his "midnight darlings" in Lamb's essay "New Year's Eve" (Lamb 1903, 2:30). The books he collected, read, marked, arranged, lent, reclaimed, and (if we are to believe James Henry Leigh Hunt) kissed, stood out against the bourgeois idea of "the literary" as an idealized category of legitimate culture that could be commodified, marketed, and subjected to universal standards of taste.[7] Lamb's books had precisely that kind of character that diminished them in a bookseller's eyes but that raised their value immeasurably in the economy of sentimental book-collecting that Lamb himself practised. His interests differed from Dibdin's focus on typeface, paper, publisher, issue, edition, and other bibliographical elements of the old books.

Just as the books in Leonora's library in *Spectator* 37 contained silk patches and hairpins as marks of gendered reading, Lamb's books contained (equally telling) residues of the bibliomaniacal reader. They spoke of the everyday doings of a literary essayist and man of letters, having "their constitution hardened by the fumigation of tobacco" and their "dry worm-eaten leaves moistened with ale as a libation" ([Duyckinck], 1). In a letter to Coleridge that accompanied a box of books he lent his friend, Lamb remarked:

> If you find the Miltons in certain parts dirtied and soiled with a crumb of right Gloucester blacked in the candle (my usual supper), or peradventure a stray ash of tobacco wafted into the crevices, look to that passage more especially: depend upon it, it contains good matter. (Lamb 1935, 1:328, 4 November 1802)

The crumbs of Gloucester cheese, like the tobacco from Lamb's pipe, were place-markers derived from accidental, everyday living, now permanently integrated with the text. More importantly, as Lamb insists, they were marks of taste, indicating Miltonic beauties through the lens of his own literary-critical judgement.

In addition to crumbs and stains, Lamb and Coleridge both left much spilt ink in the margins of Lamb's books in the form of autograph writing. Coleridge occasionally added postscripts to his notes, and successive postscripts to his postscripts. In Lamb's copy of Sir Thomas Browne's *Pseudodoxia Epidemica*, he even left a key to his marginalia:

•	a profound or at least solid and judicious observation
=	*majesty* of conception or style
//	sublimity
X	brilliance or ingenuity
Q	characteristic quaintness
F	an *error* in fact or philosophy (Coleridge)

---

7   James Henry Leigh Hunt remarks "how natural it was in C. L. to give a kiss to an old folio, as I once saw him do to Chapman's Homer" (Hunt 49).

Contrasting the homogeneity of commodity culture, which would privilege an untouched, pristine copy of the book, Lamb's copy of *Pseudodoxia Epidemica* speaks to the singularity of lived literary experience. As a literary historical object, a book like this is generative of narrative, and the older the book, or the more signs of life it contains, the greater the potential for the stories it can tell beyond the substance of its own textual content. But only a sentimental collector – or transgressive man of taste – can rate such books at their true value.

By dribbling cheese along with commentary into his books, a bibliophile like Lamb turns a commodity back into an object that is precious to the degree that it defies the kind of market value associated with an untouched book. The dilapidated volumes from his bookshelves, in blatant transgression of all rules of gentlemanly, middle-class taste, have since become enshrined in various Temples of Culture, from the British Museum to the Beinecke Rare Book and Manuscript Library at Yale University, to the rare-book reading rooms of the Henry W. and Albert A. Berg Collection of English and American Literature in the New York Public Library. They have become, in a word, transgressive insiders, redefining the category of literary taste from their (relatively) untouchable position in book museums: special collections and rare book rooms of circulating and research libraries guided by protocol intended to preserve the book in the form it took when it entered the library.

Lamb's copy of *[John] Cleaveland Revived* in the Berg Collection, to take one example, has a cracked back, loose covers, flaking leather, missing leaves, and torn pages. But that did not stop William Thomas Hildrup Howe, former Yale professor and President of the American Book Company, from proudly pasting his bookplate inside the front cover.

Fig. 7. Inside cover of Charles Lamb's copy of *J. Cleaveland Revived: Poems, Orations, Epistles, and Other of his Genuine Incomparable Pieces* (1668).

Another of Lamb's copies of Cleaveland's poetry found its way to the Fifth Avenue mansion of Gilded-Era millionaire Ogden Goelet in New York City before entering the New York Public. Goelet had his equally threadbare copy of Lamb's Cleaveland rebound. That copy, titled *Poems by John Cleaveland*, now has gilded leather covers with floral borders. Its formerly broken spine has raised ornamental bands, gilt panels, and lettering that proclaims not only the title and date of the book, but the fact that it was "CHARLES / LAMB'S / COPY". Lamb, the former owner, takes precedence over the author as the name that gives the book its value.

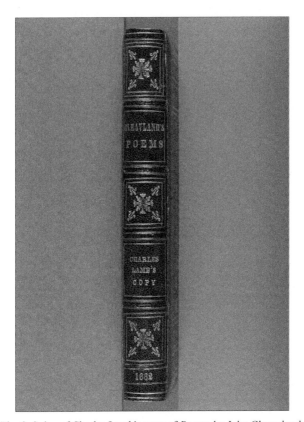

Fig. 8. Spine of Charles Lamb's copy of *Poems by John Cleaveland;*
with additions never before Printed (London: printed for W. Shears, 1662).

Yet, what are we to make of the fact that both books from Lamb's shabby library now have institutional resources devoted to their safety, preservation, and the maintenance of the hallowed atmosphere surrounding them? Of the two, Howe's copy of *J. Cleaveland Revived* from Lamb's library, still in its overworn habiliments, forms the greater contrast with the tasteful conditions of the space surrounding it in this inner sanctum of culture. It sits like a museum piece on its foam cradle, to be handled only under supervision and according to house rules. One might say, with Bourdieu, that such a book has crossed the "sacred frontier" from the everyday world of commerce into culture. Or perhaps, we might consider this beggarly insider a testament to the fact that such a frontier never really existed.

Works Cited

Addison, Joseph et al. *The Spectator*. Ed. Donald F. Bond. 5 vols. Oxford: Clarendon Press, 1965.

---. *The Guardian* 101. July 7, 1713. *The British Essayists*. Ed. James Ferguson, vols. 13-16. London: J. Richardson, 1832.

Bourdieu, Pierre. *Distinction: A Social Critique of the Judgement of Taste*. Trans. Richard Nice. Cambridge, MA: Harvard UP, 1984.

Cannadine, David. *Ornamentalism: How the British Saw Their Empire*. Oxford: Oxford UP, 2001.

Cheng, Anne Anlin. *Ornamentalism*. Oxford: Oxford UP, 2019.

Coleridge, Samuel Taylor. Manuscript note dated 10 March 1804, on front flyleaf of Thomas Brown, *Pseudodoxia Epidemica: or Enquiries into Very Many Received Tenets, and Commonly Presumed Truths*, 3rd ed. London: Nathaniel Ekins, 1658. Henry W. and Albert A. Berg Collection of English and American Literature, New York Public Library.

Crabb Robinson, Henry. *The Diary of Henry Crabb Robinson: An Abridgement*. Ed. Derek Hudson. London: Oxford UP, 1967.

Duyckinck, Evert Augustus. Unpublished letter to George Long Duyckinck, 9 February 1848. Duyckinck Family Papers, The New York Public Library.

[---.] "Charles Lamb's Books at Auction". *The Literary World: A Journal of American and Foreign Literature, Science, and Art*, 3:40, November 4, 1848.

Edwards, Edward. *Libraries and Founders of Libraries*. London: Trübner and Co., 1864.

---. *Memoirs of Libraries; Including a Handbook of Library Economy*. 2 vols. London: Trübner & Co., 1859.

Gigante, Denise. "Transgressions in Taste: Libraries Ornamental, Gastronomical, and Bibliomaniacal". *The Persistence of Taste: Art, Museums and Everyday Life Since Bourdieu*. Ed. Dave Beech, Michael Lehnert, Malcolm Quinn, Carol Tulloch, and Stephen Wilson. London: Routledge, 2018. 35-48.

---, ed. *Gusto: Essential Writings in Nineteenth-Century Gastronomy*. New York: Routledge, 2005.

---. *Taste: A Literary History*. New Haven: Yale UP, 2005.

Grimod de la Reynière, Alexandre Balthazar Laurent. *Almanach des gourmands*. 8 vols. Paris: Maradan, 1803-12.

Hazlitt, William. *The Round Table*, 40. *The Examiner*, 439, 26 May 1816. 332-33.

Hunt, James Henry Leigh. *Essays*. London: Edward Moxon, 1841.

Jones, Erasmus. *The Man of Manners; or Plebeian Polished*, reprint of 3rd London edition, 1737. Sandy Hook CT: Hendrickson Group, 1993.

Kant, Immanuel. *Critique of Judgement*. Trans. Werner Pluhar. Indianapolis: Hackett, 1987.

Kitchiner, William. *The Cook's Oracle; Containing Receipts for Plain Cookery, on the Most Economical Plan for Private Families*. London: Robert Cadell, 1831.

Lamb, Charles and Mary Lamb. *The Letters of Charles Lamb to which are added those of his sister Mary Lamb*. Ed. E. V. Lucas. 3 vols. New Haven: Yale UP, 1935.

---. *The Works of Charles and Mary Lamb*. Ed. E. V. Lucas. 7 vols. London: Methuen, 1903.

[Livermore, George]. "Public Libraries". *North American Review* 71 (1850): 185-221.

Lockhart, John Gibson. *Memoirs of the Life of Sir Walter Scott, Bart*. 10 vols. Edinburgh: Adam and Charles Black, 1862.

Robinson, Henry Crabb. *The Diary of Henry Crabb Robinson: An Abridgement*. Ed. Derek Hudson. London: Oxford UP, 1967

Said, Edward. *Orientalism*. London: Penguin, 1977.

Spang, Rebecca L. *The Invention of the Restaurant: Paris and Modern Gastronomic Culture*. Cambridge, MA: Harvard UP, 2000.

Stolnitz, Jerome. "The Aesthetic Attitude in the Rise of Modern Aesthetics". *Journal of Aesthetics and Art Criticism* 36 (1977-78): 409-22.

---. "On the Origins of Aesthetic Disinterestedness". *Journal of Aesthetics and Art Criticism* 10 (1961-62): 131-42.

---."Beauty: Some Stages in the History of an Idea". *Journal of the History of Ideas* 22 (1961): 185-204.

Sturgeon, Launcelot [pseud.]. *Essays, Moral, Philosophical, and Stomachical, on the Important Science of Good-Living*. 2nd ed. London: G. & W. Whittaker, 1823.

Wordsworth, William. *Prose Works*. Ed. J. B. Owen and Jane Worthington Smyser, vol. 1. Oxford: Clarendon Press, 1974.

Richard C. Sha

Can Transgression Be Meaningful Even After It Is Required or Expected?

When transgression becomes required or expected, can it remain an effective or meaningful tool against the norm? This question becomes more urgent given that Literary Studies has valued violations of the law or of the norm or of boundaries to the point of their banality. One way it has done so, as Peter Starr has so carefully demonstrated in his *Logics of Failed Revolt*, is to make literary language itself the site in which transgression is most fully realized, so much so that politics becomes by comparison bankrupt (Starr 158-63). In this view, for Barthes, Lacan, and Kristeva, after the failed revolutions of 1968, only a poetic language of deferral can compete with and counter a modern politics of narcissism, as deferral functions to sap egoism of its powers. But this is to essentialize literary language as transgressive, a move that ultimately risks liquidating much if not all of its transgressive force, for who is comforted when literary language becomes the prime venue for transgression? With regard to the Romantic period, otherwise known as the Age of Revolution, the idea of transgression has had such significant force in shaping the criticism, that it risks triviality.[1] To wit, the German *die Transgression* refers to the erosion of land by the sea, and frames transgression as a quotidian natural process (Clason 3). That the violation of nature has so easily become nature should give us pause.

To help us think about how required or expected transgression can remain meaningful, and what such an answer would entail, I turn to the Kuhnian paradigm for scientific revolutions, Queer Theory, and finally Byron's *Don Juan*. Kuhn offers a curious choice of opening, but I submit that by tracking how his concept of scientific revolution paradoxically actively discourages transgressions yet makes the agent of change the anomaly, we learn something about how change is theorized and made visible. I then turn to the ways in which Queer Theory operationalizes yet contains transgression. Finally, I examine transgression in terms of form, in Byron's case, *ottava rima*, and how the form leverages the emotion of surprise for transgressive effects. The fact that Byron's verse functions continually to generate surprise against systems and the heroic self even within a poetic system suggests that surprise may be the embodied form par excellence of transgression. Hence it is high time to think more about how it works.

---

1   A May 1, 2020 *JSTOR* advanced search with the keywords "Romanticism" and "Transgression" turns up over 4,000 entries. A 2018 study edited by Clason on Romantic transgression, for example, looks at the works of E.T.A. Hoffmann, and how they defy categorization. Heartfelt thanks to Norbert Lennartz, for inviting me to Vechta to give this talk, and for his gracious and warm hospitality.

Combined, these approaches suggest that in considering how transgression can remain meaningful, one must theorize how to set criteria for transgression that can be evaluated; one has to confront how the aesthetics of transgression make it visible but potentially undermine transgressiveness; one must deal with the fact that getting rid of any one particular set of norms neither abolishes normativity itself, nor our need for normativity to compel us; and one must distinguish effects from agency so as not to be misled by transgression's implicit promise that the breaking of a rule is tantamount to its abolishment. In this view, transgression thus is about the fantasy of agency, and too often, the crediting of the desire as the accomplishment.

Warding off Transgression: Scientific Revolutions and the Kuhnian Paradigm

When Thomas Kuhn sought to explain scientific revolutions in terms of paradigm change, he put front and centre the problem of how to narrativize change within science. According to Kuhn, "though the world does not change with a change of paradigm, the scientist afterwards works in a different world" (Kuhn 2012, 121). He adds "To reject one paradigm without simultaneously substituting another is to reject science itself" (Kuhn 2012, 79). Kuhn grants the paradigm stunning constitutive powers: it is the monolithic structure without which science does not exist. But does science have a structure, or is this monolith a fantasy of scientific instrumentality? Margaret Masterman famously documented the twenty-one different ways in which Kuhn had used the term 'paradigm' (Masterman 61-65), capturing the difficulty of specifying a structure that encompasses all that goes under the umbrella of scientific work. Given how 'structure' has today lost any diagnostic powers, what was the source of its power? As we shall see, 'structure' made change itself intelligible while 'anomaly' made that change essentially conservative and anti-transgressive.[2] The problem is that to register as an anomaly, one has to notice a transgression of the norm.

To make visible this work of structure, consider what a structure of ecological change would look like, and why we today do not consider the absence of structure to be a problem. Our present fascination with ecology frames change more dynamically, and thus raises the issue of how to imagine a structure that could possibly encompass such

---

2   Watkins notes that for Popper, Kuhn's normal science would be unscientific (Watkins 28). Popper thought that science was about continual revolution. Watkins helps reinforce the conservatism behind Kuhn's paradigms. He also praises Popper's narrower criteria of falsifiability over the vaguer Kuhnian notion of "puzzle-solving tradition" (Watkins 30). In thinking about why Kuhn values normal over extraordinary science, Watkins argues that Kuhn was responding to how much scientific work is the less exciting mopping up varietal (Watkins 32), and that Kuhn was reinforcing a parallel between scientific and religious communities (Watkins 33). Reisch situates Kuhn within his work on general education in the time of the Cold War: he shows how Kuhn had used 'dogma' and 'ideology' in the place the paradigm (Reisch 23-27).

insistent dynamism. Furthermore, under dynamism, which insists on webs of relation-ships, who or what are the agents of change, and how does one tell the difference be-tween the norm and its violation, much less cause and effect?[3] All these things must be legible for transgression to have a purchase. Hence, I suggest ecology is a solvent of evidence of human agency and therefore of evidence of transgression. Coupled with a posthumanism that is, on the one hand, fuelled by a concept of the Anthropocene which frames human change in terms of planetary catastrophe, and, on the other hand, wary of how much human agency sucks attention away from competing agencies – this move to ecological understanding diffuses change by making it the work of the system and also preventing us from seeing the incoherence between Posthumanism's maximalist and minimalist accounts of human agency.[4] Embedded here are different theories of agency which in their mutual resistance to empirical evidence remain theories that defer evi-dence. Because of the numerous points of reference, the required scale for evidence of agency challenges our ability to make sense of it. Yet can system changes be controlled, and if not, can system-level changes be considered transgressions? To ask the question this way is to worry about what system and ecology do to human agency, and the degree to which, in the Anthropocene, ecology allows us to hold onto human agency even after we have purged the human of its aggrandizing powers. It is also to ask the degree to which the specification of limits that structure entails allows the transgression to appear. Foucault submits that transgression is our remaining technology for finding the empti-ness of the sacred, and in this view, transgression is where we can find cultural value. He writes, "profanation in a world that no longer recognizes any positive meaning in the sacred – is that not more or less what we may call transgression" (Foucault 1998, 70). In our secular age transgression and art console us for the loss of the sacred. With its growing powers of consolation, transgression orients itself towards fantasy and away from action and evidence.

In her reappraisal of Kuhn, Daston notes that 'structure' in the humanities has been re-placed by 'culture', 'context', and 'thick description', words that eschew generalization (Daston 2016, 117). Transgression traffics in generalization when it serves up what may be a microaggression as a revolution. Kuhn's key term for the change that will foment a revolution is not transgression but rather 'anomaly'. When the terms are compared, we can see that transgression often assumes the value of its difference, where anomaly brackets its difference as an exception to the rule. The former carries an intent to defy the norm, while the latter eschews and actively resists the possibility of transgression by minimizing ruptures of the norm as exceptions. But how then does the anomaly earn its revolutionary power, especially since not all anomalies prompt revolution? Crucially, in Kuhn's view, the scientist neither aims for novelty nor anomaly, but as he recognized, revolution can paradoxically stem from the confirmation of existing theories, as better articulations of the theory come out (Hacking 2012, xvi-xvii). While this framing grants

---

3   On systems thinking, see Capra and Luisi 80-83.

4   On the challenges of all that traffics under posthumanism, see Cary Wolfe.

the veridical power of science the ability to foment revolution – it makes transgression a by-product of collective scientific work, not its aim. Here's Kuhn's account of how anomaly works:

> discovery commences with the awareness of anomaly, i.e., with the recognition that nature has somehow violated the paradigm-induced expectations that govern normal science. It then continues with a more or less extended exploration of the area of anomaly. And it closes only when the paradigm theory has been adjusted so that the anomalous has become the expected. (Kuhn 2012, 53)

Through the anomaly, scientific discovery flirts with transgression but always goes home with a norm: a norm is challenged by its opposite and gradually replaces the old norm with a new one. Note, however, that Kuhn points his finger at 'nature' as having done the violating or transgressing, not the individual perceiving scientist, despite his acknowledgment that anomalies must "enter ... the consciousness of scientists" (Kuhn 2012, 54). In this view, once again nature paradoxically works against nature. Kuhn argues that the gauge of a scientific revolution is the extent to which an anomaly ultimately sweeps away the previous paradigm (Kuhn 2012, 97). How does an anomaly go from something outside the paradigm to having the power to deflate it? Kuhn concedes that minor paradigm changes such as Herschel's discovery of Uranus help prepare the way for larger ones (Kuhn 2012, 115-16). To heighten the anomaly's objective status, Kuhn goes so far as to suggest the anomaly moves beyond mere interpretation. As he puts it, "no ordinary sense of the term 'interpretation' fits these flashes of intuition through which a new paradigm is born" (Kuhn 2012, 122-23). Here, Kuhn, a trained physicist mindful of quantum physics and its uncertainty principle, insulates the anomaly from the lone interpreter, moving it in the direction of a collective objective fact and new norm.[5] One might even say that in this view, the anomaly becomes a transgression from nowhere and by no individual one, as history moves from norm to norm. In exiling interpretation, Kuhn allows nature to be the author of the anomaly, and in this way science structures an ideal of normativity that withstands any particular revolution.

Kuhn further immunizes science from transgression when he insists

> though such intuitions depend upon the experience, both anomalous and congruent, gained with the old paradigm, they are not logically or piecemeal linked to particular items of that experience as interpretation would be. Instead, they gather up large portions of that experience and transform them to the rather different bundle of experience ... (Kuhn 2012, 123)

In this view, the scientific paradigm is paradoxically the bundler of experience, since interpretation is unqualified to do so. The totality of the paradigm speaks to the encompassing nature of science, and interpretation, by contrast with the paradigm, can only offer synecdoche. In anticipation of Latour, Kuhn's anomalous object objects to the pre-

---

5   Kuhn proffers the switch from Newtonian to Einsteinian paradigms as his central exhibit for his theory of revolution (Kuhn 2012, 101-03). In Peter Dear's account of scientific revolution, seventeenth-century natural philosophy orients itself to instrumentalism.

vious paradigm, but demurely. That nature or science itself authorizes the revolution, thus makes these anomalies fundamentally conservative. In his later *The Essential Tension*, Kuhn continues to limit anomaly's power by separating the basic scientist from the inventor and innovator, and by chiding the Americans in the audience for their preference for the latter over the former (Kuhn 1977, 239). When the anomaly somehow overturns a paradigm, it is not because it has been valued over and above normal scientific work. At issue then in the gamut from anomaly to transgression is a theory of agency.

Let us also reflect upon what kind of piercing of the norm might have the power actually to deflate the norm, thereby changing the very nature of experience itself.[6] What is the tipping point between an anomaly that functions as an irritant and one that requires paradigm shift? What enables the anomaly to goad science away from its normative "mopp[ing] up" as Kuhn puts it (Kuhn 2012, 24), of the difference between theory and fact?[7] Even more worrisome, and from the other direction, does 'revolution' package merely a symptom of a norm for the norm itself? In this regard, the ability of proponents of the norm to cite various, even competing versions of nature, suggests a resilience that will at least give transgression pause. My point here is that if deferral in the form of difference is the engine of transgression, it is available to nature, too. Evolution, for instance, exploits genetic variation, but crucially does not know in advance which differences will confer survivability. In a word, checkmate.

Given the current rise of pluralistic understandings of science, the problem of making change visible has only become larger. Moreover, who gets to stand in as the poster boys or girls of change? Pluralistic understandings exist in part to combat what traditional histories of science have left out: where Kuhn privileged theory over experiment, Galison has argued for three separate areas of scientific research – theory, experiment, and instrument (Hacking 2012, xvi). Would Kuhn's paradigm shift be able to account for three, not two, dimensions of change? Historians of Science, moreover, are increasingly focusing on understudied areas like Africa and the Caribbean, thus making Western science more of an anomaly, and thereby provincializing any of its revolutionary powers and rightly so. My point here is that 'human' agency itself is the problem.

Daston highlights the fact that unlike structure, Kuhn's 'revolution' has taken off like wildfire (Daston 2016, 117). Revolution turns to political change to help us to understand epistemological change, but like transgression it is a promissory note that one often never fully cashes out. There is also the problem of whether or not epistemological

---

6   In *Against Nature*, Daston distinguishes between historical norms, which have been different across time, and normativity itself, or the preconditions required to stipulate any ideal of the norm at all. Too often the norm masks itself as normativity (Daston 2019, 44-45). As she points out, our disagreements with particular norms do not address the ideal of normativity itself, which is bound up with the human, and our need for order and to be compelled by some larger ought.

7   Kuhn cautions his audience away from thinking about science in terms of divergent thought, instead preferring "convergence" (Kuhn 1977, 226). Again and again, he privileges identity over difference, narrowing the space for transgression within science.

change functions anything like political revolution. Ian Hacking wrote long ago that there can never be a sufficient articulation of the why behind revolution (Hacking 1979, 47), and this implies that 'revolution' is a signifier of a change that can never quite deliver the empirical goods. When Foucault made 'savoir' (knowledge) unconscious, he opened it to the explanatory powers of psychoanalysis to compensate for what empirical arguments could not deliver. His historiographical emphasis upon discontinuities, dubbed by some as 'history with a saw', simultaneously threatened to subdue all possible transgressions under a generalized power insofar as the abrupt about-face within any discourse was power's signature. In much the same way as Kuhn's paradigm of science as housekeeping contains anomaly,[8] Foucault's discourse contained transgression: as he insisted, the role of transgression was "to measure the excessive distance that it opens at the heart of the limit and to trace the flashing line that causes the limit to arise" (Foucault 1998, 74). Here, transgression paradoxically contents itself by measuring and tracing the seam between epistemes even as the subsequent episteme acquires the explosive power to overturn its predecessor. Foucault adds:

> Transgression … affirms limited being – affirms the limitlessness into which it leaps as it opens this zone to existence for the first time. But, correspondingly, this affirmation contains nothing positive: no content can bind it, since by definition, no limit can possibly restrict it. (Foucault 1998, 74)

As a limitlessness that paradoxically articulates and affirms the limit, transgression lacks content because content requires limits. In this way, transgression structures discourse and tells us where its borders are, but at the huge cost of evacuating it of essential content. The limitlessness that transgression reaches towards threatens to dissolve discourse by dissolving the ability of structure to contain content. Perhaps that structuring power comes at too high a price. Perhaps this helps explain why structure now lies in the humanities' dustbin.

In keeping with the idea that pluralism and ecology make evidence for transgression harder to find and track, Daniel Garber has recently argued that there was no Kuhnian scientific revolution, and instead insists that the paradigm of revolution has come at the expense of competing scientific narratives which cohere for him around a turn to innovation and a turn against authority. Garber implies then that the narrative of revolution turns to a linear or cyclical narrative to document cause and effect. Instead of revolution, Garber highlights a litany of changes: theoretical, structural, educational, economic (Garber 135). He sums up that what Kuhn called a scientific revolution "looks less like a real revolution – an old regime that enters into crisis before being replaced by a new regime – and more like a Protestant Reformation, with its decentralization of religious authority" (Garber 142). In this view, Kuhn's scientific revolution has chosen the wrong political label, and the choice of trope reminds us that transgression contained through the anomaly is not the only form of historical change and agency. Decentralization or

---

8   Paola Mayer, by contrast, suggests that Romantic science "is inherently transgressive, meaning by this a hubristic attempt to change reality by manipulating a border", i.e., the one between life and death (Mayer 65-67). Mayer's view of science is closer to Popper's.

even reformation of authority may be more accurate ways to think about how change comes about. Of course, under the widening aperture of multiple historical frames what counts as an anomaly too, fractures and dissipates, facilitating a turn to system that turns to relationality to make fungible evidence for human agency. If only evidence for human change were more empirically obvious.

Queer Theory and Radical Transgression

My focus on how scientific revolutions help us to think about transgression has prepared us to see how structure, narrative and form shape how and what kinds of transgression can become visible, and to think about whether historical change and agency should be thought about in terms of violations of norms or decentralization or reformation. How a theorist becomes an authority on transgression – how she shows us how and where to look for it – screens choices concerning agency and the very nature of change. I turn now to how Queer Theory helps us to rethink these issues. Like the anomaly, queerness names an instability or ambivalence that is believed to have the power to rupture norms. Unlike its shyer and more retiring cousin, the anomaly, queerness thrives by insisting that its various instabilities have the power to rupture/transgress ways of being. There are several obstacles to the ability of queerness to deliver upon its promised ruptures: the instability it relies upon needs first to be perceived. Such perception must then overcome the human capacity for denial. And the instability must have sufficient force to wreak the larger havoc it promises. Too often evidence for instability has been construed as mission accomplished. It is not as if the norm lacks flexibility and resilience: one reason why the norm repeatedly turns to nature for a foundation is that nature offers so many versions of order for us to draw upon.[9] And yet, as Daston submits, to get rid of one set of norms is not to get rid of the appeal of normativity itself because normativity is largely about order (Daston 2019, 48). To wit, as queerness reverses heteronormativity, it threatens to replace one norm with a homonormativity.

The sceptic thus wonders how often an instability has actually done away with the norm. When has the by now well-documented precarity of patriarchy expunged it? And when has deconstruction actually provided a clear end of shelf life to a binary opposition? The sceptic further wonders since these ruptures are often predicated upon linguistic deferral, whether the effectivity or performativity of the gap in the world is being presumed. The gap, then, can only be the initial evidence for transgression, not its closing exhibit. Then again, perhaps total erasure is too high a standard for transgression, one that threatens to make any transgression invisible. At issue is how to correct for the tendency of transgression to promise more revolution and liberation than it delivers, to make its chew commensurate with its bite.

---

9   See Daston, *Against Nature*. See also Joan Roughgarden, *Evolution's Rainbow*, which
     argues for the naturalness of homosexuality – its prevalence within nature – and suggests
     that Darwinian evolution works through cooperation, not the survival of the fittest.

At its best, Queer Theory calls out claims of transgression that do not quite live up to the hype and thus gives us more thoughtful forms of it. Leo Bersani, for example, recognizes the degree to which models of intractable sexual desire can be fundamentally conservative (Bersani 1995, 124), and the ways in which "homosexuality can be a privileged model of sameness" (Bersani 1995, 6). The moral here is what is done in the name of transgression may turn out to be fundamentally conservative. To guard against this eventuality, Bersani radicalizes homo-ness so that it represents a necessary withdrawal from society as we know it.[10] Bersani writes, "the most politically disruptive aspect of the homo-ness I will be exploring in gay desire is a redefinition of sociality so radical that it may appear to require a provisional withdrawal from relationality itself" (Bersani 1995, 7). Moving deliberately against any kind of respect that homosexuality has purchased in recent decades, Bersani focuses our attention on the specificities of homosexuality that resist societal inclusion, what he calls the "politically unacceptable and politically indispensable choice of an outlaw existence" (Bersani 1995, 76). In so doing, he considers the costs of respectability, which he argues has been tantamount to a degaying of gayness, and grants transgression the power continually to challenge the very basis of sociality itself. For Bersani, the Queer Theorist's version of homophobia is the screening of gay fucking by a queer politics. Hence his vision is for nothing less than an outlaw politics that upends politics as we now know it.

Lee Edelman makes a similar radicalizing move in *No Future*. In thinking about the ways in which the child "carries the burden of signifying futurity" (Edelman 13), Edelman questions whether there can be a future that does not normalize heterosexual reproduction. Just as Bersani questions sociality itself, Edelman urges Queer Theory to give up on the future because a future inseparable from reproduction is in his view not worth having. Insofar as both make transgression work against anything like a desire that could be embodied in something like a subject, but transform it into a drive, they pit a subjective desire against a psychoanalytic drive, and in this way help us to think about what it means to limit transgression to desire. They take from Lacan and Freud the notion that desire is fated to be unfulfilled, in part because its objects and acts are never commensurate with desire. Freud submits that because desire encapsulates the history of the subject, it is necessarily fractured among its past and present objects: otherwise how would transference between the patient and analyst come to be?[11]

---

10   Bersani puts it this way in his *October* interview: "the problem with queer politics as we now define it is that, however broad its reach may be, it is still a micropolitics focused on numerous particular issues which there is no reason to believe will ever be exhausted if the fundamental types of community and relationality out of which such issues spring are not themselves questioned or attacked" (Bersani 1997, 11).

11   See Adam Phillips, *Becoming Freud*, 123-31. Phillips' superb study shows how Freud frames biography as the enemy to psychoanalysis, since only the subject knows the truth of his/her desire.

But are the radical transgressions Bersani and Edelman offer worth the price? On the plus side, society and the future are so cherished parts of our mental furniture that getting rid of them would seem to make our world the equivalent of living on the Titanic without deckchairs. There is also little danger here of these versions of queerness being co-opted or normalized by society in general.[12] On the minus side, is the struggle worth it, and in the end ultimately defeating? Bersani and Edelman frame the drive as the engine of an unstoppable transgression of the pleasure principle – a kind of death drive – but in process, transgression has become an endless looping whose very interminability perforce guarantees the rupture of anything like a hetero or homonormative self, which, in turn, puts pressure on the very nature of sociality. In Foucauldian terms, the transgression escapes the horizon of its limit by looping itself into the future, but in so doing reduces itself to an ordinary process not unlike German erosion. The loop/algorithm ironically becomes the queer future, but how is this qualitatively different from a reproductive futurity? Why the death drive seems to offer a sexier monotony is the question.[13] Moreover, any agency that accompanies the transgression is undermined by the algorithmic engine subsuming it.[14] Here, effectivity comes at the price of an agency without the subject.

Stephen Best in *None Like Us: Blackness, Belonging, Aesthetic Life* provides a more nuanced lens through which to examine these questions.[15] He examines queerness at the intersection between race and homosexuality, and he worries about what does it mean to be compelled to belong to an African American history – an afterlife of slavery – that would extinguish his very self. Rather than considering the future as queerness's central problem, he focuses upon history. In articulating his considerable ambivalence about what it means to belong to a history of subjection, Best weighs the costs and benefits of the communitarianism behind African-American Studies, and he concludes that a transgressive disaffiliation is necessary. Yet his acknowledgement of the layers of ambivalence, coupled with an intersectional treatment of queerness between race and sexuality, allows disaffiliation to be the outcome of deliberation, instead of a transgressive drive. We experience the push and pull of its vexed and mixed emotions and intersectionality, most memorably when Best describes the pride making his father sick (Best 4) at his son's college graduation. The father could not sit through the ceremony because such success implies a turning of one's back against one's collective history. Best thus urges

---

12 As Robyn Wiegman shrewdly points out, Edelman refutes critics who insist on his nihilism by showing how negativity is part of society, not external to it (Wiegman 221).

13 Ultimately, it is sexier because it erodes notions of the subject rather than contributes to subjectification. Lacan also frames the plural drives as essentially metonymic, thereby preventing them from organizing a subject. See Evans, 46-50.

14 Ed Finn defines the algorithm as "culture machines that operate in the gap between code and culture" (Finn 47). Since we already have algorithmic intimacy, Finn urges us to become better readers of algorithms, so that we do not merely prostrate ourselves before them.

15 My thanks to my colleague, Dustin Friedman, for suggesting I read Best.

that the imperative of the collective be dismantled. However, does that disaffiliation return us to the false triumphalism of neo-liberal individualism, and what does the emptiness of collectivity now mean? Nonetheless, Best takes us through the psychological experience of his meandering road to disaffiliation, and in so doing, helps make transgression an embodied versus abstract experience, one that offers a kind of empirical evidence for itself. In this way, transgression's embodiment can offer more than a compelling theory.

Before leaving Queer Theory in the rear-view mirror, I focus briefly on Lacan because he raises the problem of the ethics of transgression.[16] Where Bersani traffics in Freud, Edelman traffics in Lacan, who is always trafficking in his version of Freud. As a psychoanalyst, Lacan worried especially about the analyst's ethical responsibility in the wake of the coercive norm. Lacan thought that Freud's entire body of work could be understood within the dialectic of transgression and the death drive (Lacan 2-3). Where Freud considered civilization to be co-extensive with sublimation, Lacan's project then was to keep his patient true to the excessiveness of desire, since those desires by virtue of their excess resisted any taming by the norm, here captured as "sublimation".[17] This norm includes any subject, since desire exceeds any form of the subject, and since the Lacanian subject is inseparable from an entry into signification. How then in psychoanalytic practice to preserve the space for this excess? Lacan addresses this problem squarely in his 1960 seminar, "The Jouissance of Transgression", included in *The Ethics of Psychoanalysis*. Lacan submits that "does it go without saying that to trample sacred laws under foot … itself excites some form of jouissance" (Lacan 195). Yet this jouissance is bound up with cruelty and obsession and even boredom, in part because jouissance prompts the superego to contain it, and such containment introduces aggression. Because jouissance is inseparable from aggression, it is easy to accept its sublimations for jouissance itself.

Consequently, what Lacan admires in Sade is his ability to cut the subject "loose from his psychosocial moorings – or to be more precise, from all psychosocial appreciation of the sublimation involved" (Lacan 201). When the boredom of the repetitive random acts of Sadean sex unites with the obsessive aggressive fury of desire, one "appreciates" fully sublimation along with its limits, so much so that, for Lacan, such sublimation becomes a dead end rather than a strategy of civilization. To counter sublimation, and also to surpass Freud, Lacan suggests a severing of moorings so complete that one could no longer appreciate sublimation at all. Lacan's ethical imperative, then, is to keep the patient's jouissance alive in the plural and excessive forms of its signification – running

---

16   Foucault insisted that transgression had to be "detached from its questionable association to ethics" (1998, 74).

17   I have been influenced here by Finkelde's study of how excess is leveraged by Kant, Hegel, and Lacan, to provide a dynamic foundation for ethics. Libbrecht offers a powerful analysis how Lacanian desire is tied to the Other: the desire of the analyst only has one object, which is desire itself (Libbrecht 78-79).

the gamut from the death drive, through aggression, and to pleasure – making impossible any unitary "subject".[18] We are again confronted with the problem of whether the costs of this radical transgressive excess surmount its benefits, especially since the *moi* or ego now begins its work. At the same time, once transgression itself becomes ethical, has the violation so co-opted the norm that it becomes feckless? And if a kind of algorithmic repetition satisfies ethics, returning ethics to an obeisance to rules in the form of a drive, then is this a transgressive ethics anyone should want?

Romanticism, *Don Juan*, and Transgressive Contingency

Don Juan (*DJ*) returns us to all the challenges raised herein: the degree to which pluralism / ecology makes transgressive acts difficult if not impossible to track; the ways in which aesthetic form makes transgression visible but also contains it; the difficulty of preventing transgression from merely setting a new norm or even containing that norm is something like a subject; and the gap between an instability and a change. There is also the issue of how desire, the drive, the algorithm – transgression's vehicles (often mechanisms) – thereby cancel out any agency lent by the transgression. Here, transgression often offers liberation under the guise of a different master. Briefly, I submit that Byron transgresses the epic by structuring reality around a radical contingency that ironizes any notion of a hero or heroine. In his "Detached Thoughts", Byron mused that man is merely "a sad jar of atoms" (Byron qtd. in Marchand 278), and in the *ottava rima* form, Byron would find the ideal jar. But this is a transgressive radical contingency that no one wants, simply because this contingency gives the lie to social constructionism. Although social construction claims to bypass the determinism of nature, it is a constructionism that we all suffer. Far from liberating us, the turn from the natural to the social merely provides us with new masters, and new forms of contingency. Through the form of *ottava rima*, Byron weaponizes contingency against forms of egoism and agency that would aggrandize any self into heroism. Because it is a lesson we never can quite take on board, especially in the epic form where heroism is the genre's oxygen, we witness our continual surprise, line after line, canto after canto, along with the power of narcissism to vacuum difference.[19] Through *ottava rima*, then, Byron repeatedly lever-

---

18 Foucault anticipates Lacan when he argues that Sade writes "the form of desire, of repetitive desire, unlimited desire, desire without law, without restriction, without an exterior, and it is the suppression of exteriority with respect to desire" (Foucault 2015, 114). In this view, literature writes desire as transgression beyond limits and beyond content.

19 Miller argues that the eighteenth century distinguished between violent and pleasurable senses of surprise, and began to associate surprise especially with the novel. For Miller, Wordsworth distinguished between good lyric surprise (because cognitive and renewable) and bad novelistic surprise (mere emotional stimulation). My interest in this essay has to do with the cognitive benefits of surprise in Byron, and how rhyme within *ottava rima* must work to remain novel, and can do so only when it prompts cognitive reappraisals. For Byron, since *ottava rima* helps generate narrative, I do not think he thinks there

ages surprise to push a self beyond itself, to question its beliefs, and in the process, reveals heroism to be an empty container and the self to be an effectively inert one. In this way we come to know the ego or Byronic hero as drive and feel the costs of that drive as our collective vulnerability.[20]

It was Kuhn who argued that the Romantic period participates in a scientific revolution of its own. Kuhn credited the period for enabling heat, light, electricity and magnetism to acquire paradigms (Hacking 2012, xiii). Hence Byron witnesses not one paradigm shift, but two. The first is a move away from Newtonian corpuscles to a dynamism that can account for magnetic and electrical materiality. Byron alludes to this when he compares Johnson's soul to "(Galvanism upon the dead)" (*DJ* 8.41). Where the current moment seeks to substitute the theological soul with Galvanism and animal electricity, Byron's simile and bracketing parentheses make clear that all it actually has done is to make the dead move. In this way the so-called paradigm shift merely returns us to the fact of our beholdenness to contingency. The second is a rethinking of bodily health that moves away from the rational and calculable circulation of the heart and towards the surprising plasticity of the nervous system, and the manifold ways in which sensation makes us hostage to our immediate environments. Byron's contribution is to make human contingency a repeatedly felt experience, one with the power repeatedly to puncture egoism in an epic form predicated on egoism.[21]

Don Juan, moreover, raises important questions for Queer Theory, since the contingencies it fulsomely generates ultimately overwhelms what might be leveraged for a queer politics. When there is such excess contingency, how can a select contingency prevail over others? Not even doubt offers any ultimate respite from the relentlessness of particularity. Byron comments, "So little do we know what we're about in / This world. I doubt if doubt itself be doubting" (*DJ* 9.135-36). In the first line of the concluding couplet, the poet severs any connection between intention and knowledge by making aboutness beyond knowledge, while the second line revels in a triple internal rhyme riche. The net effect is that despite the fact that doubt should in keeping with its name doubt itself, it offers the very last refuge for a certainty (in the stability of a rhyme that stays in place) that can ground selfhood, as did Descartes when he posited "I think,

---

is a split between narrative and poetic forms of surprise. I thank Denise Gigante for pointing me to Miller's study.

20   Steinbock connects surprise to the need to re-evaluate a belief as in I am now believing what I could not believe at first (Steinbock 6). Although Steinbock offers much insight, he unfortunately emphasizes the pre-reflective over the deliberative side of surprise. Although it seems to have become consensus that our brain functions to minimize surprise, Clark asks why some seek novelty or exploration (Clark 265-68). He hypothesizes in a world of uneven distribution, exploration reduces the value of a state the longer the state is occupied. Cooper shrewdly thinks about Byron's *ottava rima* as a "miniature vortex" (Cooper 258), but resolves Byron's scepticism into a "perpetual process of pragmatic adjustment" (Cooper 262). I am less optimistic that pragmatism triumphs over contingency.

21   Byron ends Canto 9 with the nervous system: fancies whirling in his brain (verse 85).

therefore, I am". Yet Byron's calculated lowering of expectations allows us to be less frustrated by the negative, and more surprised by any positive outcome. At the same time, by highlighting through rhyme riche the fact that doubt goes against its very nature when it refuses to turn against itself, the poet recognizes the human desire for certainty in a world which prevents it. In this way Byron advertizes how doubt functions as a kind of self-protection, and thereby undermines its very compensations. Thus, when Owen Wynn claims that Byron uses *ottava rima* to celebrate doubt, he tells only half the story.

Let us look closely at the complex ways in which Byron's rhymes leverage and sustain surprise to reveal the self as lack, an inert container whose predictions are riddled with error. Before doing so, the work of Nobel-prize winning scientist Eric Kandel may help suggest why surprise can be so effective. In his study of sea-slugs, Kandel isolated the neural circuits for short-term and long-term memory. Kandel writes,

> we observed that when we produced habituation by touching the skin repeatedly, the amplitude of the gill-withdrawal reflex decreased progressively. This learned change in behavior was paralleled by a progressive weakening of the synaptic connections. Conversely, when we produced sensitization by applying a shock to the animal's tail or head, the enhanced gill-withdrawal reflex was accompanied by a strengthening of the synaptic connections. (Kandel 201)

Greater sensitization or more surprise/shock impacted, for example, the numbers of synapses available to learning: the number of synaptic terminals doubles from 1300-2700, the percentage of active synapses increases from 40 to 60% (Kandel 213-15), and a new protein was synthesized. With long-term memory, anatomical change had occurred, and he later discovered that this protein synthesis was essential to the making of new synapses. Neuroscientist Stanislaus Dehaene adds that "learning is active and depends on the degree of surprise linked to the violation of our expectations" (Dehaene 203). Now while Byron could not have known this, he recognized the transformative power of surprise, despite claiming that he himself was so cosmopolitan that he was immune to it (Miller 8). Joseph Addison anticipates Kandel and Dehaene when Addison recognizes how the surprising is actually empirically more memorable (Miller 24).

I focus here on a few early stanzas of Byron's Canto 9 (1823). Through rhyme, Byron pits contingency against heroism/agency, and overwhelms any self that would contain it.[22] The Canto is book ended by Wellington and Catherine the Great, and so there is a lot of overwhelming to do. When he defines Wellington's actions, those of the reigning British hero, in terms of having "repaired Legitimacy's crutch, –" (*DJ* 9.19), Byron deflates any transgressive heroism by highlighting Wellington's fundamental conservatism with the verb "repair". In this way, his self-functions as an inert container, and we are reminded of Garber's reading of Kuhn: what looks like revolution to some, looks like reformation to others. The comparison of Waterloo to the repair of legitimacy's crutch,

---

22   Recall here Bill Keach's reminder that Byron was schooled in the *ottava rima* written by Murray's Tory friends. Keach submits that through *ottava rima*, Byron "sounds the political syllables both ways" (Keach 552).

frames Wellington's martial success as addressing a symptom, not the cause, even as the crutch takes away legitimacy's legitimacy. When Byron rhymes "crutch" with "Dutch", he alludes to how Wellington's victory was propped up by Dutch soldiers, without whose help there may not have been a victory at all. What seems heroism from another vantage becomes dumb luck, what Byron will call a "lucky blunder" (*DJ* 9.38). No wonder Kuhn sought to immunize the scientific anomaly from interpretation. Byron's rhyme here encourages a second look, so that the emotion can help disrupt patterns of thought.

Byron considered himself like Sylla: "I have always believed that all things depend upon Fortune, and nothing on ourselves" (Byron qtd. in Marchand 277). Byron parallels Wellington with Sylla's life thusly: "Called 'Saviour of the Nations' – not yet saved; / And Europe's Liberator – still enslaved" (*DJ* 9.39-40). By contrasting the names versus reality, and by puncturing the name within both lines of the couplet, the poet surprises because each line in the couplet functions as its own sledge hammer. Even better, the fact that he uses the last two feet of each pentameter line to dissipate what took three feet to build only underscores the hollowness of heroism, and by extension both the self, along with the nation that relies upon it. In this way, Byron exploits the machinic force of rhyme to confront the epic's need to confirm heroism, itself now understood as a kind of crutch that usually supports nations. Byron also highlights how varying time scales shift the interpretation: what we now label saving becomes in a longer time frame merely another form of enslavement. The ease with which saving becomes enslaving reminds us that what passes as a transgression today looks like a reformation tomorrow. Rhyme as the play of similarity and difference, asks us to evaluate difference so that we can distinguish between claims of significance from actual significance. And the temporality of rhyme pushes the evaluation of the achievement into the future, showing the scalar limits of transgression.

When sound drives the narrative movement, Byron's rhymes move everything into the column of contingency, but this system casts doubt on whether our lowering of expectations actually creates meaningful agency or simply has us feel better. Canto 9, stanza 18, offers an illustration.

> It is a pleasant voyage perhaps to float,
> Like Pyrrho, on a sea of speculation;
> But what if carrying sail capsize the boat?
> Your wise men don't know much of navigation;
> And swimming long in the abyss of thought
> Is apt to tire: a calm and shallow station
> Well nigh the shore, where one stoops down and gathers
> Some pretty shell, is best for moderate bathers. (*DJ* 9.137-44)

Byron's target here is Pyrrhonic scepticism, which insists that the suspension of judgement fosters tranquillity, and thus attempts thereby to cure unease. The consonance of 'p' sounds – pleasant, perhaps, Pyrrho – distils this cure into speculation. Note, however, the barb in "perhaps", which foists scepticism against itself, and thus suspends any palliative force of scepticism in a world besieged by doubt. In ancient scepticism there is no end to doubt, but all that can be hoped for is an alleviation of its disease. For Byron, however, Pyrrho is not much of a hero because such suspension/contingency becomes simultaneously a lack of ground, entailing not an allaying of unease but rather a different unease that accompanies the endless suspension of judgement. When all is suspended, there is cognitive suicide. After all, what can be known, and why bother trying to know? While Byron acknowledges that it is perhaps pleasant to float upon such suspension, the problem is that too much air might cause the boat to capsize, and that swimming ceaselessly is exhausting. Hence his a-rhymes pair float/boat/thought, thus hovering between figure and ground, while any power of the rhyme to ground is strained by Byron's awkward stretching of the sound of "boat" into "thought" even as his boat evaporates into thought. At the same time his b-rhymes speculation/navigation/station extend the enjambed sea of speculation, creating a taste for the material shell as something to be desperately gathered. So much for any tranquillity!

Yet if Pyrrho is the zero masked as a hero, Byron's shell offers no firmer alternative. First, the shell is an empty home, and although it can be gathered, it functions in this stanza more like a red herring or shiny object, given to distract the reader from the hollowness of the tiny sanctuary it offers. To the extent that Pyrrho left no traces of his own, but whose philosophy became known through the writings of Sextus Empiricus, Timon, and Diogenes, among others, the shell as figure for Pyrrho, highlights a missing centre. Second, the shell only consoles moderate bathers – those preferring shallow or deep bathing are bound to be disappointed. Byron's larger point is that only those capable of or given to moderation could be satisfied by this form of scepticism. Third, the "station" is not on the shore but near it, and we are still partly submerged under water. The enjambment between the sestet and the final couplet merely extends the suspension, whose consolation is really only a temporary albeit pretty distraction. The eye rhyme of the final couplet, moreover, – "gathers" does not really rhyme with "bathers" – a fact underscored by the asymmetrical rhyming of a verb with a noun – once again underscores both the deception of appearances and the inability of appearances to offer any lasting consolation. If the nature epitomized in the shell provides any refuge from contingency, whatever agency it offers here is tiny in scale, hollow, and ill equipped to solve the larger problem. The shell is emphatically not a shore, despite their consonance. At the same time, while we have scaled down our hopes and scepticism has done its work, Byron's medial caesuras – three in the last three lines – and his extended caesura in the form of a medial clause that begins with "where" – returns us to the pleasures of suspension but not those from judgement, which amounts to cognitive suicide, but from relentless contingency. Crucially, Byron's verb is "gather", not possession: in 1821, he wrote, "I allow sixteen minutes, though I never counted them, to any given or supposed possession" (Byron qtd. in Marchand 248). Fittingly, his lines measure the gathers of any possession or shore, even as one line erodes the previous one. *Die Transgression* indeed.

What, then, does Byron show us about transgression? Literary language itself is not transgressive, but requires embodiment through surprise. Transgression does its most powerful work when we feel its price, when its theoretical promises can be tensed and evaluated against its actual practices, and its fantasmic structure thereby loses its siren call.[23] It also works most effectively to redefine and limit agency through its ability to confront the self with surprise. In this view, surprise throws down the gauntlet to agency by insisting on its limits. Agency and transgression therefore no longer take the form of an arc between mentality and action, a kind of linear causality, but is transformed into the mind's ability to second guess itself, and thereby to contain its narcissism. Through rhyme, Byron must repeatedly help us to feel the loss of heroism, to experience ultimately the very lack that structures the self as a crutch, and to get us to reflect upon why his surprise does not become equivalent to tickling oneself, an impossibility because surprise has been circumvented.[24] Through surprise, Byron has us experience ourselves as weak containers with very limited predictive powers, which cannot overcome contingency because there is so much of it. In Byron, transgression can never remain the basis for feeling good because no heroism can shield us from our essential vulnerability. Without the false consolation of feeling good, we can never grow smug in our transgressions, and surprise thus generates humility since one's previous self is powerless to overcome surprise through prediction and must therefore be revised. Experienced over thousands of rhymes, the lack reveals the self to be a drive from which suspension is sometimes necessary if not welcome or even pleasurable. As Byron's insistent British mangling of the Spanish declares, in *Don Juan*, then, there has never been or never will be a true one.

Works Cited

Bernstein, Charles. "The Body of the Poem". *Critical Inquiry* 44 (2018): 582-85.

Bersani, Leo. *Homos*. Cambridge, MA: Harvard UP, 1995.

---. "A Conversation with Leo Bersani". Interviewed by Tim Dean, Kaja Silverman, and Hal Foster. *October* 82 (1997): 3-16.

Best, Stephen. *None Like Us: Blackness, Belonging, Aesthetic Life*. Durham, NC: Duke UP, 2018.

Byron, Lord [George Gordon]. *The Complete Poetical Works*. Ed. Jerome J. McGann, vol. 5: *Don Juan*. Oxford: Clarendon Press, 1986.

Capra, Fritjof and Pier Luigi Luisi. *The Systems View of Life*. Cambridge: Cambridge UP, 2014.

---

23 I here allude to Charles Bernstein's concept of "aesthetic justice": "aesthetic justice occurs when intuitive preferences outfox rationalist principles" (Bernstein 582). Since one rationalist principle is the principle of order, I would modify him to say aesthetic justice can occur when intuitive preferences challenge rationalist principles. This revision does not presume the winner in advance.

24 Neuroscientists have become fascinated by why we cannot tickle ourselves, and they point to the need for surprise. Schizophrenics have been shown to be more vulnerable to self-tickling.

Clark, Andy. *Surfing Uncertainty: Prediction, Action and the Embodied Mind*. Oxford: Oxford UP, 2016.

Clason, Christopher R. "Introduction". *E.T.A. Hoffmann: Transgressive Romanticism*. Ed. Christopher R. Clason. Liverpool: Liverpool UP, 2018. 1-15.

Clason, Christopher R., ed. *E.T.A. Hoffmann: Transgressive Romanticism*. Liverpool: Liverpool UP, 2018.

Cooper, Andrew. "Shipwreck and Skepticism: Don Juan Canto II". *Recent Romantic Revisionary Poetry Criticism*. Ed. Karl Kroeber and Gene Ruoff. New Brunswick: Rutgers UP, 1993. 253-66.

Daston, Lorraine. "History of Science without *Structure*." *Kuhn's Structure of Scientific Revolutions at Fifty*. Ed. Robert J. Richards and Lorraine Daston. Chicago: University of Chicago Press, 2016. 115-32.

---. *Against Nature*. Cambridge: MIT Press, 2019.

Dear, Peter. *Revolutionizing the Sciences: European Knowledge and Its Ambitions, 1500-1700*. Chicago: University of Chicago Press, 2009.

Dehaene, Stanislaus. *How We Learn*. New York: Viking, 2020.

Edelman, Lee. *No Future: Queer Theory and the Death Drive*. Durham, NC: Duke UP, 2004.

Evans, Dylan. *An Introductory Dictionary of Lacanian Psychoanalysis*. London: Routledge, 1996.

Finkelde, Dominik. *Excessive Subjectivity*. New York: Columbia UP, 2015.

Finn, Ed. *What Algorithms Want*. Cambridge: MIT Press, 2017.

Foucault, Michel. "Preface to Transgression". *Foucault: Aesthetics, Method, and Epistemology*. Ed. James D. Faubion. New York: New Press, 1998. 69-87.

---. "Why Did Sade Write". *On Literature: Language, Madness, and Desire*. Trans. Robert Bononno. Minneapolis: University of Minnesota Press, 2015. 97-114.

Garber, Daniel. "Why the Scientific Revolution Wasn't a Scientific Revolution, and Why It Matters". *Kuhn's Structure of Scientific Revolutions at Fifty*. Ed. Robert J. Richards and Lorraine Daston. Chicago: University of Chicago Press, 2016. 133-50.

Hacking, Ian. "Michel Foucault's Immature Science". *Nous* 13/1 (1979): 39-51.

---. "Introductory Essay". *The Structure of Scientific Revolutions*. Ed. Thomas Kuhn. Chicago: University of Chicago Press, 2012. vii-xxxvii.

Kandel, Eric. *In Search of Memory: The Emergence of a New Science of Mind*. New York: W. W. Norton, 2006.

Keach, William. "Political Inflection in Byron's Ottava Rima". *Studies in Romanticism* 27/4 (1988): 551-62.

Kuhn, Thomas. "The Essential Tension: Tradition and Innovation in Scientific Research". *The Essential Tension*. Chicago: University of Chicago Press, 1977. 225-39.

---. *The Structure of Scientific Revolutions*. Chicago: University of Chicago Press, 2012.

Lacan, Jacques. *The Ethics of Psychoanalysis, 1959-60*. Ed. Jacques-Alain Miller. Trans. Dennis Porter. New York: W. W. Norton, 1992.

Libbrecht, Katrien. "Desire of the Analyst". *Key Concepts of Lacanian Psychoanalysis*. Ed. Danny Nobus. New York: Other Press, 1999. 75-100.

Marchand, Leslie, ed. *Lord Byron: Selected Letters and Journals*. Cambridge, MA: Harvard UP, 1982.

Masterman, Margaret. "The Nature of a Paradigm". *Criticism and the Growth of Knowledge*. Ed. Imre Lakatos and Alan Musgrave. Cambridge: Cambridge UP, 1970. 59-90.

Mayer, Paola. "Transgressive Science in E.T.A. Hoffmann's Fantastic Tales". *E.T.A. Hoffmann: Transgressive Romanticism*. Ed. Christopher R. Clason. Liverpool: Liverpool UP, 2018. 65-80.

Miller, Christopher R. *Surprise: The Poetics of the Unexpected from Milton to Austen*. Ithaca: Cornell UP, 2015.

Phillips, Adam. *Becoming Freud: The Making of a Psychoanalyst*. New Haven: Yale UP, 2014.

Reisch, George A. "Aristotle in the Cold War". *Kuhn's Structure of Scientific Revolutions at Fifty*. Ed. Robert J. Richards and Lorraine Daston. Chicago: University of Chicago Press, 2016. 12-29.

Roughgarden, Joan. *Evolution's Rainbow*. Berkeley: University of California Press, 2003.

Starr, Peter. *Logics of Failed Revolt: French Theory after May '68*. Stanford: Stanford UP, 1995.

Steinbock, Anthony J. "Surprise as Emotion: Between Startle and Humility". *Surprise: An Emotion?* Ed. Natalie Depraz and Anthony J. Steinbock. Cham: Springer, 2018. 3-21.

Watkins, John. "Against 'Normal Science'". *Criticism and the Growth of Knowledge*. Ed. Imre Lakatos and Alan Musgrave. Cambridge: Cambridge UP, 1970. 25-37.

Wiegman, Robyn. "Sex and Negativity; Or, What Queer Theory Has for You". *Cultural Critique* 95 (2017): 219-43.

Wolfe, Cary. *What is Posthumanism?* Minneapolis: University of Minnesota Press, 2010.

Wynn, Owen. "Order and Disorder in the Ottava Rima of Shelley and Byron". *Essays in Criticism* 67/1 (2017): 1-19.

Nicholas Roe

Transgressive Biography

Shortly before the publication of my biography *John Keats. A New Life* I was called by a journalist from the *Guardian* newspaper, asking for some new details about Keats for an article. I suggested some possibilities, and the journalist later called me back to say "we're going with opium" – I had mentioned Keats's opium habit as a "commonplace" in Regency England. The article appeared, "John Keats was an Opium Addict, claims a new biography of the poet" (Hill), and a few days later I received a curious email:

> Dear Professor: I have read of your book, and although I have not read it wanted to say that the Keats, I love was an English poet of nightingales and autumn gold, not opium. Why do you professorise on his poetry without enjoying it? …

What interests me about this is how the "detail" that I had supplied about opium and Keats's moods of indolence had irritated this person (I would have said "reader" except that they hadn't read the book). The episode focuses one of my concerns in this essay: how and why biography can appeal strongly to some readers and, simultaneously, offend others.

In her essay on "The Art of Biography", Virginia Woolf reminds us that "biography, compared with the arts of poetry and fiction, is a young art": "Interest in our selves and in other people's selves is a late development of the human mind. Not until the eighteenth century in England did that curiosity express itself in writing the lives of private people" (*Death of the Moth* 120). With Johnson's *Lives of the English Poets* and Boswell's *Life of Samuel Johnson* the eighteenth century witnessed a new genre emerging, and by the nineteenth century, Woolf contends, "biography [was] fully grown and prolific" (*Art of Biography* 120). Leon Edel, biographer of Henry James, cited Boswell's book as "the first great modern biography", and it was Boswell's concern for intimate personal life that signalled the new direction: in his book "what [Johnson] privately wrote, and said, and thought" make up a narrative that offers readers the "minute particulars" of Johnson's life (Boswell 4, 7).

Private. Minute. Particular. Those three words constitute what I call biography's transgressive allure, its doubled capacity to delight and also to disgust. And we keep on reading. Top of the Amazon US non-fiction bestsellers in September 2019 was a biography, Harold Schechter's *Hell's Princess: The Mystery of Belle Gunness, Butcher of Men*. According to the *NYRB* the book is a "deeply researched and morbidly fascinating chronicle of one of America's most notorious female killers" (Stasio). Not far behind was *An American Princess: The Many Lives of Allene Tew*, the biography of a rural all-American girl who, in the late 1900s, reinvented herself first as a high society New York doyenne and then as European royalty. According to Hilary Mantel, this book is so lightweight that it "dances through a century of history" (Mantel). I hasten to add that I have not read either of these bestsellers, nor will "mystery" and "many lives" entice me, although they have allowed me to put into play the phrase 'morbid fascination', a phrase that strikes closest to my concern in this essay. In a word, biographies have a strange capacity to enthral and appal us – but why should the private, the minute and the particular be of such searching interest yet also distasteful and even repulsive? What explains the transgressive allure of modern biography?

Biography's developing preoccupation with what Johnson called "domestick privacies" (*Rambler* 60), with an inner world of thoughts, feelings, and intuitions, is characteristic of what we might now recognize as a Romantic sensibility (*Rambler* 346). Modern biography is a Romantic genre, as Richard Holmes has often reminded us, and the popularity of biography was thought to be a regrettable characteristic of the age now associated with European Romanticism. In 1794 the *Critical Review* referred to "this time, when a taste for biography is more than usually prevalent" (*Critical Review* 83). Ten years later the *Annual Review* noted that "[t]here is no species of literature which has been received of late with such distinguished favour by the public as biography" (*Annual Review* 470). But not everyone was so keen. The author of *Lives of the Novelists* and *The Life of Napoleon Buonaparte* noted with alarm "a desire, or rather a rage, for literary anecdote and private history" (Scott 1:1). Coleridge deplored "the age of personality" as a form of "mania" (*Prefatory Observation* 339). John Lockhart noted with contempt that "England expects every driveller to do his Memorabilia", sneered at the public's "mania for this garbage of Confessions, and Recollections, and Reminiscences", and then put pen to paper and wrote his seven-volume *Memoirs of the Life of Sir Walter Scott* (*Quarterly Review* 149, 164).

Often poorly written, pretentious, and inaccurate, biography nevertheless continues to attract readers with its promise to reveal what has been kept from the public eye or otherwise off-limits – hidden, silenced, or suppressed. For about one hundred years biography has endeavoured to cut across, to deface, or to defamiliarize what we think we already know; its technique is to claim new perspectives, to present different angles, to offer fresh evidence, to deliver the "authentic" account: so Andrew Morton's notorious book, *Diana: Her True Story*, was said by its publisher to have "exposed life inside the royal family and [shaken] the Establishment to its foundations" (Blackwell's). Michael Wolff's *Fire and Fury: Inside the Trump White House* claims to deploy "off-the-record interviews" and "deep background material"; in Wolff's pages we will discover "the meaning of working for Donald Trump". We are told that Morton's story was "done in secret" and that Wolff's narrative is based upon "extraordinary access to the West Wing [and] what happened behind-the-scenes" (Ross; Wolff). Taken together these two books claim to reveal what is off-record, deep, behind-the-scenes, secret and, by implication, "true"; publishers know all too well that readers will relish the transgressive frisson and read on, spellbound or, better word, enthralled. But how did this come about? Clearly there is a continuity between Boswell writing of what Johnson did 'privately', and Wolff's "behind-the-scenes" in the Trump White House. But why in our self-absorbed and cynical times should biography continue to engage and unsettle?

One answer might be that in the age of Google, Selfies, Instagram, Wikileaks and Wiki-pedia, biography has an unrivalled potential to probe and to disclose complex human dimensions – at its best evoking a unique individuality that for centuries used to be identified with soul or spirit, be that virtuous, tarnished, tainted, or tormented. And this link with a Christian tradition that includes confessional narratives and spiritual diaries can, I think, help to explain why biography has always had a questionable and contro-versial aspect. This is perhaps primarily because biography claims to divine aspects of a self (deep, secret, hidden) that were formerly known only to God "unto whom all hearts be open, all desires known, and from whom no secrets are hid" (*Book of Common Prayer*). Instead, biography bids to open up all hearts, all desires, and all secrets for the delectation of its readers; in so doing it provokes curiosity and combines the delight of discovery with what might be described as a lingering dread of sacrilege, the thrill of the forbidden.

With some exceptions such as Godwin's *Memoirs* of Mary Wollstonecraft, eighteenth- and nineteenth-century life narratives tended to polish and protect, ignoring and over-looking so as to idealize, commemorating in what Lytton Strachey termed a "tone of tedious panegyric" (Strachey 6). As one would expect, the words alcohol, opium, lau-danum, passion, sex, transgress, transgressive and transgression are absent from Eliza-beth Gaskell's *Life of Charlotte Brontë*. The watchwords were "cover up" and "omit", and the result, as Virginia Woolf noted, was as often as not "biographies ... like the wax figures now preserved in Westminster Abbey ... effigies that have only a smooth super-ficial likeness to the body in the coffin" (*Art of Biography* 121). Wordsworth's French lover Annette Vallon was successfully kept from public knowledge for one hundred and twenty-five years, and Keats's relationship with Fanny Brawne was suppressed for fifty-seven years until their letters were published in 1878. Southey's *Life of Nelson* gives us the prevailing tone:

> The most triumphant death is that of the martyr; the most awful that of the martyred pa-triot; the most splendid that of the hero in the hour of victory: and if the chariot and the horses of fire had been vouchsafed for Nelson's translation, he could scarcely have de-parted in a brighter blaze of glory. He has left us, not indeed his mantle of inspiration, but a name and an example, which are at this hour inspiring thousands of the youth of Eng-land. (*The Life of Nelson* 2:274-75)

Needless to say, apart from a single glance at Nelson's "private feelings" for Emma Hamilton, their notorious affair goes without mention in Southey's book (*The Life of Nelson* 2:262)

But times change. In *The Silent Woman: Sylvia Plath and Ted Hughes*, Janet Malcolm says:

> The transgressive nature of biography is rarely acknowledged, but it is the only explana-tion for biography's status as a popular genre ... The reader's amazing tolerance ... makes sense only when seen as a kind of collusion [with] the biographer in an excitingly forbid-den undertaking: tiptoeing down the corridor together, to stand in front of the bedroom door and try to peep through the keyhole. (Malcolm 9)

There are several aspects of this extract that intrigue me: biography's invitation to collude in a "forbidden undertaking", and the stealthy endeavour to "peep through a keyhole" into another person's life – by implication, their sex life. The echoes of Book 9 of *Paradise Lost*, and Eve's "rash" collusion with Satan, are perhaps sufficiently evident: "Why then was this forbid? … / … in the day / Ye eat thereof, your eyes … / … shall perfectly be then / Opened and cleared" (*Paradise Lost* 9:703-08). Lucasta Miller approaches her new biography of Letitia Landon with the intention of opening eyes and clearing sight, aiming to challenge the nineteenth-century myth that Landon was "animated by the purest sense of duty"; that her "virtuous feeling and amiable temper" attracted "among the aristocracy … several persons dignified alike by virtue and talent, who delighted to call her friend" (Blanchard 1:282, 265, 273). Instead of "duty" and "virtue" Miller gives us a modern story: the teenage L.E.L. "gearing up for … mutual seduction" with her publisher William Jerdan, in a story that involves furtive confidences, voyeurism, illicit sex, serial illegitimacy, newspaper scandal, and a mysterious death in West Africa (Miller chap. 4)

As a modern literary biography, Miller's book ticks every box. With satanic tact, some biographers now tempt readers by promising to disclose the unexpected, the strange, the shocking, the illicit and the off-limits: Larkin's collection of pornography; the exhumation of Elizabeth Siddal; why Coleridge was "a loathsome bedfellow"; the "cruel streak" in Dorothy Wordsworth; Keats's opium habit, or Keats's venereal disease; Kipling's racism; Joyce's coprophilia; a glimpse of Swinburne sliding naked down a bannister, squealing "whip me!"; T.E. Lawrence's sado-masochism – and so on. What cannot be counted on, what cannot be guaranteed, however, is how reviews and readers will respond – how the balance between enthral and appal will tip. Jonathan Bate deliberately pitched his fine albeit "unauthorised" biography of Ted Hughes as (in part) a story of the poet's sexual sadism, detailing Hughes's sexual exploits on the night of Monday 11 February 1963 – that is, the night that Sylvia Plath committed suicide. Tasked with reviewing the book in the *Spectator* was Craig Raine, poet and a former poetry editor at Faber, the publisher of Hughes and Plath, to whom Bate's book was originally contracted before the Hughes estate withdrew its cooperation. The upshot was predictable – Raine went on the attack, and did so with such verbal relish it's clear that – whatever he might say to the contrary – Bate's book had him hooked (Raine). In our own times, it seems, biography continues to generate such curiously mingled responses – in Virginia Woolf's phrase, "anger and laughter mixed".

The phenomenon is not new. As early as April 1716 Joseph Addison had remarked that

> *Grub-street* Biographers, … watch for the death of a great man, like so many undertakers, on purpose to make a penny of him. He is no sooner laid in his grave, but he falls into the hands of an Historian; … This manner of exposing the private concerns of families and sacrificing the secrets of the dead to the curiosity of the living, is one of those licentious practices which might well deserve the animadversions of our Government. (*The Freeholder* 262-63)

Addison is playing here on two senses of the word "undertaker" – one whose concern is to arrange funerals and, secondly, a literary undertaker, or Grub-Street hack, who writes shilling lives to turn a penny. Another thread in this passage takes us closer to the concerns of this essay, in that Addison's idea of biography alludes to the transgressive business of grave-robbing to provide bodies for dissection in the medical schools. So, the "great man ... laid in his grave ... falls into the hands of an Historian" who then, as if anatomizing a body's inner organs on a dissection table, "exposes the private concerns ... and ... the secrets of the dead" in a grub-street biography.

As Addison suggests, there are curious parallels between biography and the anatomical tradition in western medical history. Eighteenth-century anatomical science increasingly saw human beings as autonomous individuals actuated by the physical organs of the body and subject to material contingencies of the world. The stakes were high, and vigorous quarrels continued into the following century in the "vitality debate" between John Abernethy and William Lawrence that provided the scientific hinterland for *Frankenstein*. The biographer's pen and the surgeon's scalpel were transgressive implements that helped invent a modern, secular idea of humanity, and biography's mission was to open up the life (as a surgeon anatomizes a body) to disclose its human significance. To that endeavour can, I think, be traced biography's potential to appeal and offend.

One hundred years after Addison, Robert Southey also objected to biographical resurrection and the consequent degradation of "greatness". "Great men of every description are in ... danger from their biographers", Southey contends, "a race of Resurrection-men against whom neither laws nor patent coffins afford any protection. ... [T]hese hungry flesh-flies ... collect, enshrine, and hold out to public view all that ought to have been laid ... in the grave" (*Biography* 2:233-34). From the early eighteenth century, Southey suggests, ideas of bodily resurrection, dissection, and display – an appalling process, for most people the stuff of nightmares – have provided a figurative analogy for the biographer's investigative methods. A sense of grotesque bodily violation was carried over from the sphere of anatomy to infect biography, and the idea of biography as a contaminated art has persisted to this day.

We can see now why Addison and Southey both imply that what the biographer will produce is not an ideal likeness of a "great" subject, but a narrative that will stand in "horrid contrast" to what was intended – much as the creature Victor Frankenstein created as "beautiful" turned out to be a disfigured "wretch" (Shelley 39). Like Victor raiding the vaults and charnel houses, biography takes what "ought to have been laid ... in the grave" as material from which to create its subject. The result, Addison and Southey imply, is the equivalent of Victor's "breathless horror and disgust" as he contemplates the monstrous creature that he has brought to life.

So it is that like the resurrection men, like Victor Frankenstein, biographers have long been associated with what is off-limits, forbidden, or taboo – even though the manner of eighteenth- and nineteenth-century life writing was largely eulogistic. The twentieth century, by contrast, brought an alteration in the temper and texture of life narratives –

a willingness to test boundaries that earlier generations would have been reluctant to transgress. It may not be a coincidence that George McLean Harper's book revealing Wordsworth's relationship with Annette Vallon was published in 1918, the year in which modern biography was invented by Lytton Strachey's *Eminent Victorians*. With the First World War at an end, the time was right for a fresh conflict on a different front: the modern biographer, Strachey writes, "will attack his subject in unexpected places; he will fall upon the flank, or the rear; he will shoot a sudden, revealing searchlight into obscure recesses ..." (Strachey 5). From now on biography would leap out of its bunker, on the offensive, assertively transgressive and, as Strachey implies, going in for the kill "to show them as they really were".

With its new liberties biography's revisionary campaign extended to matters of form, for instance in fracturing conventional "cradle to grave" or "womb to tomb" narratives; biographers have devised narratives that begin midway through; that focus on a single year; or that view the subject through possessions or personal effects (this last in the wake of Neil MacGregor's phenomenally successful *History of the World in a Hundred Objects*). While there might be reasons to avoid chronology in lives where little is known about the subject – Shakespeare is a good example – or where there are significant periods of silence – Jane Austen, for instance – there is often a good case for keeping a more traditional narrative as, for instance, in Richard Holmes's masterpiece *Shelley: The Pursuit*.

Holmes interweaves biography and pathology in his technique of 'foot-stepping' that is, painstakingly following his subject as it moves through its life-places and landscapes: "the serious biographer", Holmes tells us, must

> physically pursue his subject ... Not just the birth-place, or the blue-plaque place, but the temporary places, the lost places, the dream places ... looking for clues, for the visible and the invisible. He must feel how they once were ... must be alert to "unknown modes of being". He must step back, step down, step inside the story. (Holmes 2016, 5, 6)

Wordsworth's "dim and undetermined sense / Of unknown modes of being" was won through transgression, arising, Wordsworth tells us, after "an act of stealth / And troubled pleasure" had animated the landscape such that "like a living thing" it "[s]trode after him" (*Prelude* 1805, 1:419-20; 388-89; 411-12). By implication, then, a biographer who is "alert to 'unknown modes of being'" is also aware of the transgressive potential of his or her art and, furthermore, that footstepping may lead into uncanny territory where a seemingly familiar subject acquires a strange and alienated presence.

Holmes's forensic endeavour to "step inside the story" also had an earlier currency, as Addison's idea of the biographer/surgeon has already suggested. As biography was an eighteenth-century invention, so, too, did autopsy come of age during that century with Giovanni Morgagni's 1761 treatise *On the Seats and Causes of Diseases as Investigated by Anatomy* – a foundational text of modern anatomical pathology. During the 1830s, both biographical and surgical modes of "stepping inside" were implicated in the development of Coleridge's biography. Aware of biography's pathological energies, Coleridge sought to rebuff accusations that "'all his complaints are owing to the use of opium'": "my Complaints", Coleridge explained, "were antecedent to my unfortunate (but, God knows! most innocent) Resort to that Palliative" and, with an eye to posterity, he expressed a wish "to be present while my Viscera [are] laid open!" (*Letters of Samuel Taylor Coleridge* 3:578). When, eventually, Coleridge's body was dissected, the inside story revealed heart failure and lung disease but little evidence that laudanum addiction caused physical damage that had led to his death – a discovery that had some remarkable consequences. It enabled Coleridge's first biographer, James Gillman, to polish Coleridge's life as a model of "extraordinary patience and resignation" in confronting "disease" with various stimulants: Coleridge "*began* the use of opium from bodily pain (rheumatism), and for the same reason continued it" – he was thus "an object of commiseration and interest" (Gillman 172, 245, 271). In *Coleridge: Early Visions* Richard Holmes tells approximately the same story, but adds some Coleridgean details that Gillman had left in silence: in Holmes's version of the life we hear of Coleridge's

> … rheumatic fevers, swollen leg joints, boils, agonising nephritic pains, … a swollen testicle … labyrinthine literary schemes, shadowy metaphysical castles … pain and anxiety … prostration and procrastination … the Disgust and Loathing, … & no doubt in part too the use of Brandy & Laudanum which they rendered necessary … (Holmes 1989, 297, 298).

Holmes's brilliant evocation of Coleridge's addiction updates Gillman's while also remaining dependent on an autopsy that had taken place at Highgate back in 1834.

Foot-stepping into a life can provide shape and structure, the life and its narrative sequenced as a journey; equally, however, foot-stepping can lead the biographer astray as in the wayward narrative of *Tristram Shandy* when Tristram discovers that his determination to trace the intricacies of cause and effect means that he is living 365 times faster than he can write. Telling the story of his life and opinions will literally be the death of him. It was more than a Shandean irony that shortly after his burial Sterne's body was disinterred and sold to a Professor of Anatomy at Cambridge for dissection. In one account Sterne's skull was said to have remained at Cambridge, prompting his nineteenth-century biographer, Percy Fitzgerald, to remark: "there were people who might have taken the skull of a second Yorick into their hand, as the Prince of Denmark did that of the first, and have moralised over it sadly. They might have thought of his life, [and] weighed his character … as I have striven to do in this memoir to the best of my ability" (Fitzgerald 2:408-09). Once again, a biographer is depicted contemplating the skull, not the author of 'life narrative' but – like Tristram, like Hamlet – a "historian of death", whose footsteps have led to the edge of an opened grave. The idea of "weighing character" is also, I think, a knowing allusion to autopsy, and the weighing of internal bodily organs during a post-mortem.

One lesson of Sterne's book is that at some point, a biographer must decide what thresholds not to cross, what steps not to take, what paths not to pursue. The imperative is to select and arrange material to form a coherent narrative. The most basic narrative option might be "this happened and then that happened" – and there are books that proceed as if life is a mechanical process; a more sophisticated narrative will deploy colour, imagery, music, weather – a kind of poetry – to orchestrate the effect of life lived within a web of chance. In its doomed attempt to capture cause and effect in Tristram's "Life and Opinions", Sterne's narrative becomes more and more distracted, further and further from the "inside story" it is attempting to tell. In so doing, it presents an ironic commentary on an age preoccupied by the systematic arrangement of knowledge in books like Burton's *Anatomy of Melancholy*, the French *Encyclopédie*, Linnaeus's *Systema Naturae*, Johnson's Dictionary, and the *Encyclopaedia Britannica*. Eighteenth-century anatomists, likewise, were attempting a systematic explanation of what was called "the vital principle": they dissected and displayed the organic mechanisms of a human body – brain, heart, lungs, muscles, veins, blood – in an endeavour to understand the inside story of life, although the fundamental cause, the essential "vivifying principle" – be it soul, spark, or what John Thelwall called "a something" – remained as elusive as the completion of *Tristram Shandy* (Thelwall 20-21). Leibniz had tried to solve the anatomists' dilemma by positing the body as a kind of "divine machine"; William Blake offered a Romantic counter-intuition, "everything that lives is holy". In this way the eighteenth-century culture of physical anatomy was accompanied by intense debate about a "vital principle" that was analogous to and as elusive as the "inside story" that Richard Holmes identifies as the goal of the modern biographer. Does vitality arise from "the mighty power of God, that made the mountains rise" in Isaac Watts's hymn? Or from an invisible all-pervading medium? – Christopher Smart's "Electrical fire ... which God sends from heaven to sustain the bodies both of man and beast" ("For I will consider my cat Jeoffry"); Shelley's "secret strength of things" ("Mont Blanc"); Coleridge's "creative Deity" that "Roll[s] thro' the ... material mass / In organizing surge!" ("Religious Musings"); Wordsworth's mysterious "motion and spirit" ("Tintern Abbey"). Or, is life contingent merely on the material arrangement of body parts, what Mary Wollstonecraft daringly and dangerously described as "organized dust" (Wollstonecraft 97)?

Vitality, as Denise Gigante remarks, was "the distinguishing feature, of Romantic aesthetics" (Gigante 4), and I want to suggest that Romantic biography also reflects vitalist arguments in its organization of material particulars, what Samuel Johnson called "minute history", in its perilous quest to re-animate an individual – to make its subject seem to live again in a life narrative. The problem of this endeavour, for eighteenth-century anatomists and biographers alike, was that it risked the stigma of atheism: if life is indeed the contingency of "organised dust", and life-narrative an amalgam of minute circumstances and "privacies", the role of a fundamental cause – God – disappears. This, I think, is the horror that lurked in Addison's and Southey's identification of biographers as resurrection men who treated "the secrets of the dead" as material goods to be sold on; and if that was true more than two centuries ago, we can see the same dynamic informing responses to modern biographies.

Particulars, privacies, and minute history have been a preserve of biography since Johnson's time, yet they have also exacted a penalty. According to the *OED*, "minuteness" registers progressive insignificance, becoming "trifling", "tedious" and "despicable" –

literally "to be looked down upon". Godwin's *Memoirs of the Author of a Vindication of the Rights of Woman* tells of Wollstonecraft's "ardent affection" for Henry Fuseli; her "[giving] loose to all the sensibilities of her nature"; her civil "certificate" of connection with Imlay; her "cool and deliberate" suicide attempt; and finally her marriage to the anti-matrimonial philosopher, William Godwin (Godwin 90, 108, 114, 157). The reviews were, perhaps, only to be expected: "It will be read with disgust", opined the *European Magazine*, "by every female who has any pretensions to delicacy; with detestation by everyone attached to the interests of religion and morality; and with indignation by anyone who might feel any regard for the unhappy woman, whose frailties should have been buried in oblivion". This review also cautioned readers about the "very minute, and in some particulars ... disgusting, narrative ... of her illness" (Anon. *European Magazine* 251). A letter to *The Gentleman's Magazine* complained that Godwin "minutely marks the various events of her life ... [disclosing] *some circumstances* which one might have supposed delicacy would have prompted him to conceal" ('Philaletes' 186-87), and *The Monthly Review* noted that "the particulars of her death [are related] with more than necessary minuteness (Anon. *The Monthly Review* 324). If detail was disgusting in 1798, it continues to be controversial in our own time: Kenneth Johnston's *The Hidden Wordsworth: Poet, Lover, Rebel, Spy* was censured by Jonathan Bate in the *Sunday Telegraph* not for its daringly speculative account of the poet, but because of what Bate termed the book's "extreme minuteness" (Bate).

Why should "minute particulars", "details of daily life", "incidents" and "domestic Privacies" have proved so detestably, so disgustingly more than necessary? The explanation may have less to do with the material in Godwin's book than with the seventeenth-century's discovery of the "minute". "Working downwards", Addison remarks, the imagination contemplates a dizzying recession of minuteness that ultimately baffles its powers in "endeavouring after the idea of an Atome". The "Immensity of the Void" so revealed, Addison says, might be "capable of being spun out into another Universe", in which with Gulliverian logic the "smallest particle" might appear immense while the "greatest object" can attain atomic minuteness. Hitherto invisible lifeforms were discovered through microscopes, and telescopes revealed new planets and the vastness of the heavens: human beings were correspondingly diminished, rendered insignificant, suspended in an atomized universe that Addison feared might be a "void". When the *European Magazine* said that Godwin's *Memoirs* would be read "with detestation by everyone attached to the interests of religion and morality" (251) it captured the transgressive modernity of Godwin's book but omitted to explain the implications of Godwin's minutely materialistic narrative: Mary Wollstonecraft had been anatomized, and atomized, by her biographer.

What I have been doing so far is to sketch some intellectual and cultural backdrops to the rise and reception of modern biography, to try to explain why the form has often seemed so appealing and yet simultaneously so offensively transgressive. I have also attempted to suggest how in particular instances, as with Addison's and Southey's remarks, and in the reception of Godwin's *Memoirs*, biographies have tapped into much deeper causes, anxieties, and fears that may be related, I have argued, to controversial material understandings of humankind: the entwining of biography and the anatomical tradition illustrates this particularly strikingly.

Biographers go to a poet's life in an endeavour to explain the works that flowed from it; so, Coleridge's opium addiction may help decode the imagery of "Kubla Khan", and Keats's birth at Moorfields in the City of London can explain his so-called "cockney" rhymes. But Keats himself saw things differently, preferring to find in a poet's works a figurative representation of the life. So, he heard in Burns's passionately humane poems the voice of an abundant genius who had been constrained by the circumstances of his life – "he talked with Bitches – he drank with Blackguards, he was miserable – We can see horribly clear in the works of such a man his whole life" (Keats *Letters* 1:325). In much the same manner, the extraordinary volubility of Keats's poetry was sounded out of a life of strangled possibilities – orphaned, fractured, disappointed, often despondent, depressive in some extremes of his moods. The full Keatsian music, all bosomy ripeness, was sounded from a dissonant and diminished actuality, and it is in this sense, not in any Cockney cockiness, that Keats's poetry is most compellingly transgressive as the signature of a poet who had no public voice. The biographer's task is to try to feel into a life adequate to a poet's words, to the sound of their poetry – hence, perhaps, many poets' reluctance to account for their art; hence too, perhaps, Seamus Heaney's vigilance in policing biography with the interviews in *Stepping Stones* that run to some 470 pages. That's the authorized Heaney, and Heaney's authorized biographer, Fintan O'Toole, has already been commissioned: one wonders who will be brave enough to write an unauthorized life of Seamus Heaney and step around the substantial palisade that the poet has put in place.

I want to finish by offering a few reflections on my own experiences as a biographer. I came to Keats through writing about him in my biography of Leigh Hunt, and my starting point was the pattern of rising and falling that often appears in his poems. This alternating movement is there in the earliest surviving Keats poem that we have, his "Imitation of Spenser": the sun rises as a rill of water "did down distill"; the king-fisher looks down to see its plumage reflected "below", as light from the "golden scales" of fish is "Cast [light] upward"; "on high, / ... [are] clouds of fleecy white" while "Slopings of verdure" dip "luxuriously" (Keats *Poems* 27-28). In "Sleep and Poetry" we encounter "A laughing school-boy ... / Riding the springy branches of an elm" (rising and falling as he does so) and in "To Autumn" are "the small gnats ... / ... borne aloft / Or sinking as the light wind lives or dies". The "Sleep and Poetry" moment is bright and energetic – quite literally springy; the one in "To Autumn" is elegiac and autumnal. I wanted to read these lines back into the life of their poet, by presenting a more vigorous yet also a more moody – even bipolar – Keats than I thought had been on offer in existing biographies of him. Hardly a transgressive aim, although it did in fact prove so.

I adopted for my own narrative the feckless orphan, "five feet hight", who Geoffrey Matthews once claimed was a "classic case history of a delinquent" – that is, from the

Latin *dēlinquĕre*, meaning failed, lacking, at fault, offensive, and guilty (Matthews 28). In a word: transgressive. Delinquent Keats had been brought up in a murky underworld of financial speculation, sexual intrigue, dodgy property deals, booze, quarrels, drugs, disease and madness. His mother was a man-hungry teenager; his father – one could never be sure – was a livery-stable manager on the make. Their eldest son John Keats, the school bully, grew into a Hampstead whorehound, an opium-addled dandy who dressed like Lord Byron, scribbled bawdy rhymes, got burned by gonorrhoea and poisoned himself with mercury. Delinquent Keats was in the front row at bloody prize-fights – a prohibited sport – and he measured his "reach" as a poet like a boxer landing a punch.

Nothing in that portrait is fictional. Every detail arises in Keats's letters or contemporary accounts of him, where we can also discover contrary aspects of his personality – the Keats who could sink into indecision, unresponsive, in a hurry to be gone. While there is some correspondence between Keats's delinquency and his impatience with what he called the "French" school of poetry, his most distinctive poetry emerged from a strange mingling of delinquent energy and diffidence – his poems are so linguistically and formally transgressive (we might say, original) that they enraged critics while the poet himself often doubted his own capacity to succeed.

Here then, was the embodiment of Keats's bipolar temperament that I had detected in the rising and falling dynamic of the poems: the poet's art read back into the life. These emotional extremes and instabilities may be traced to his parents' untimely deaths and earlier tragedies and insecurities, and we can sense how those formative losses may have shaped the intense ambition and forlorn awareness of his poems. Beyond those events, however, Keats's power as a poet has seemed to draw upon circumstances sealed-off in his childhood and lost to posterity. Keats's letters mean that we know a great deal about much of his life, sometimes with day-to-day and even hour-by-hour precision, but there are still significant gaps and puzzles. It is very difficult to say anything new about Keatsian matters that are already familiar, however minute and particular they may be. As a consequence, I started to investigate patterns of behaviour that informed his creative life and might provide a structure for my own narrative from within the story I was attempting to tell.

As a boy he had lived on an edge where the metropolis of London merged with surrounding meadows and market gardens. At the beginning of his story Thomas Keates, his father, was killed in a riding accident – a formative loss to which Keats would return as he set out in April 1817 to begin *Endymion*. Thomas's son grew up in villages at Edmonton and Enfield in a changeful landscape that allowed him to find a voice for his unsettled, orphaned nature. Time after time Keats ventured across this edgy suburban terrain, finding in its most unconsidered corners material for his poems – a shadowy brook, a minnow, sugary cherries, snail-horns, sounds of footsteps on gravel, a gold-finch, puddles in rain, a broken bottle. Throughout his life he was drawn to summits and shorelines, streams, beaches, chasms, and caverns. I began the book with Keats waking up one morning in July 1818 amid a wild fastness of crags, rocks, and rivers in Glen More, remotest heartland of the Isle of Mull; at the end of his story, death delays coming to him at Rome until late on Friday 23 February, the Roman festival of *Terminalia*, sacred to the limits and extremities the poet had so often sought and created from. In such landscapes, and at such searching extremities, Keats's bi-polar patterns of intense activity, lethargy and inertia found their appropriate places. No longer confined to Cockney coteries, my Keats is a creature drawn to edges and peripheries, glimpsed, as he tells us, "round many western islands".

Water provides a connecting image that flows through my narrative from the stream Keats heard while breakfasting at the "Mansion" Derry-na-Cullen on Mull to the "writ in water" on his gravestone (Keats *Letters* 1:346-47). "[P]lenty of Water thank heaven" was his comment on Oxford, where he was writing the third book of *Endymion* (Keats *Letters* 1:149). *The Eve of St Agnes* was composed on an island between fresh water and sea water at the Old Mill House in Bedhampton, a watery situation that seemed to me to suggest the contrasts and oppositions that colour and animate that poem, and also, incidentally, some of the mingled sweet and salt of Keats's life situation in January 1819.

Finally, I became fascinated by Keats's lunary instinct: his poems repeatedly invoke the sun and moon, planets and stars, and constellations from his early sonnet "To my Brother George" to the "Dian skies" and "maturing sun" of "To Autumn". His proof corrections for *Endymion* followed the lunar cycle, with corrected copy for each book of the poem dispatched from Teignmouth at the full moon.

None of this was of any purpose to the *Guardian* journalist asking for interesting new details about Keats. They opted for Keats and opium despite my pointing-out that a laudanum habit was commonplace at the time and had little transgressive relish. Far stranger, I think, are the details of Keats's moods and his edginess, his attraction to watery places, and his susceptibility to "the Queen Moon". It may be, then, that the transgressive nature of biography is no longer to be found in exposing details of sexuality, addiction, disease, sado-masochism and the like, but in more occult 'terrain' such as moods and moon phases, the sun, planets, and stars, tidal ebb and flow, astrology and other agencies of a secret or mysterious nature. And my surgical-anatomical analogy for biography holds true for this new transgressive allure: an occult disease is hidden, concealed, unaccompanied by readily discernible signs or symptoms. Century by century physicians and anatomists have invented new surgical methods and techniques, so it may seem likely that biographers will adopt new methods for inquiring into "secrets of the dead" of which we currently have, perhaps, little or no apprehension.

Works Cited

Addison, Joseph. *The Freeholder* 35, 20 April 1716.

Anon. "Chalmers' Life of Ruddiman". *The Critical Review; or, Annals of Literature.* London: Simpkin and Marshall, 1794. 83-89.

---. "Godwin's Memoir of Mrs. Godwin". *The Monthly Review; or Literary Journal.* London: R. Griffiths, 1798. 321-24.

---. "Memoirs of the Author of a Vindication of the Rights of Woman". *European Magazine, and London Review*. London: J. Fielding, 1798. 246-51.

---. "Biography and Correspondence". *The Annual Review, and History of Literature; for 1804.* London: Longman and Rees, 1805. 470.

---. "Autobiography". *The Quarterly Review* 35, January. London: John Murray, 1827. 148-65.

Bate, Jonathan. "Did the Poet Wander Lonely as a Spy?" *Daily Telegraph*, 11 July 1998. London: Telegraph Media Group.

Blackwell's. "Publisher's Synopsis". https://blackwells.co.uk/bookshop/product/Diana-by-Andrew-Morton-author/9781843177159 (accessed 25 June 2020).

Blanchard, Laman. *Life and Literary Remains of L.E.L.* 2 vols. London: Colburn, 1841.

Book of Common Prayer. "The Collect. The Lord's Supper or Holy Communion". https://www.churchofengland.org/prayer-and-worship/worship-texts-and-resources/book-common-prayer/lords-supper-or-holy-communion (accessed 9 June 2020).

Boswell, James. *The Life of Samuel Johnson, LL.D.* 5 vols. London: Baldwin and Dilly, 1791.

Coleridge, Samuel Taylor. "A Prefatory Observation on Modern Biography". *The Friend; A Literary, Moral and Political Weekly Paper.* Penrith: J. Brown, 1810. 337-40.

---. *Letters of Samuel Taylor Coleridge.* Ed. Earl Leslie Griggs. 5 vols. Oxford: Oxford UP, 1956-71.

Fitzgerald, Percy. *The Life of Laurence Sterne.* 2 vols. London: Chapman and Hall, 1864.

Gigante, Denise. *Life: Organic Form and Romanticism.* New Haven and London: Yale UP, 2009.

Gill, Stephen. *William Wordsworth.* Oxford: Oxford UP, 2010.

Gillman, James. *The Life of Samuel Taylor Coleridge.* London: William Pickering, 1838.

Godwin, William. *Memoirs of the Author of a Vindication of the Rights of Woman.* London: Johnson and Robinson, 1798.

Hill, Amelia. "John Keats was an opium addict, claims a new biography of the poet". *The Guardian Online*, 21 September 2012. https://www.theguardian.com/books/2012/sep/21/john-keats-opium-addict (accessed 18 June 2020).

Holmes, Richard. *Coleridge. Early Visions.* London: Hodder and Stoughton, 1989.

---. *This Long Pursuit: Reflections of a Romantic Biographer.* London: Pantheon, 2016.

Johnson, Samuel. "The Dignity and Usefulness of Biography". *The Rambler* 60, Saturday, October 13, 1750. 3 vols. London: Rivington, 1816. 1:343-48.

Keats, John. *The Letters of John Keats, 1814-1821.* Ed. Hyder Edward Rollins. 2 vols. Cambridge, MA: Harvard UP, 1972

---. *The Poems of John Keats.* Ed. Jack Stillinger. London: Heinemann, 1978.

Lockhart, John. *Memoirs of the Life of Sir Walter Scott.* 7 vols. Edinburgh: R. Cadell, 1837-38.

Malcolm, Janet. *The Silent Woman: Sylvia Plath and Ted Hughes.* London: Granta, 1995.

Mantel, Hilary. "Best Books of 2018". *The Guardian,* 3 December 2018. https://www.theguardian.com/books/2018/dec/03/best-books-of-2018-hilary-mantel-yuval-noah-harari-and-more-pick-their-favourites (accessed 25 August 2020).

Matthews, Geoffrey. "The Living Keats." *New York Review of Books.* 7 November 1968. 28.

Miller, Lucasta. *L.E.L.: The Lost Life and Scandalous Death of Letitia Elizabeth Landon, the Celebrated 'Female Byron'.* London: Jonathan Cape, 2019.

Milton, John. *The Poems of John Milton.* Ed. John Carey and Alastair Fowler. London and New York: Longman, 1980.

Morton, Andrew. *Diana: Her True Story.* https://books.google.co.uk/books/about/Diana.html?id=sibdAgAAQBAJ&redir_esc=y (accessed 9 June 2020).

'Philalethes'. "Remarks on the Life of Mrs. Godwin". *The Gentleman's Magazine and Historical Chronicle.* London: John Nichols, 1798. 186-87.

Raine, Craig. "Poet as Predator". *The Spectator,* 3 October 2015.

Ross, Deborah. "Interview: Andrew Morton". https://www.independent.co.uk/life-style/interview-andrew-morton-he-couldnt-shout-diana-was-in-on-this-she-trusted-me-it-would-have-been-a-1286288.html (accessed 9 June 2020).

Shelley, Mary. *Frankenstein or The Modern Prometheus, the 1818 Text.* Ed. Marilyn Butler. Oxford: Oxford UP, 2008.

Southey, Robert. "Biography". *Omniana, or Horæ Otiosiores.* London: Longman, Hurst, Rees, Orme, and Brown, 1812.

---. *The Life of Nelson.* London: John Murray, 1813.

Stasio, Marilyn. "True Crime". *The New York Times Summer Reading,* 1 June 2018. https://www.nytimes.com/interactive/2018/books/review/summer-reading-true-crime.html (accessed 25 August 2020).

Strachey, Lytton. *Eminent Victorians.* Ed. John Sutherland. Oxford: Oxford UP, 2003.

Thelwall, John. *An Essay Towards the Definition of Animal Vitality.* London: Robinson, Debrett, and Cox, 1793.

Wolff, Michael. *Fire and Fury: Inside the Trump White House*. https://books.google.co.uk/books/about/Fire_and_Fury.html?id=E3M-DwAAQBAJ&redir_esc=y (accessed 9 June 2020).

Wollstonecraft, Mary. *Letters Written During a Short Residence in Sweden, Norway, and Denmark*. London: Johnson, 1796.

Woolf, Virginia. "The Art of Biography". *The Death of the Moth and Other Essays*. London: Reader's Union, 1943.

---. *The Death of the Moth and Other Essays*. London: Reader's Union, 1943.

Wordsworth, William. *The Prelude*. Ed. Stephen Gill. Oxford: Oxford UP, 2010.

Kasahara Yorimichi

Croly's Dying Warrior: The Roman Gladiator That Crossed the Boundary and Turned into Arminius

Byron's Dying Gladiator in *Childe Harold's Pilgrimage*, Canto 4 (hereafter *CHP* 4) is undoubtedly one of the highlights of the entire poem. Yet it should not blind us to the fact that there are other Dying Gladiator poems produced in the English Romantic period. William Hayley, George Robert Chinnery, Felicia Hemans, and William Sotheby, for example, all made poems or lines based on the statue of *Dying Gaul* or *Gladiator*, now housed in the Capitoline Museums in Rome (Kasahara 44-48). Seen in this context, Byron's Dying Gladiator may be just one of them. George Croly's Dying Warrior, too, is yet another. But it is unique in several points. First, his Dying Warrior in *Paris in 1815*, as its title suggests, captures the statue when it was on display in the Louvre as one of the trophies of Napoleon's conquest of Continental Europe. What makes Croly's descriptions further unique is its model. The man who is now about to die is not a gladiator fighting in the Roman coliseum. It is Arminius or, as some Germans later came to call him, Hermann,[1] who, at the head of the anti-Roman alliance, fought fierce battles against Roman legions led by Varus in the Teutoburg Forest in the year AD 9. What I aim to do in this article is first to give a brief biographical sketch of the poet Croly, along with an overview of the poem. I will then, in the next section, devote a few paragraphs to the close reading of the earlier version of Croly's stanzas on this Germanic hero, and compare it with the later version. These two versions happen to cross the chronological border of 1818, the year when *CHP* 4 was published: the earlier version written before 1818, and the other after. By so doing, I hope to see the significance of Croly's transgression of the 1818 borderline on his revision of his picture of this ancient Germanic hero who crossed the boundary geographically, chronologically and thematically.

Croly's Life and an Overview of *Paris in 1815* (1817)

For George Croly, who was born in Dublin in 1780, educated at Harrow, then at Trinity College, Dublin, the crossing of boundaries seemed nothing out of the ordinary. In 1804 he was ordained in the Church of Ireland, but soon abandoning the clerical profession, crossed the Irish Sea once again, this time with his two unmarried sisters and his mother – now a widow – and settled in London. By 1813, says David Hanson in the *Oxford*

---

1   Since Croly uses no particular name in the poem, nor in the endnote, I will, throughout the present article, use the name "Arminius" which the Kalkriese Museum adopts to refer to this hero. One of the originators of "Hermann" is Martin Luther. See footnote 4 below.

Dictionary of National Biography, the only reliable source available today, Croly had emerged as a theatre critic for *The Times* (Hanson).

In April 1813 *The Times* assigned him as a foreign correspondent to Hamburg and Paris. The crossing of the English Channel and the French-German boundaries seems to have served as a basic formative experience to the composition of *Paris in 1815.* It gave him chances to see and feel what was actually happening on the Continent just when the Congress danced, or the Vienna System was being contemplated for the post-Napoleonic balance of power in Europe. Croly was fortunate enough to be a living witness to all that took place in the French capital from the time when the French army lost the Battle of Waterloo in June 1815, all through the time when the Louvre was being cleared of Napoleon's trophies once looted from all over Europe. He wrote the First Part of *Paris in 1815* and had it published anonymously by John Murray's in 1817 (hereafter abbreviated as *P 1815* (1817) 1).

This is a poem in which the poet narrator pays visits to various places in the city and makes outspoken Byronic comments here and there, just like those in *CHP*. The poem begins as the poet places himself upon a vantage ground, like the narrating poets of eighteenth-century prospect poems. The narrator first goes up Montmartre, overlooks St Cloud, Sèvres, Meudon, and other villages, and goes on to describe what he sees with meditative comments. Here is one of these views:

> The gale has come, at once the fleecy haze
> Floats up, – then stands a purple canopy,
> Shading th' imperial city from the blaze.
> Glorious the vision! tower and temple lie
> Beneath the morn, like waves of ivory,
> With many an azure streak and gush of green,
> As grove and garden on the dazzled eye
> Rise in successive beauty, and between
>   Flows into sudden light the long, slow, serpent Seine. (*P 1815* (1817) 1:14.1-9)

> For Paris now. – Now farewell hill and vale,
> And silence sweet, fresh blooms, and dewy sky!
> Farewell the gentle moral of the gale,
> The wisdom written in the rose's dye!
> I go to meet the wizard city's eye,
> That puts on splendour but to dim the soul.
> A thousand years of crime beneath me lie!
> One glance! – I stand as on a mighty mole,
>   Around whose base not waves, but evil ages roll. (*P 1815* (1817) 1:15.1-9)

Here Croly first presents the view of the "imperial city" against the backgrounds of a quick succession of changing weather, contrasting it with the unmoving "tower and temple" – reminiscent of Wordsworth's prospect of London in "Composed upon Westminster Bridge, Sept. 3, 1802" (Wordsworth 147). He then concludes Stanza 14 with the moral sinuousness of the Seine, again, contrasting it with Wordsworth's tranquillity of the Thames in the same sonnet. In Stanza 15, Croly goes on to parody Byron's meditation upon the Rhine in *CHP* 3, making the waves roll against the base as "evil ages", instead of "wash[ing] down the blood of yesterday" (*CHP* 3:51.5). Very Byronic indeed. But how quick Croly is to catch the best of Byron from *CHP* 3, published in November 1816, and incorporate it into the 1817 edition of *Paris in 1815*!

What makes Croly's Byronism different from that of *CHP*, however, is that his comments are mainly made from anti-revolutionary and pro-English viewpoints supporting Church-and-State. In other words, it is a conservative version of *CHP*. Here is another example: the poet, descending Montmartre (*P 1815* (1817) 1:22.1), takes a worm's-eye view of the city, and pays a visit to a gorgeous mass held at Notre-Dame, saying, "Low at the altar, forms in cope and hood / Superb with gold-wrought cross and diamond twine, / As in the pile – alone with life endued, / Toss their untiring censers round the shrine, / Where on her throne of clouds the Virgin sits divine" (*P 1815* (1817) 1:43.5-9), and comments later:

> Gorgeous! – but love I not such pomp of prayer;
> Ill bends the heart 'mid mortal luxury.
> Rather let me the meek devotion share,
> Where, in their silent glens and thickets high,
> England, thy lone and lowly chapels lie.
> The spotless table by the eastern wall,
> The marble, rudely traced with names gone by,
> The pale-eyed pastor's simple, fervent call;
>   Those deeper wake the heart, where heart is all in all. (*P 1815* (1817) 1:45.1-9)

True, it is a conservative version of *CHP*, but one does not have to be "a staunch de-fender of Church and King" with "the Tory viewpoint" as Reiman characterizes the poet in his "Introduction" to Garland's facsimile edition of *Paris in 1815* (Reiman v) to cher-ish this love of "lone and lowly chapels" of the English countryside (though Croly is of Irish origin). Those who can sympathize with Gray's "rude Forefathers of the hamlet" in his "Elegy Written in a Country Church Yard" (Gray 38) will not fail to appreciate the humble dignity of "[t]he marble, rudely traced with names gone by".

The volume of *Paris in 1815* as published in 1817 carries no mention of its being the "First Part" on the title page, but ends as "The End of the First Part". This suggests that Croly, who had started the poem with a single-volume plan, began entertaining the idea of continuing it towards the final stage of printing, and had just time enough to add a few words at the end. In fact, Croly himself states in the "Preface" to the 1821 edition (hereafter abbreviated as *P 1815* (1821) 2) that he had continued writing a "considerable number of stanzas", which were meant to be published immediately following the 1817 edition, but some causes that were "unimportant to the reader" delayed its publication (*P 1815* (1821) 2: Preface iii). He further comments that he mentions the circumstance "only to avoid the appearance of plagiarism", and continues, "[t]he lines on the Louvre Statues, and Pictures, were written before the publication of that Canto of *Childe Har-old*, in which the same subjects are described" (*P 1815* (1821) 2: Preface iii). It was in this 1821 edition that the Dying Warrior stanzas were first published as part of the Second Part of *Paris in 1815*.[2]

The 1821 Edition and After

In the Second Part of *Paris in 1815* published in 1821, the poet becomes more liberated from the constraints of actual time and place. He becomes ekphrastic and gives descriptions of works of art amassed in the French capital. He first speaks of *The Triumphal Quadriga*, or the Roman bronze statue of horses, then temporarily placed on the Arc Triomphe de Carrousel in Paris, now returned to St Mark's Basilica in Venice. The works of art in the Louvre he mentions are, in the order of the poem, Guido Reni's *Penitence of St Peter*, Raphael's *Transfiguration*, Titian's *Peter Martyr*, Correggio's *The Marriage of St Catherine*, and statues of *Apollo Belvedere*, the *Laocoön* Group, *Dying Gladiator*, and *Venus de Medici*. The poet then touches upon the public execution of King Louis XVI, Napoleon's Russian campaign and his retreat in the harsh winter of 1812, his exile on St Helena, his defeat at Waterloo, and the late years and funeral of King George III, etc., before he finishes the Second Part.

Croly keeps revising the poem after the publication of the Second Part in 1821. Then in 1830 *The Collected Works of Croly* comes out, in which is given the revised version of the First and Second Parts of *Paris in 1815* (hereafter abbreviated as *P 1815* (1830) 1 or 2). What I intend to examine below is the Dying Warrior stanzas of the 1821 edition claimed to have been written before the publication of *CHP* 4 or the 1818 borderline, and those of the revised 1830 version.

What the Endnote Tells Us

All editions of *Paris in 1815* are appended with endnotes. The notes relating to the Dying Warrior stanzas are identical regardless of editions, and will be hereafter quoted from the 1821 version. There are three main points in the interpretation of the Dying Warrior stanzas.

Chinnery's Dying Gladiator Criticized

Croly begins the endnote with a criticism of the expression "[c]ollecting all his energies to die" in "an Oxford prize-poem on the *Dying Gladiator*". He says "[t]he Dying Gladiator is *collecting no energies*. His strength is totally gone ..." (*P 1815* (1821) 2:80-81, Croly's italics). Croly does not mention the poet's name, but if what he means is George Robert Chinnery's "The Statue of the Dying Gladiator" that won the Newdigate Prize of

---

2   "The Dying Warrior" is my coinage, based upon (1) Byron's "Dying Gladiator", and (2) Croly's phrase "Beside him sinks a warrior on his shield".

the University of Oxford in 1810, the original passage runs as follows: "... rally life's whole energy – to die!" (Chinnery l. 18) and not "collecting" as Croly defiantly criticizes.[3] We cannot help thinking that either Croly was too confident of his memory to take the trouble of checking the original, or simply the book was not near at hand.

Battle of the Teutoburg Forest, and the Expedition of Germanicus in AD 9

The second and third paragraphs of the endnote, compared with the first, are extremely laconic but of far greater importance. This is all that Croly says:

> This statue, of the highest excellence in its style of strong expression, is generally supposed to represent, not a gladiator but a German dying on the field.

> The allusions in the stanzas refer to the celebrated description of the march of the Roman army, to find the remains of Varus and his legions. "Igitur cupido Caesarem invadit solvendi suprema militibus," &c. – *Tacitus, Annal. Lib.* 1 [sic]. (*P 1815* (1821) 2:80-81, Croly's italics)

The Latin quotation at the end is taken from the beginning of Section 61, Book 1 of Tacitus's *Annals*, which describes the expedition of Germanicus conducted in the year AD 15. Croly's actual source, however, is not confined to this part of *The Annals*. He also takes from other volumes and other sections as well as from other writers, notably from Velleius Paterculus, whose account of Varus's severed head carried "o'er many a hill and fen" (*P 1815* (1821) 2:56.8) proves indispensable in the interpretation of the latter part of Stanza 56. Again, Croly does not seem have paid much attention to the accuracy of citation. Or perhaps Croly, assuming that everyone was familiar with Arminius's surprise attack of AD 9, and trying to remind us that his stanzas were concerned with two separate battles, pointed out only the lesser known one in the note.

Whichever the case, here is the basic historical background reconstructed from Arminius-related narratives by various authors:[4] the first major event to note is what is called the Battle of the Teutoburg Forest in the year AD 9. In this battle, the chieftain of the Germanic Cherusci tribe, whom Romans called Arminius, stood at the head of the anti-Roman alliance, fought fierce battles against three Roman legions led by Publius Quinctilius Varus in the Teutoburg Forest, and forced the Roman commander Varus to commit suicide. According to Velleius Paterculus, "The body of Varus, partially burned, was mangled by the enemy in their barbarity; his head was cut off and taken to Maroboduus

---

3   For Chinnery's complete poem, see Kasahara, pp. 44-45. It should be noted that the poem accessible on the internet, starting "Imperial Rome and trophied Greece ..." (as of 13 Jan. 2021) is a different poem.

4   Since all the ancient narratives were written by Roman historians, I have much benefitted from Harnecker's summary of the battle in *Arminius, Varus and the Battlefield at Kalkriese*, and from the following two websites: Jona Lendering, *Livius.org: Articles on Ancient History*, and *Varusschlacht*, the official museum website, all written from neutral or non-Roman viewpoints.

and was sent by him to Caesar; but in spite of the disaster, it was honoured by burial in the tomb of his family" (Paterculus 2:119). In the year 15, Germanicus, nephew and adopted son of the Roman emperor Tiberius, in one of his punitive campaigns crossing the Rhine, came near the Teutoburg Forest. And "[t]here came upon the Caesar, therefore, a passionate desire to pay the last tribute to the fallen and their leader" (Tacitus 1:61), as Tacitus says in the very passage which Croly mentions in the endnote. In this campaign Germanicus pursues Arminius with much difficulty. "It was a night of unrest", writes Tacitus, and "the barbarians, in high carousal, filled the low-lying valleys and echoing woods with chants of triumph or fierce vociferations" (Tacitus 1:65). Thus, Arminius finally succeeded in foiling the Romans. The end of Arminius does not occupy much space in Tacitus. It happened much later in the year AD 21 as a result of an intertribal conflict (Tacitus 2:88). Yet, this is the very moment that Croly captures at the beginning of the Dying Warrior stanzas, where the "heart" (*P 1815* (1821) 2:55.2) of the dying warrior alone tells as the remembrance of past events.

Dying Warrior Stanzas in the 1821 Version

> Beside him[5] sinks a warrior on his shield,
> Whose history the heart alone must tell!
> Now, dim in eve – he looks, as on the field,
> Where when he fell, his country with him fell.
> Death sickens all his soul, the blood-drops steal
> Slow from his breast, congealing round the wound;
> His strong arm shakes, his chest has lost its swell,
> 'Tis his last breath, – his eye-ball glares profound,
>   His heavy forehead glooms, bends, plunges, to the ground! (*P 1815* (1821) 2:55.1-9)

The first stanza begins with what appears to be an ekphrastic description of the statue. We need, of course, to read it on the assumption that it is not a gladiator but a German dying on the field that is depicted. The second line gives the overall framework of the following lines: what follows is the history which the warrior's heart alone tells, in other words, readers will be shown as a dying vision of a warrior what he witnessed in the past and had kept only in his heart. We are told in the poem that he is a warrior on the shield, and that he is looking onto the field "[w]here when he fell, his country with him fell" (55.4).

As we read on, the statue gets incarnated and becomes flesh with the description of a minute-by-minute movement of this dying man: "blood-drops" (2:55.5), presumably having gushed out for some time, have already begun to slow down, "congealing round the wound; / His strong arm shakes, his chest has lost its swell" (2:55.6-7). The narrating poet, hearing the dying man's breathing, thinks out loud "'[t]is his last breath" (2:55.8). There is glaring in his eye-ball, which speaks of profoundness, perhaps, in thought, feeling, and his entire existence. There is gloom across his forehead. The head gradually

---

5   A reference to Laocoön in the preceding stanza.

begins to bend, and suddenly no longer able to sustain itself, "plunges, to the ground" (2:55.9). This is a wonderful verbal rendition of the last moment of the dying German, with all the movements, feelings, and thoughts condensed in the static marble statue. The succession of three verbs "glooms, bends, plunges" (2:55.9) skilfully captures the very frozen moment of the dying man full of potential energy.

> Yet had he high revenge, if Roman tears
> For Roman slaughter could rejoice his soul.
> Did he not hear the crashing of the spears?
> When like a midnight tide, his warriors stole
> Around the slumbering legions – till the roll
> Of the wild forest-drum awoke the glen;
> And all was havoc; – and the German pole
> Bore Varus' head o'er many a hill and fen.
> > Chains and the spear are chaff, when Heaven gives hearts to men! (*P 1815* (1821) 2:56.1-9)

In this stanza, the narrator describes the battle that took place in the Teutoburg Forest in the year AD 9, within the framework of vengeance, which Arminius would have felt, if – synonymous with "since" in this context – Roman tears shed for the slaughter of Romans, could rejoice Arminius's soul. Croly next speaks of "Roman slaughter" (2:56.2) or the Romans slaughtered in a German ambush. In this attack, German warriors took advantage of the terrain, and "like a midnight tide ... stole / Around the slumbering [Roman] legions" (2:56.4-5) causing havoc all round. Soon the head of Varus was severed, borne on a "German pole" (2:56.7) and carried "o'er many a hill and fen" (2:56.8). This surprise attack, the poet comments at the beginning of the stanza, would have fulfilled Arminius' revenge – "had he high revenge" (2:56.1) – if there were Romans who shed tears for this slaughter.

Between Stanza 56 and Stanza 57, we need to assume the passage of six years.

> Had not that glance the fuller, haughtier joy,
> To see the Caesar stand a weeper there?
> Fated Germanicus! when, years gone by,
> The Legions came the funeral pile to rear;
> With silent march, bare head, and trailing spear,
> Piercing the forest o'er the slaughter grown;
> In horror finding chief and comrade dear
> In wolf-torn graves, and haggard piles of bone
> > Along the ramparts' ruins, and marshy trenches strown. (*P 1815* (1821) 2:57.1-9)

> Still frown'd the fatal altars, now in robes
> Of giant weeds that sheeted down the boughs
> Of the brown pines. There had the thronging globes
> Of German warriors held the night's carouse,
> And groans of death, and Magic's fearful vows
> Startled the moon. But now the murder'd lay,
> The human hecatomb! in ghastly rows,
> The leaders still unmix'd with meaner clay
> > Tribune and consul stretch'd in white and wild decay. (*P 1815* (1821) 2:58.1-9)

These two stanzas are based, as Croly himself mentions in his endnote, on Tacitus's account of Germanicus's expedition in the year AD 15. In fact, Croly's lines roughly correspond with the account of Tacitus: legions led by Germanicus trying to find the site of the Roman encampment, the remains of the slaughter being clearly visible even to altars and bones (*P 1815* (1821) 2:57), and those of soldiers and officers being in separate places (*P 1815* (1821) 2:58), all in Section 61 of Tacitus' *Annals*; and German warriors holding the night's carouse (*P 1815* (1821) 2:58) in Section 65.

The 1830 Version Compared with the 1821 Version

The Dying Warrior episode of the later version begins with the same ekphrastic description of the statue as that of the earlier version. In fact, Stanza 51 of 1830 is identical with Stanza 55 of 1821. The next stanza (Stanza 52) includes an expression that suggests a very important change of direction in the 1830 version:

> Yet had the bold barbarian joy; if tears
> For Roman slaughter could rejoice his soul.
> Did he not hear the crashing of the spears?
> When like a midnight tide, his warriors stole
> Around the slumb'ring legions – till the roll
> Of the wild forest-drum awoke the glen;
> And every blow let loose a Roman soul.
> So let them sting the lion in his den;
> > Chains and the spear are chaff, when Heaven gives hearts to men! (*P 1815* (1830) 2:52.1-9)

The first sentence "Yet had the bold barbarian joy" (*P 1815* (1830) 2:52.1) had originally been "Yet had he high revenge" (*P 1815* (1821) 2:56.1) in the earlier version. The substitution of "revenge" with "joy" through the process of revision is to be carried on to the next stanza, where an entirely new concept "shame" appears:

> Had not that with'ring lip quaff'd long and deep,
> The cup that vengeance for the patriot fills;
> When swords instinctive from their scabbards leap,
> When the dim forests, and the mighty hills,
> And the lone gushings of the mountain rills,
> All utter to the soul a cry of shame;
> And shame, like drops of molten brass, distils
> On the bare head and bosom of the tame,
> > Till the whole fetter'd man, heart, blood, and brain, is flame. (*P 1815* (1830) 2:53. 1-9)

> Then there were lightnings in that clouded eye,
> And sounds of triumph in that heavy ear;
> Aye, and that icy limb was bounding nigh,
> Tracking the Roman with the bow and spear,
> As through the live-long night the death-march drear
> Pierced the deep forests o'er the slaughter grown;

Seeking for ancient chief and comrade dear,
Through wolf-torn graves and haggard piles of bone,
    Along the rampart ruins, and marshy trenches strown. (*P 1815* (1830) 2:54.1-9)

We need to note in the first place that Stanza 53 has no corresponding lines in the earlier version. It begins with the narrator's confirmation to the reader, in the form of a negative interrogation, that Arminius surely did drink from the cup filled by the personified vengeance for the patriot Arminius (2:53.1-2), which would certainly be the cause of the sense of shame he next feels in the latter half of this stanza. The key word here is "shame," (2:53.6, 7) a new concept in the 1830 version. Shame, the narrator tells us, distils "like drops of molten brass" (2:53.7), and works magic on the mind and heart of the tame German, and he, in turn, is set aflame (cf. 2:53.9) with this distilled sense of shame. What we are looking at here is the reversal of emotive direction. Vengeance, a negative feeling directed towards outside, is transformed into a negative feeling directed towards oneself or inward: shame.

We should also note that this change of direction is caused by Arminius's contact with nature. He hears the cry of shame in the natural environment, or to be more precise, it is "the dim forests, and the mighty hills, / And the lone gushings of the mountain rills" (2:53.4-5) that utter a cry of shame to the soul of Arminius. Here nature seems to be acting of its own will upon our Germanic hero. The 1830 addition makes vengeance capable of making the person susceptible to nature when internalized, which in turn causes the negative feeling formerly directed towards the outside to change direction and turn into shame. Vengeance is thus mitigated and transformed into shame in the 1830 version.

In the 1821 version, Arminius is referred to with no particular name. He is first mentioned as "a warrior" (2:55.1), and the following references are all made by the use of the third person pronoun. In the 1830 version, Arminius still remains unnamed, but is, instead, referred to with various rhetorical alterations such as "the bold barbarian" (2:52.1), "the patriot" (2:53.2), "the tame" (2:53.8), and "the ... fetter'd man" (2:53.9). He is furthermore given references to various parts of his body: "that with'ring lip" (2:53.1), "the bare head and bosom" (2:53.8), "that clouded eye" (2:54.1), "that heavy ear" (2:54.2) and "that icy limb" (2:54.3), none of which has any corresponding expressions in the earlier version. All in all, we are able to visualize more clearly what he would physically have been with these parts of the body mentioned, and what he would have been inside with these different designations.[6]

---

6   Why the hero constantly remains nameless throughout the revisions is a big question that would require a full-length thesis. The facts are that Croly does not use the Latin name "Arminius", nor does he use its German version "Hermann", which had, by Croly's time, come to be popularized, as Benario points out, by Klopstock's trilogy: *Hermanns Schlacht* (1769); *Hermann und die Fürsten* (1784); *Hermanns Tod* (1787). It may not go beyond speculation but Croly's use of the word "warrior" may have something common with what Martin Luther writes in his discussion of the Psalm 82, "Herman [sic], whom the Latins

In spite of the fact that Arminius remains nameless in both versions, his antagonists are introduced with distinctive names in the earlier version: "the German pole / Bore Varus' head o'er many a hill and fen. ... Fated Germanicus!" (2:56.7-8; 2:57.3) In the 1830 version, Varus and Germanicus are gone, and all that is left are racial appellations: German and Roman. In addition, the episode of Varus's severed head carried "o'er many a hill and fen" (2:56.8) disappears in the 1830 version along with the name Varus. Thus, in the 1830 version, while Arminius becomes more vivid physically as well as inwardly, all the personal antagonism is somehow substituted by, or sublimated into, the racial consciousness, German *vs.* Roman, with vengeance internalized and personal names gone.

The 1830 Version Compared with Byron

Between the 1830 version of *Paris in 1815* and the 1821 version which, Croly declares in its "Preface", was written immediately after the 1817 version, comes the publication of *CHP* 4 in 1818. One of the most characteristic features of Byron's Dying Gladiator stanzas, perhaps, would be the dying man's vision of his wife and children.

> I see before me the Gladiator lie:
> He leans upon his hand – his manly brow
> Consents to death, but conquers agony,
> And his drooped head sinks gradually low –
> And through his side the last drops, ebbing slow
> From the red gash, fall heavy, one by one,
> Like the first of a thunder-shower; and now
> The arena swims around him – he is gone,
>   Ere ceased the inhuman shout which hail'd the wretch who won. (*CHP* 4:140.1-9)

> He heard it, but he heeded not – his eyes
> Were with his heart and that was far away;
> He recked not of the life he lost nor prize,
> But where his rude but by the Danube lay,
> *There* were his young barbarians all at play,
> *There* was their Dacian mother – he, their sire,
> Butcher'd to make a Roman holiday –
> All this rush'd with his blood – Shall he expire
>   And unavenged? – Arise! ye Goths, and glut your ire! (*CHP* 4:141.1-9)

Stanza 140 begins with what first appears to be an ekphrastic description of the statue, "I see before me the Gladiator lie". This gradually turns into an imagined realistic description of the gladiator dying in the coliseum with expressions indicating clear movement: "... sinks gradually low ... the last drops, ebbing slow ... fall heavy, one by one". And with the next passage "now / The arena swims around him", the narrator's eye becomes one with that of the gladiator. The arena swims around him, as well as the narrator

---

treat badly and call Ariminius [sic], is actually *ein Heer man* (an army man)" (Benario 87-88).

and the reader. From this line onwards, the narrator goes inside the consciousness of the gladiator.

He "heard" the inhuman shout, in the next stanza, but he "heeded not". The roaring spectators in the coliseum are no longer capable of penetrating into the gladiator's heart. There is something more precious than his own life at the innermost core of his heart: "his rude hut ... his young barbarians ... their Dacian mother". This final dying vision of the gladiator lies at the innermost core of his consciousness. Then revives the self-consciousness: "he, their sire, / Butcher'd to make a Roman holiday". We are not exactly sure whether this is the gladiator thinking about himself, or the narrator commenting on the ancient gladiatorial show. In any case, we are no longer at the innermost core of the gladiator's consciousness, we have moved one step outward. With the next phrase "All this rush'd with his blood", the narrator further zooms out and describes the imagined death of the gladiator, as he had done in the preceding stanza. Thus, Byron in his description of the statue, moves on to the imagined gladiatorial show in the ancient Roman period, goes inside the gladiator's heart, sees what he might have seen, and then comes out of this sacred shrine of his heart.

We can see that both Byron's Gladiator lines and Croly's 1830 revised version of the Dying Warrior stanzas are characterized by the narrator intently looking inward: one describing the most intimately private moment of his domestic life with his wife and children before he was taken prisoner, the other describing the minute process of forests, hills, and mountain rills uttering a cry of shame to the soul of Arminius, and the process of shame being distilled compared to a very slow movement of molten brass dripping drop by drop on the head and bosom of the tame German warrior.

After this, the narrating poet, in strong sympathy with the gladiator, apostrophically comments, "Shall he expire / And unavenged? – Arise! ye Goths, and glut your ire!" If there is anything common in this vengeful outburst of Byron's narrator with Croly's lines, it is the racial consciousness that has come to the fore, rather than personal vengeance. Byron's narrator, in order to avenge one particular gladiator from Dacia, is calling onto the entire Goths to arise and destroy the whole Roman Empire, which indeed was the real course of history. Gladiator's personal vengeance is sublimated in Goth-Roman antagonism.

This final sublimation of vengeance at the end of the Dying Gladiator stanzas (*CHP* 4:140-41) is in fact the culmination of the entire Coliseum stanzas (*CHP* 4:128-45) as well. From the very beginning, the narrating poet, meditating in the coliseum at night, calls on to "Time, the avenger", saying "unto thee I lift / My hands, and eyes, and heart, and crave of thee a gift" (*CHP* 4:130). He then calls on to Nemesis, saying, "*thou* shalt take / The vengeance" (*CHP* 4:133, Byron's italics), yet when he thinks of his own future poetic composition, and how "a far hour shall wreak / The deep prophetic fulness of this verse" (*CHP* 4:134), he turns the direction of his vengeful outburst to the opposite direction, and assumes a deliberately careless attitude, saying, "That curse shall be Forgiveness" (*CHP* 4:135). The reason for this sudden affected change, says the narrator, is that he knows how he has "suffered things to be forgiven ... had ... Life's life lied away" (*CHP* 4:135), and still was able to keep calm, because he knows he is "not altogether of such clay / As rots into the souls of those whom" he surveys (*CHP* 4:135). What we see here is a man, burning with vengeance, trying to strike a balance with the thought of his future fame and his feigned superiority over his enemies, and finally forcing out the word of "forgiveness" hardly inseparable from "curse". It is the recognition of "that within me which shall tire / Torture and Time, and breathe when I expire" (*CHP* 4:137), that puts an end to his vengeful outburst, enables him to "become a part of what has been, / And grow upon the spot – all-seeing but unseen" (*CHP* 4:138), and finally allows him to see before him "the Gladiator lie" (*CHP* 4:140). Introspective contemplation that is capable of overcoming vengeance is an indispensable prerequisite for Byron's Dying Gladiator stanzas.

Conclusion

Some of the characteristic features of Croly's 1830 revision of *Paris in 1815*, as far as the Dying Warrior stanzas are concerned, can thus be seen as a product of the transgression of the 1818 borderline, the year *CHP* 4 was published. The features I discussed are, first of all, an introspective orientation, exemplified in the Gladiator's final vision of his wife and children, preceded by the recognition of something that is within oneself in Byron (cf. "that within me" (*CHP* 4:137)), and the German warrior's crude sense of vengeance transformed into shame in contact with nature, and gradually distilled in his heart until it sets his heart on fire. The second feature is an emphasis on racial antagonism rather than on personal conflict, exemplified in the narrator's apostrophic call to the Goths to arise and glut their ire in Byron, and in Croly manifested in the disappearance of proper nouns, Varus and Germanicus, from the later edition. The ancient Germanic hero's transgression of the 1818 borderline has clearly brought the later version thematically closer to Byron. Croly's Dying Warrior in the 1830 version of *Paris in 1815*, Part 2 is Byron's Roman Gladiator that crossed the boundary and turned into Arminius, with vengeance distilled into shame, and with personal antagonism sublimated into racial consciousness.

Works Cited

"Ancient Authors on the Issue of the Varus Battle". *Varusschlacht im Osnabrücker Land: Museum und Park Kalkriese.* https://www.kalkriese-varusschlacht.de (accessed 13 January 2021).

Benario, Herbert W. "Arminius into Hermann: History into Legend". *Greece & Rome* 51.1 (2004): 83-94.

Byron, Lord [George Gordon]. *The Complete Poetical Works.* Ed. Jerome J. McGann, vol. 2. Oxford: Oxford UP, 1980.

Chinnery, Robert. *The Statue of the Dying Gladiator: A Prize Poem, Recited in the Theatre, Oxford July 3*. Oxford: Collingwood, 1810.

[Croly, George]. *Paris in 1815: A Poem*. London: John Murray, 1817.

Croly, George. *Paris in 1815, with Other Poems*. London: J. Warren, 1821.

---. *The Poetical Works*. 2 vols. London: H. Colburn & R. Bentley, 1830.

Gray, Thomas. *The Complete Poems of Thomas Gray: English, Latin, and Greek*. Ed. H. W. Starr and J. R. Hendrickson. Oxford: Clarendon Press, 1966.

Hanson, David C. "George Croly". *Oxford Dictionary of National Biography*. Oxford: Oxford UP, 2004.

Harnecker, Joachim. *Arminius, Varus and the Battlefield at Kalkriese*. Trans. Erika Strenski. Bramsche: Rasch, 2004.

Kasahara Yorimichi. "Byron's Dying Gladiator in Context". *The Wordsworth Circle* 40.1 (2009): 44-51.

Lendering, Jona. "The Battle in the Teutoburg Forest". *Livius.org: Articles on Ancient History*. Livius.org (accessed 13 January 2021).

---. "Paterculus on the Battle in the Teutoburg Forest". *Livius.org: Articles on Ancient History*. Livius.org (accessed 13 January 2021).

Paterculus, Velleius. *Compendium of Roman History / Res Gestae Divi Augusti*. Trans. Frederick W. Shipley. London: Heinemann, 1924. Loeb Library.

Reiman, Donald H. "Introduction". George Croly, *Paris in 1815 [...] Paris in 1815, Second Part [...]*. Ed. Donald H. Reiman. New York: Garland, 1977.

Tacitus. *The Annals. The Histories, IV-V & The Annals, I-III*. Trans. Clifford H. Moore and John Jackson. Cambridge, MA: Harvard UP and London: Heinemann, 1931.

"The Myth Arminius – Hermann". *Varusschlacht im Osnabrücker Land: Museum und Park Kalkriese.* https://www.kalkriese-varusschlacht.de (accessed 13 January 2021).

Wordsworth, William. *Poems, in Two Volumes, and Other Poems, 1800-1807*. Ed. Jared Curtis. Ithaca: Cornell UP, 1983.

List of Contributors

ALEXANDRA BÖHM studied German, English and American Literature at the University of Erlangen-Nürnberg, the University of Glasgow and the University of Gießen. She achieved her PhD in 2010 with a comparative study on Heine and Byron, which focused on their interventionist poetics between 1815 and 1830. Since 2015, she has been working as research assistant at the Department of German Literature of the University of Erlangen-Nürnberg. Her present research focuses on narratives of empathy in human-animal encounters since 1750. She is co-editor of the volumes *Tiere erzählen* (2019), *Tiergeschichten* (2019) and *Animal Encounters. Contact, Interaction, and Relationality* (2019).

SEBASTIAN DOMSCH teaches Anglophone Literatures at the University of Greifswald. He holds a PhD from Bamberg University, and a Habilitation from the Ludwig-Maximilians-University in Munich. His major fields of interest are Romantic literature and eighteenth-century literature, graphic novels, as well as the history and theory of literary criticism. He is the author of books on Robert Coover (2005) and Cormac McCarthy (2012), as well as on criticism (2014) and video games (2013).

IAN DUNCAN is Florence Green Bixby Chair in English at the University of California, Berkeley. He is the author of *Human Forms: The Novel in the Age of Evolution* (Princeton UP, 2019), *Scott's Shadow: The Novel in Romantic Edinburgh* (Princeton UP, 2007), and *Modern Romance and Transformations of the Novel: The Gothic, Scott, Dickens* (Cambridge UP, 1992). He has co-edited essay collections on Scottish Romantic-period writing, and edited several works of nineteenth-century Scottish fiction. He is a general editor of the *Collected Works of James Hogg* (Edinburgh) and *Edinburgh Critical Studies in Romanticism* (Edinburgh).

DENISE GIGANTE, Sadie Dernham Patek Professor of Humanities at Stanford University, is the author, most recently, of *Book Madness: A Story of Book Collectors in America*, currently in production with Yale UP. Other publications relevant to this essay include *Taste: A Literary History* and *Gusto: Essential Writings in Nineteenth-Century Gastronomy*, both published in 2005. Less relevant, but currently in the works, are *The Mental Traveller: William Blake*, forthcoming from Oxford UP, and *The Cambridge History of the British Essay*, co-edited with Jason Childs and forthcoming from Cambridge UP.

JONATHAN GROSS is the author of *Byron: The Erotic Liberal* (2001) and *Anne Damer: Portrait of a Regency Artist* (2012). A specialist in the lives of Regency women, he has edited *Byron's "Corbeau Blanc": The Life and Letters of Lady Melbourne and Belmour*, *The Sylph*, and *Emma, or the Unfortunate Attachment*. He has received awards from the Huntington Library, the Virginia Foundation for the Humanities, and the American Antiquarian Society, for several projects, including *Thomas Jefferson's Scrapbooks: Poems of Nation, Family, and Romantic Love*. He is currently Joint-President of the International Association of Byron Societies.

KASAHARA YORIMICHI is Professor at Meisei University, Tokyo, Japan. Studies widely on English Romanticism. President of Japan Association of English Romanticism (2012-16). Editor/Co-author of *From John Denham to Romanticism: How Arose the Lyric from Loco-descriptive Poetry* (Meisei UP, 2004) [in Japanese]. Author of "Byron's Dying Gladiator in Context", *The Wordsworth Circle* (2009). Editor/Translator of *Byron's Poems: Parallel Translation* (Tokyo: Iwanami-shoten, 2009) [in Japanese]. Author of "P. B. Shelley, *terza rima*, and Italy: Con-fusion of Voices, Persons, and Poetic Forms", *POETICA* (2014). Author/Designer of the website "Shakespeare in Silver" (Meisei University, 2020), https://kenkyu. hino.meisei-u.ac.jp/vase-sh/.

RICHARD LANSDOWN is Professor of Modern English Literature and Culture at the University of Groningen in the Netherlands. He is the author of *Byron's Historical Dramas* (Oxford UP, 1992), the *Cambridge Introduction to Byron* (Cambridge UP, 2012), and *Byron's Letters and Journals: A New Selection* (Oxford UP, 2015). He is also the author of *A New Scene of Thought: Studies in Romantic Realism* and *Literature and Truth: Imaginative Writing as a Medium for Ideas*, published by Brill-Rodopi in 2016 and 2018, respectively.

NORBERT LENNARTZ is Professor of English Literature at the University of Vechta in Germany. Among his major publications are a book on the deconstruction of eroticism in seventeenth-century British poetry and two collections of essays on Romantic literature, one on *Lord Byron and Marginality* (with Edinburgh UP in 2018) and another on *The Lost Romantics* (with Palgrave in 2020). He has just finished a full-length monograph on the literary and cultural history of tears, fluids and porous bodies (about to be published with Bloomsbury in 2021) and is currently working on a book covering open and submerged discourses of Germanophilia and Germanophobia in nineteenth-century British fiction.

SWANTJE VAN MARK is currently working as research assistant at the chair of English Literature at the University of Vechta and working on her PhD on the depiction of dandy figures in late nineteenth-century literature. Her research interests include literature of the nineteenth-century, Gothic writing, vampire literature, detective fiction and intertextuality.

SOPHIA MÖLLERS is working as research assistant at the chair of British Cultural Studies at TU Dortmund and holds a Master's degree in German and English Studies. She is currently writing her PhD which focuses on inheritance, filial duty, and the redefinition of value in William Godwin's later novels. Her research interests include the Long Eighteenth Century, Romantic and Gothic writing, the origins of Psychiatry/Psychoanalysis, and the Godwin-Shelley Circle.

MARVIN REIMANN received his Master's degree in English Literatures and Cultures at the University of Bonn in 2018. He is currently a second-year doctoral student and research assistant at the DFG Graduate School 2291 "Contemporary/Literature. History, Theory, and Praxeology" at the same university. His dissertation follows an interdisciplinary approach as it consists in a comparative analysis of selected philosophical texts

(Novalis, Schelling) and poems (Wordsworth, Shelley, Keats) with respect to their conceptions of temporality and time consciousness. As the subject of his thesis already suggests, his research interests mainly lie in the interrelationship between philosophy and literature, with a particular focus on English Romanticism, Transcendentalism, German Idealism, and Early German Romanticism.

NICHOLAS ROE is Wardlaw Professor of English Literature at the University of St Andrews, Scotland. He is a Fellow of the British Academy and of the Royal Society of Edinburgh, and an Honorary Fellow of the English Association. His recent publications include *John Keats. A New Life* (2012) and, as editor, *John Keats and the Medical Imagination* (2017). He is a founding editor of the scholarly journal *Romanticism*.

DIEGO SAGLIA is Professor of English Literature at the University of Parma, Italy. His research centres upon Romantic-period literature and culture, and particularly such themes as exoticism and orientalism, Gothic, national identity and gender, and several central figures including Jane Austen, Lord Byron, Felicia Hemans and Walter Scott. He is a member of the advisory committee of the Byron Museum in Ravenna, and some of his latest publications are *Byron and Italy* (coedited with Alan Rawes, 2017), *Spain and British Romanticism 1800-1840* (coedited with Ian Haywood, 2018), and the monograph *European Literatures in Britain, 1815-1832: Romantic Translations* (2019).

LEONORE SELL has studied Art History, German Studies and British Studies at Leipzig University. She is currently teaching English Literature at the University of Vechta and working on her PhD dissertation on the reception and biofictional treatment of the life and works of Edith Nesbit. Her main fields of research constitute speculative fiction, children's literature, adaptation studies and women writers as well as intertextual currents between nineteenth-century literature and Postmodernism.

ALEXANDER SCHLUTZ is Associate Professor of English at John Jay College and the CUNY Graduate School and University Center. He is the author of *Mind's World. Imagination and Subjectivity from Descartes to Romanticism* (University of Washington Press, 2009) and associate editor of the journal *Essays in Romanticism*. His work on E.T.A. Hoffmann has appeared in edited collections, academic journals in the US and Germany, and on the online *E.T.A. Hoffmann Portal* of the Staatsbibliothek Berlin.

RICHARD C. SHA is Professor of Literature at American University in Washington, D.C., where he is also an affiliate of the Center for Behavioral Neuroscience. His most recent book is *Imagination and Science in Romanticism* (Johns Hopkins UP 2018), which won the Jean Pierre Barricelli Prize in that year. Previously he published *Perverse Romanticism: Aesthetics and Sexuality in Britain, 1750-1850*, also with Johns Hopkins UP. With Joel Faflak, he will publish *Romanticism and Consciousness Revisted* with Edinburgh UP. Recent and forthcoming articles are on Trauma Theory and the Nanjing Massacre, Blake and the hard problem of experience; data, science, and the sublime; and a piece on George Sand's transgressive sexuality.

Studien zur englischen Romantik

Herausgegeben von Christoph Bode, Jens Martin Gurr und Frank Erik Pointner

22　Pascal Fischer, Christoph Houswitschka (Eds.): **The Politics of Romanticism. Selected Papers from the Bamberg Conference of the German Society for English Romanticism**
Aus dem Inhalt: A. J. Harding: Romanticism and the Politics of Dissent: From Religious Liberty to Romantic Radicalism · R. Lessenich †: Millennial Hope Shattered: William Godwin's Travels of St Leonand Romantic Scepticism · K. J. Harris: Ill-Starr'd Wanderers: Exile, Refuge, and Charlotte Smith's The Emigrants · K. Röder: Hospitality as a Precarious Ethico-Political Practice in Charlotte Smith's The Young Philosopher · N. Roe: Placing Displacement: Wordsworth and Coleridge in the 1790s · J. Lloyd: "far in some sequester'd dell": The Politics of Retirement in the Poetic Dialogue of John Thelwall and Samuel Taylor Coleridge · I. Duncan: Don Giovanni Automaton · T. Rajan: Godwin's Fleetwood and the Persistence of Dissensus · D. Weißenfels: Body Politic and National Body: Political Myth-Making and Romantic Nationalism in John Bull's Bible · G. Sourgen: The Revolt of Islam and the Politics of Form · S. Fricke: Barbary Captivity in the Romantic Age · P. J. Kitson: Romantic Nationalism, De Quincey and the Public Debate about the First Opium War, 1839-42 · M. Modrzewska, G. B. Tomaszewska: The Institution of Romanticism in Polish Culture: Trends and Politics · M. Irimia: Decebalus's Ancestral Voice Prophesying National Unity: Romanian Romanticism and the Politics of Ethno-Genetic Identity · M. Nabugodi: Allegorical Realism: Bertolt Brecht and Walter Benjamin's Reading of Percy Bysshe Shelley's Political Verse · F. Burwick: Shelley's Oedipus Tyrannus; or, Swellfoot the Tyrant: George IV and the Adultery Trial of Queen Caroline · A. Esterhammer: Political Economy and Narrative Performance in John Galt's The Entail · J. Thompson: 'Affiance on Affiance Multiply': John Thelwall and the Hope of Future Time　　**ISBN 978-3-86821-802-2, 222 S., kt., € 29,50 (2019)**

21　Christoph Bode (Ed.): **Romanticism and the Forms of Discontent**
If, as Sigmund Freud argues, to be in culture is the same as to feel a kind of unease, a kind of discontent, then what is the specific, historically differentiated place of Romanticism in the cultural history of unease? What are the forms that discontent takes in an age of increasing, indeed unprecedented pressure on the individual, an age that, at the same time, offers a new space in which such discontent can be voiced and visions of a non-repressive existence can be sketched – in the realm of the aesthetic? Blending theory with close textual analysis, this volume offers a series of case studies that, while identifying a concrete historical moment, also point to some deep continuities between Romanticism and the society we live in today.　　**ISBN 978-3-86821-739-1, 216 S., kt., € 26,50 (2017)**

20　Sebastian Domsch, Christoph Reinfandt, Katharina Rennhak (Eds.): **Romantic Ambiguities. Abodes of the Modern**
Aus dem Inhalt: M. J. Bruhn: Ambiguity in Affect: The Modernity of Wordsworth's Lyrical Ballads · N. Halmi: Two Types of Wordsworthian Ambiguity · R. Haekel: 'The earth is all before me': Contingency and Ambiguity in Milton's Paradise Lost and Wordsworth's The Prelude · F. E. Pointner, D. Weißenfels: From Childe Harold to Don Juan: Narrative Ambiguity in Byron's Major Works · J. M. Gurr: Views on Violence in Shelley's Post-Peterloo Prose and Poetry: Contradiction, Ambivalence, Ambiguity? · J. Vigus: A 'Romantic State of Uncertainty': William Hazlitt's 'On Going a Journey' · C. Duffy: Ambiguity and the Value of 'Literature': Thomas De Quincey's Modernist Commodities · G. Sedlmayr: The Ambiguous Nature of the Romantic Scientification of Literary Knowledge · P. J. Kitson: 'Unexpected Affinities' and 'Fatal Errors': Ambiguities in the Romantic Reception of Confucius · F. Burwick: The Ambiguity of Time in Romantic Drama · A. Esterhammer: Ambiguous Identities in Hogg's Private Memoirs and Confessions of a Justified Sinner and Its Late-Romantic Contexts · M. Procházka: Internalized Apocalypse? Ambiguities of Transcendentalism in Melville's Pierre; or, The Ambiguities · I. Duncan: The Novel and the Romantic 'Moment' · P. Fischer: The Sublime: A Category of Ambiguity · M. Modrzewska, S. Modrzewski: Navigational Approximations in Joseph Conrad's World at Sea S. Fricke: Losing and Gaining Ambiguities: First Impressions, Pride and Prejudice and The Lizzie Bennet Diaries · C. Reinfandt: The Romantic Paradigm: Ambiguity, Then and Now　　**ISBN 978-3-86821-727-8, 308 S., 12 Abb., kt., € 35,00 (2017)**

Wissenschaftlicher Verlag Trier · Bergstraße 27 · 54295 Trier
Tel.: 0651/41503 · Fax: 0651/41504 · www.wvttrier.de · wvt@wvttrier.de